T0160970

The Wild Kindness

The Wild

Kindness

A Psilocybin Odyssey

BETT WILLIAMS

dottir
press
NEW YORK CITY

Published in 2020 by Dottir Press
33 Fifth Avenue
New York, NY 10003

Dottirpress.com

FIRST EDITION
Second printing, June 2021

Cover illustration by Mike Perry
Illustration on page 255 by Elizabeth Daggar
Design and production by Drew Stevens

The Wild Kindness is set in Adobe Caslon, which was designed in 1990 by Carol
Twombly, and Montserrat, which was designed in 2012 by Julieta Ulanovsky.

Trade distribution by Consortium Book Sales and Distribution, www.cbsd.com.

Library of Congress Cataloging-in-Publication Data is available for this title.
ISBN 978-1-9483-4031-1

MANUFACTURED IN THE UNITED STATES OF AMERICA, JUNE 2020

PREFACE

PSYCHEDELICS HAVE HIT the mainstream. Strangers seek me out regularly, asking if I know of a therapist who can guide them on a psilocybin mushroom journey. Self-proclaimed experts preach evangelically about the miraculous benefits gleaned by those who've done it in this way: in a clinical setting, with a trained professional.

"I do know of a therapist," I respond. "They're called a mushroom. Eat them and ask them for help."

It's much too simple a prescription for most. For me, it has been an act of decolonization to arrive to the mushrooms on their own terms, without the burden of expectations or the concepts put upon them by others. It is not in the nature of the Western psyche to give such power directly to a plant, let alone an unruly fungus. We want babysitters, esoteric prophets, shamans, and scientists to act as gatekeepers in the realm of the incomprehensible. Fair enough. After all, what is the psychedelic but a private drama that, for all its profundity, only holds meaning and significance to others when framed in a specific cultural context? Up until recently, the celebrated psychedelic culture makers were predominantly white men. I have my own opinions as to how this has affected our collective imagination, but I suggest you look into it yourself.

Three to five grams of dried psilocybin mushrooms should be sufficient to achieve clear-sightedness. Keep your wits and don't do anything stupid. When you land solidly back to earth, you will have had the only psychedelic experience that really matters—the one that is your own.

1

"Before Wasson, nobody used the children
only to find God. They were always taken to
cure the sick."

—MARÍA SABINA

I WAS BORN in Santa Barbara, where bougainvillea grows
like weeds, its delicate paper flowers in red and pink spill
over walls and tangle in hedges along with night-blooming
jasmine and toxic oleander bushes. Trees planted by settlers from the far corners of the earth bear strange flowers
that smell of urine, burning campfires, and honey, all of
which mingle with the holy scent of ocean mist.

Now my house where I live in New Mexico, is surrounded by juniper trees on all sides. They are always in my
sightline. For decades I hadn't given them much thought,
being that the pinion trees outside are much more famous.
They're older and occasionally produce pine nuts, and the
wood is better for burning. In the late nineties, a bark beetle scourge took out a massive percentage of the pinions
in northern New Mexico—thirteen trees on my land. The
bark beetle carries a blue stain fungus in its mouth that
lodges itself under the bark of a pinion tree and weakens

the resin, its natural defense. The junipers were immune to this attack. There are a lot of things suffering in this world, myself included, but if there's one thing that's not suffering at all, it's the juniper trees. They go on for miles.

Now that I think of it, juniper has been around since the very beginning. Juniper kind of tried to kill my mother. Her allergies left her bedridden throughout my childhood and adolescence.

"It's the juniper," she would say, in a state of total collapse. "It's killing me."

It was the juniper—not depression, not my father, not the cigarettes. Still, she insisted on planting even more juniper bushes in our yard, unearthing the perfectly fine ground cover that came before. Juniper was sturdy and drought-tolerant and didn't require tending. She planted it everywhere, vast swaths arranged in graded tiers that formed a maze of underground tunnels beneath the scratchy, slightly psychoactive branches. Juniper was a bleak underworld labyrinth I crawled through on my hands and knees with my dog, as if on a personal dare. The juniper tunnels were where Charlie, my demure sheltie, chose to relieve himself. I navigated around the dried shit piles to where the juniper fields ended at the skylight window of the guesthouse. One of my brother's friends was renting the space and sometimes I would get lucky and catch him jerking off.

Juniper provided my mother with what she needed most—a thing she could blame her Victorian illnesses on. Her commitment to juniper could've been a secret rebellion, a return to her Lubbock roots, where nothing grows from the desolate, sandy ground except the strongest, most determined of plants. Juniper was just like her—fucking alive and fucking irritating.

It occurred to me that the junipers might be what herbal medicine people would call my ally plant. Psilocybin mushrooms have been my gateway drug to LSD and San Pedro cactus; they've also been my gateway drug to yarrow, rose, mullein, and the juniper trees. The mushrooms roll their eyes at the fact that it took a substance as unsubtle and hardcore as a mushroom to wake me up to the rest of the natural world.

I ATE MUSHROOMS for the first time at age fifteen, in 1983, with a pale and haunted girl who wandered into my life for only this purpose before disappearing. We walked under the full moon through crumbling Greek architecture in Montecito, California, and kissed for a short while like Victorian ladies. It was everything one would want from a first-time experience. After having visions of insects and dirt, I went to sleep blissfully, tears streaming down my face in gratitude.

The next day I had plans to visit a juvenile detention center as part of a teen outreach program facilitated by a twenty-eight-year-old woman with whom I was having an intense and very secret sexual relationship. The volunteers gathered in the parking lot. While we were standing around, I told the facilitator what I had done the night before, that I had eaten mushrooms with a girl and it had been beautiful. She fired me on the spot. I waited in the car, sobbing hysterically, while the rest of the group was inside for nearly two hours. It was stupid of me to tell her. I loved the teen outreach program and I also loved the facilitator. She broke my little mushroom heart.

It's possible I associated that traumatic experience directly with the mushrooms without meaning to, because I avoided them after that. In the late 1990s, I moved up the road from a tiny coal town in rural New Mexico and began to frequent a shop that sold candles, antiques, blown glass, and handmade ironwork. The owner, Denise, had red hair and wore leather pants and seemed to really like me. We talked a lot on my frequent visits to the store. Once we got in full gossip mode, we couldn't shut up. When parting, it was always with the promise that we would eventually get together for a real hangout.

One day she casually mentioned, "Sometimes I take a little bit of mushroom before work. I've been doing it every few days for a while. It makes the tourists a lot easier to handle."

In one beat, her homey, witchy little shop became a drug den. The candles suddenly looked dirty, the stained glass mediocre and sad, the woven shawls and figurines made of car metal scraps now detritus of a wayward hippie life. I made up a lie about forgetting an appointment and left. I never returned. Her comment completely freaked me out.

Over twenty years later, I found myself in a dangerous downward swirl. Having published a novel in my late twenties that received strong reviews, I was creatively blocked. I wasn't writing, and I was completely absent from the wheel of my own destiny. Even worse, I was cool with that. The psilocybin mushrooms must have known.

It was through the body of a dying cottonwood tree that mushrooms landed in my life for good. Its branches dangled over the house where I lived with my girlfriend and her five-year-old child before our horrific breakup. My friend Sophia came over to cut the branches down before they crashed onto the roof in a storm.

Sophia and I have been friends for over twenty-five years. She was known as the cute punk girl who had made a home under a tree for a time. We once lay in bed together in the twenty-something misunderstanding that we should probably have sex because we liked each other so much. We decided not to. We saw each other rarely, but when we did there was always an exchange that marked the beginning of another chapter.

Day laborers had been knocking on my door for months, asking if I needed help cutting the tree down, but when they entered the yard and looked up at the massive thing, they said it was too big, too difficult. Sophia didn't even use a ladder. She hoisted herself up its trunk with ropes and cut the branches down with a small chainsaw. She was something to behold up there, with her piercings and strong, square body.

We both felt the whoosh of the larger limbs falling, saw the air arrange itself back into the empty space the branches left behind. Cottonwood branch gone—boom, just like that.

"Whoa," we said in unison. There was no other word

for such an event. Not everyone gets it, but air gets confused when it loses a familiar.

"I know this is a really random question, but do you have any magic mushrooms?" I asked. I didn't consciously grasp yet how miserable I was, but the nature of the body is to move toward healing, and my request came from a primal, yet-to-be-visited place within me, the way one might ask, *Do you know of a genius Jungian psychotherapist with a slightly sadistic streak? Or a remote woodland sanctuary where I could pretend I died, just for a little while?*

"Actually," she said, "yes, I do."

Our transaction played itself out in a way that is now familiar—not a lot of talk, the atmosphere thick with acknowledgment of what was occurring. I was about to meet an utterly foreign entity, a being with whom I would enter into a partnership.

IT BEGAN WITH a solitary trip by the fire three days later, with a cautious, less-than-three-gram dose. When there's nothing to lose, there's not a lot to worry about. It was easy to trust a mushroom—to trust anything outside myself and the twisted will that had landed me in this desperate clearing. I placed a small mound of tobacco at the base of a candle, a common offering I'd been practicing since I was a teenager, taught to me by herbalists and indigenous ceremonialists. I burned copal and flat cedar. Lying down on the couch under a wool blanket, I waited.

"You need to stop seeing yourself as a sick person," the mushrooms said. They spoke to me like this, in fully formed sentences heard internally, like a memory. "In your female form you are the quintessential bedridden Victorian lady on retreat."

"Yes, it's true!" I replied. "I do come from a long line of sick women. My mother had polio, tuberculosis, cancer, diphtheria, and Graves' disease. My grandmother had tuberculosis and a morphine addiction. Sickness is how I locate my ancestry."

"Oh, I am so very sick!" the mushrooms echoed, mocking me.

"You don't care that I'm sick?"

"We're just waiting for you to stop *pretending* to be sick."

"But I actually am kind of sick."

"Take as long as you like."

I wasn't sick, the mushrooms said, but the Trader Joe's frozen Greek yogurt I'd been eating daily was causing inflammation in my hips. What was going on in my hips was jacking my neck up and this somatic traffic jam was making me depressed and lethargic. The damage could be remedied with ginger.

"Ginger?"

"Yes, ginger. Will you let us show you?"

An intricate, multi-dimensional golden temple with a Moroccan silhouette arose in front of me. It was vast and bejeweled, with an empty throne at its center. As a lover of minimalist architecture, I resent having to describe its rococo attributes. I'll just say it whacked me with its beauty so thoroughly I was hyperventilating from its splendor. *The mushrooms must like me for such a thing to arise. Maybe I'm good at this*, I thought.

Personal preferences were tossed in, like my favorite shade of aqua found only in paint made from Smithsonite and contrasting garnet reds and lapis blues set side by side, emanating a lovely resonant sound. And gold, tons and tons of gold, in chunks and flowing strands and the thinnest of threads, gold forming arches and furniture, walls and handrails, cups and hairbrushes.

"This is ginger? This palace?"

"Yes, and it will help you."

"Ground or fresh?"

"Fresh is best. Keep it simple."

2

DURING ONE OF the solo trips I embarked on about every two or three weeks, I was lying in the outside bath; a red Italian contraption from the '70s I bought off Craigslist. Warm water trickled into it from a loose tube hooked up to shower. It was infused with Epsom salt, sea salt, ginger, tourmaline, magnetite, and gunpowder. I'd been bathing in this stuff regularly, thinking it would help me because I slept next to the enemy and her towering pile of clothes and the electrical circuit breaker was only inches away from my head and I had just been diagnosed with high-functioning autism by a psychiatrist in Albuquerque. I swallowed down the last of the mushrooms Sophia of the cottonwood tree had given me. My girlfriend's child must've been with her dad. My girlfriend was wherever.

I knew how I'd gotten there. Through a series of other bad choices in partners, the last one being an emotionally avoidant social justice photographer who worked in war zones, I had come to believe that because I was privileged, my value and sense of self-worth were based solely on my ability to help others. This wound was in play from the moment we hooked up. Two weeks later, I hosted a fundraiser so she could pay her rent—an agreement from which the baby daddy had shifted that had to do with child support. It was a cartoonish act of heroism meant to be a gesture of courtship. Her dad was very rich and anything she wanted from Amazon always showed up on the doorstep, yet she always said she was broke.

I had a thing for tattooed punk girls. Maybe because I'm from Santa Barbara, I didn't know that misspelled tattoos are always a red flag. (I'd say what the word was, but honestly, I'm still too afraid of her.) I didn't know there were people in the world so cruel and horrible until I read about them on the internet years later, amid her scorched-earth attack, when I would find myself facing off with her in a courtroom after over a year of no contact, being falsely accused of robbing her house in order to paint me as "dangerous and violent" and manipulate the state into giving her a restraining order.

I'd stopped writing completely. We had acquired a second dog and I was transfixed by how she played with Spanky. I ruminated *if artists like Henry Darger and Yayoi Kusama can make an art career out of their obsessions, perhaps I can do the same with Spanky and the second dog— drawing them, filming them, writing haiku about their little ways. That could be a life.* I was officially a helper girlfriend, though she didn't like the word *girl*, or *woman*. She called my small room in the back of the house the "man cave." She didn't want me to go out of the house with my hair down. The kid, when angry, would scream, "You're just the babysitter!"

Amidst my slow death, the mushrooms came to save me. Mycelium seeks out death. An artist at MIT named

Jae Rhim Lee makes mushroom suits for the dead, actual bodysuits with spores injected into the fabric that eventually colonize the corpse. A death jacket was not an unfitting metaphor for the current state of my relationship.

They came on while I lay in the bath. The sunshine hit the ginger and gunpowder in the water, creating tiny black rainbows. I stared up at the dying cottonwood tree. Pixelated elves on a mission ran along the thin white skin, metallic in the sun. *How was it that I got to see this? Was this vision payback for all the trees I hugged as a child, annoying my parents on walks, insisting we stop so I could get out of the stroller to embrace them?*

"Us trees thrive on sound," the cottonwood said. "Some sounds we like more than others. We like the sounds of birds, and the laughter of children, and Willie Nelson on a transistor radio. Not so much the passing trucks. But the sound of a dying tree is the most exquisite sound of all."

I listened. I could hear the dry, hollow crackling of wood nearly turned to dust, the subtle echoing notes tinkling, tiny little winds crushing through fast-opening microscopic crevasses. Every little sound the dying tree made could not be replicated; it was its very own signature that no other tree could copy. A dying tree is a symphony heard by all the trees around it. Later, I read that when a tree dies, the cellular information is downloaded into the mycelium at its roots. In this way, the soul of the tree lives on.

I somehow knew this, that a dying tree exists as a transmission for all the other trees around it. *Don't move a dying tree until it stops singing. The Tibetan Book of the Dead* advises pretty much the same for human beings, as death has its stages and spiritual tasks, and it is through being present with the machinations of death's liminal zones that the soul is able to transcend.

IN THE BEGINNING, my ritual was always the same. I would wait till the house was quiet or empty, and then I would light a fire, eat the mushrooms, offer tobacco, and lie under my favorite wool blanket on the couch, waiting. I burned copal and flat cedar at intervals. During one of my first trips done in this way, I felt myself getting anxious and unfocused. I intuitively pulled up Nicolás Echevarría's documentary about María Sabina on YouTube, *Mujer Espíritu*, the version without English overdubbing. The Mazatec are keepers of one of the few living traditions in which mushrooms are used ceremonially. It made sense to me to pay attention to how they did things.

María Sabina was the great mushroom curandera of Huautla de Jiménez, Mexico. She was known for her sublime ceremonial chants, otherwise known as veladas. Curandera, a woman who uses folk remedies to heal.

The film's meandering soundtrack takes its time, with long, casual conversations among friends and relatives. There's the clucking of chickens, the shucking of corn, epic fiddle-playing that serves no purpose toward forwarding the plot whatsoever, and long sequences of María's chanting during ceremonies in which participants occasionally threw up. To this day, it's the most pleasing recording I've ever heard in psychedelic space.

"She was not a poet in any ordinary sense," editor

Jerome Rothenberg characterized her in his 2003 collection of her work, *María Sabina: Selections*. She "lived out her life in the Oaxacan mountain village of Huautla de Jiménez, yet her words, always sung or spoken, have carried far and wide." Rothenberg describes her, beautifully, as "seeking cures through language—with the help of Psilocybe mushrooms, said to be the source of language itself." He quotes Henry Munn, who said that María Sabina was a "genius [who] emerge[d] from the soil of the communal, religious-therapeutic folk poetry of a native Mexican campesino people" and the Mexican poet Homero Aridjis, who called her "the greatest visionary poet in twentieth century Latin America."

I will not mention R. Gordon Wasson just yet, nor the impact of Sabina's legacy. The name María Sabina is deserving of a pause before such complications are invoked. There is time for all of that. Right here and now, I'd like to pretend it was the wondrous sound of her name— *María Sabina,* the way it rolls off the tongue—that made her a saint among healers and many great Mazatec poets, not the doings of a colonizing mushroom thief in need of a persona upon which to anchor his discoveries. For just a moment, I will pretend I do not know that all of Mexico vilified her as a neo-Malinche figure, a betrayer of Mexican nationalism, the sole monster mother of a mongrel, mestizo, counter-culture generation. María Sabina, María Sabina, Santo, Santo, Santo, my saint. I say it out loud still, and proudly.

I needed her to be a saint at that time in my life. With copal, with the tobacco that she called San Pedro, San

Pablo, she, clock woman, woman of dew, book of language woman—from the beginning, she showed me how to do things properly. Her belonging is natural, yet still a problem, a kind of theft that I can't undo alone. They burned your house down, María. You called the mushrooms *the little children*. You said the mushrooms stopped working after the white people came. You grieved the loss of them, you as La Llorona, the one who never stops weeping over her children who are gone. If there's anything I can do to change this story, let it be so.

I throw down tobacco. I burn copal. I sing, "Santo Santo Santo, San Pedro, San Pablo," when I'm high.

WHAT I GLEANED from the documentary held me to a simple ceremonial structure to which I adhered for nearly two years. *Don't go running around outside. Offer tobacco. Burn copal. Focus on prayer and healing. Let the mushrooms themselves guide the ceremony.* I managed to do a ceremony about every two or three weeks. They were so helpful in balancing out my moods that even my enemy approved. I became a person who didn't need anything.

The mushrooms speak to me, but I don't hear words like you'd hear from another person talking. It's as if language arises in my own body, though it's nothing I'd come up with on my own. Sometimes I am aware of fully formed sentences. Other times, whole systems of knowledge present themselves, devoid of any coherent words at all.

The mushrooms told me addiction starts in the feet, for instance. *Your position in the collective has been injured.* An old sheepherder set my leg on the ground. I was a foal, newly born, and my front left leg resisted contact with the earth. He stroked it until I allowed my hoof to lightly touch down. The earth's subtle electricity flowed into the ley lines of my calf, up into my hips and my neck and shoulders, giving them relief from some long-held, useless question mark.

"You are alive now. There."

"Thank you, sir."

I became him, the old man with the cane. He was not a relative, but a stranger.

When I was a little girl, I used to play that I was an old man with a cane, wandering through the town with a white dog. The image was very specific, with no variation. At that time in my life, I doodled crosses with hearts and stars in a very particular way. As an adult, while looking for the perfect cross to draw on the top of my hands with henna before a performance, I came upon that exact design. It was the veve for Papa Legba, the Haitian Loa who guards the crossroads. He takes the form of an old man with a cane and is often accompanied by a white dog.

Papa Legba, the one who opens the roads.

The mushrooms said, "Papa who? You just want to take the shape of this old man because he is slightly crippled."

"But I *am* kind of crippled."

"Get into that loop as long as you like. But really?"

"Okay, I'm not crippled. I'm just a little bit sick."

"Come as you are. But you're not sick, just saying."

"But what am I supposed to do in a healing ceremony if I'm not sick?"

I'm now living in the mushroom's wordless answer to this question, continually.

I learned how to literally suck the sickness out of my body and spit it out. I was given poses—mouth wide open, tongue out, eyes rolled all the way up into the skull. This is how one's own skull becomes that of an ancestor, ready for purification. Mushrooms showed me the resentments to which I was clinging and helped me to let them go. Sometimes I couldn't let them go and I stewed in rage and self-loathing, observing its contours with equanimity, knowing these hard emotions are a thing shared by all people. Exploring these realms of discomfort and psychic pain, I built a storehouse of compassion for myself and all of us pitiful human beings.

There were times when I landed in a gray in-between, kin to a world of cheap plastic figurines and urban street grease, where random fractal gargoyles of childhood television shows visited only to transmit the essence of mediocrity itself into my tender consciousness. This never scared me. I figured such dislocation was one of three things: a psychic detox, bad digestion, or perhaps I really *was* that two-dimensional and mediocre, and I had just succeeded at being in denial. Whatever situations arose, I approached them with a strong work ethic that was often notably absent in my real life.

Unwanted images and language forms—usually pop culture detritus, unwritten tweets, random shapes, and creepy critters—always dissipated after I gave them proper acknowledgment, offered some tobacco, and calmly set my attention elsewhere. I attribute the ability to do this to dosage. I always did roughly three grams. With this dosage, a sense of ego still remains. You can steer your own ship. Over seven or eight grams, you might become the actual ship. A very high-dose mushroom trip comes with its own teachings. I'm not uncurious, but thus far, the mushrooms have not guided me to ingest a dose higher than seven grams.

In his essay, "The Mushrooms of Language," Henry Munn explains that in the Mazatec worldview, it is important that a practitioner maintain "an ethical relationship with the real." I have taken this as mantra to live by. It's one that is likely dose-specific. Munn claims the Mazatec did not experience many hallucinations at all during ceremony, that their experiences were mostly somatic and linguistic. That is how it was for me, back when I kept it simple.

"The little children are to be eaten in pairs," María Sabina said. "They are holy and a sacrament. Don't do them in the daytime, they make you crazy. Only do them at night."

Okay, sometimes I did them in the daytime, but I tried to do them only at night. Staying close to this protocol served me well in the early days. It kept me humble.

3

THE WALK

WE COMMENCED WITH the evening's event by picking vermiculite off the slightly bruised fruits. Clement had just arrived from San Francisco. They are an old friend and creator of an animated stop-motion video about inter-dimensional deer who weigh the souls of humans who have died, while a panel of mushrooms gathers to discuss taking over the earth. My friend Brannigan was here after many months of deep ayahuasca ceremony in New York City. She and I shared a desire for the mushrooms to eventually show us the ceremonial structure that best suited their medicine, but we aren't indigenous people, so it was presumptuous to think that such a structure would look anything like a traditional peyote or ayahuasca ceremony. Our ancestors, who came before us, long ago, sat with the same open-hearted desire to do the right thing and were given directions. The old ways share more similarities than differences, yet I personally had no shame in being allied with the tribe of stoners that crowd the Erowid experience vaults with tales of jumping into swimming pools with boots on, making bras out of luncheon meat, or reaching an epiphany while watching *Broad City*. While high on something as fantastic as a mushroom, is anything really secular?

I made a point of taking a lower dose, but they came on even stronger than what I was used to, something about needing to heal from the relationship I had just ended. I prepared for my usual descent into somatic landscapes of psychodrama and body pain. Brannigan came in from outside, a beautiful shawl wrapped around her shoulders.

"It's incredible out there," Brannigan said. She'd been around the block in that huipil, her feathers in a box and her holy underground connections. We knew each other because I saw her picture on a friend's Facebook page. Taken by her beauty, I invited her over. She'd now been visiting and staying in the guestroom on and off for a couple years.

I got it together enough to step out in my pajamas and look at the stars. I stood on a spot where the rocks recede and it's just a flat expanse of soft, white clay. If you stand there looking southward, two hills slope into an arroyo right in the center of your sightline, and it's very vaginal for miles till it drops off into nothing. My legs filled with blood and lightness. Strung tight and tuned between the dirts and the stars, my body slammed back into my body. All the loops having to do with my ex disappeared.

Clem suggested we walk and visit each of the directions on the land. I agreed that it was a very good idea. Brannigan wanted to stay inside by the fire—maybe I was getting on her nerves. Our friendship was a contract I signed but never read; whatever the hidden agreements, when Brannigan says to go outside because it's amazing, you go.

I went in my bedroom to get dressed. I put on my camel hair Pendleton coat and my Stetson fedora hat.

I tied a long, narrow, red silk scarf around my neck and slipped on the silver-toed men's cowboy boots I'd bought off eBay, which are brown, pointy, and elaborate in their stitching. I put on my three rings: a hierarchical family of silver led by a bear ring with two peridot jewels set above its eyes. My oversize brass Lubbock belt buckle hung low and heavy on my waist.

Some people introduce themselves to nature through song and words and you'd think this would be my way, but no—it turns out the only time I ever care about fashion is when I am on mushrooms. What I wear becomes very important. The mushrooms seem to like it when you show up in an exaggerated, cartoonish shape. In this way I become the protagonist, joined with all the other weirdo protagonists in the zillion narratives of wonder and danger, un-gendered and without individual history. Just another dude under the stars.

I grabbed my bird wing and a jug of Bugler tobacco. Clem and I began walking up the hill on the north side of the house. Two dudes we were, now under stars. Our boots sunk into spongey dirt covered with stones the size of paws. White quartz and rocks of green and red were occasionally collected into small piles by Airbnb guests who decided against bringing them back on the plane. Side by side, I felt our sameness of spirit offset, charged by the dissonance of our shapes. My cheesy, dated, Hunter Thompson-esque aesthetic of excess moved alongside Clem's economical, Oliver-Twist-Industrial-Age newspaper boy. In their tweed cap and buttoned-up shirt, Clem was old-world knowledge to my quack Texan medicine man, and together we formed an atonal duo that brought to mind the characters in *Don Quixote*, the fat, short one and the tall, thin one. David Foster Wallace said he stole those guys from *Don Quixote* and inserted them into his novel *Infinite Jest*, so timeless and imperturbable they are upon this earth as an engine of truth-telling. A perverted take on the sacred twin theme, certain awkward arrangements have made the spirits crack up laughing since the beginning of time and we were that thing of two walking around.

"I'm really happy right now. I can't remember when I've felt this happy. This is incredible. Wow," Clem said.

I felt the same way, even though nothing hugely dramatic was happening. We stood up at the circle of stones, the highest point on the land where you can see the horizon in all directions, the glow of lights from Santa Fe in the north and Rio Rancho in the south. Homestead lights sparkled in the nearby hills. Lights from cars moved in snaky ways down dirt roads, as if floating in air before blinking into nothingness. For so many years, these lights fed into my fears of UFOs and unexplainable orbs, until over time I figured out they were just car lights on a distant hillside.

Over twenty-five years ago, I sat in this place for weeks, waiting for the cement contractors. My ancient cell phone rested next to me, the size of a concrete block. Back then, every call cost a fortune, and there was no internet. I explained all this to Clem, who was taking everything in.

"Throw some tobacco on that rock, okay?" I said.

"There?"

"Yeah, just put some tobacco on it."

"Like that?"

"Yes, perfect. Maybe we should go to the bus. I don't know."

Clem had been working in a scrapyard-salvaged, anti-hippie, minimalist-aesthetic, masochistic-writer bus for days, working on an outline for their lemur project. This 1950s school bus had been full of rat droppings when I bought it. I had it towed out to the property on a flat bed and cleaned it out myself, digging through the shit with a mask on. Inside, I'd found a pair of high heels, some vodka bottles, a few *Playboy* magazines, a stone pipe, baby pictures, and a pair of H&H riding boots—detritus of a life destroyed by substances, namely alcohol. I cleaned the death out of that bus, the tragic wrong-thinking of a fringe generational demographic. I turned it Donald Judd, aesthetically, and installed a wood stove and a futon bed.

The view out of the windows to the Ortiz mountains is sublime. Everyone who comes to visit loves working there. Nothing like a clear, clean container in a wide-open space to organize your thoughts.

"I'll go wherever," Clem said.

"You've kind of taken care of the bus, though, with all the work you've done there. We should go over to the east. There's this thing there. This thing that's —it's the reason I bought this land. Kip called it the amphitheater. He said, 'You have to see this place because there's an amphitheater on it.' You okay to go?"

"Sure. I'll follow you wherever you take me. I'm just so happy right now."

Clem was visibly bubbling over with joy. I wondered whether I would have recognized how rare a time we were having if I were alone. I saw that Clem had stepped into a real clearing, and I was in it with them. It was a space defined by what had been removed from it, those things being our useless thoughts. Trees, our feet in the dirt, the stars above us...it all existed in a soup of resonance stripped of the human language that surrounds such things, hence, everything was simply way more itself.

It's amazing, all the crap you can lay on a juniper tree at night—everything from *Isn't that juniper tree pretty* to *That juniper tree is giving me allergies. That juniper tree is a crystal hieroglyphic. That juniper tree is Lisa Bonet. That juniper tree is next to another, smaller juniper tree.* All that was gone now.

"Hello," one of us said.

Hello is the happiest word in the English language.

Our walk to the east is remembered more as a teleportation. We arrived at the amphitheater. A precarious descent down a cliff situated us in a sandy area where water tends to pool during heavy storms. I've taken mud baths there. I told Clem about the time I greeted the gravel delivery guy in my underwear, covered in mud, and he called me for weeks after, offering me deals on truckloads. The whole area is held in and contained by clay rock formations that have a distinctively fleshy way about them, compared to other rocks that are around. I mean, yes, I was seeing babies and old ones in the rocks, but it had been that way for a long time, even when visiting the place in a sober state.

This time, I noticed something new. I saw that the area was sunken deep enough into the earth that it was the only place around where you couldn't see the horizon in any direction.

"This place disappears the horizon!" I said. "That's why it's so amazing! It becomes anywhere, like fiction! I want to know what can happen here. What am I supposed to do? What are the customs of this place?"

Clem was more pragmatic, seeing the amphitheater as a possible place to film the live action sequences in their lemur film. We continued down the arroyo through a barbed wire fence that Clem had to navigate carefully, being that real lines of barbed wire were indecipherable from the hallucinated ones, giving them the sensation that they were walking through the fence miraculously.

Now, on land that wasn't my property, I noticed a slight change in the texture of things towards increased softness, humor, and delightfulness. I saw ownership of land as a web of thought forms that affect the land vibrationally. On *not my land*, the stars all had red lines connecting them to each other, creating a complex geometrical web. Real stars birthed phantom stars that fell out of them like delicate fireworks. Clem and I were seeing the same thing in the distance, the way the phantom stars dropped down into distances and into specific trees as if blessing them, as if saying, *I'm touching you, I'm tagging you and you are part of us now, this spectacular tangle.*

"Is that hill in the direction of the house?" Clem said, pointing back the other way.

"Oh. Yes," I said. "That's the arrogant, slightly narcissistic promontory that thinks it's all that. It's where we stand with our coffee looking out. It's where Elaine Amora buried her cat. I mean, I shouldn't talk that way about that hill, but it's just kind of that way."

Up on that hill looking out, suddenly we *were*. We watched the stars with the lines connecting them to each other, the stars that fell out of the stars and the dance they did around the trees and all the other things seen and unseen. I named the animals that I knew lived in this place—rabbits, mice, snakes, rats, bobcats, transient chipmunks, the occasional deer—feeling that the words naming those things accelerated the intelligence of the engine that was the web of stars. I told the story about when my dad got drunk and threw lettuce all around outside the house for the rabbits and the lettuce was gone in a day.

"It's not just over there," Clem said, nodding to where the stars were being the most flashiest.

"I know. But I don't need to think about that right now. I am going to just think that it's over there. Do you really think those lines are touching us, too?"

"It's all around us right now. You know that, right?"

"I know," I said. We were quiet for a very long time after that.

This experience became known as "The Walk." Every psychedelic writer claims their moment. Terence McKenna has his UFO in La Chorrera. Clem and I have "The Walk," where we as the archetypal, atonal, comedic duo, walked around in the night, understanding what it meant to be in "right relationship." It was really that simple. It wasn't an epiphany. Epiphanies are narratives building up into an ecstasy of vertical structure, a kind of lift-off into a realm of interconnectivity with other similar vertical structures built by human brains that may or may not be in present time. Our walk was lateral, a meandering. I know it has something to do with what makes music beautiful, in the way music stretches out time and takes you right alongside it until patterns conjure up a tangible relationship with origins. When people say *you either have it or you don't*, The Walk's got something to do with the "it" part. It's the space of becoming before a shape has been taken, crystalized, and then it's all over.

4

MUSHROOMS REPRODUCE asexually through the release of microscopic spores. They travel in the air and on the backs of birds and beasts. They can lodge in the straw hat of a farmer or the T-shirt of a tourist boarding a plane. It is said mushroom spores exist in space. They are programed to reach for the farthest yonder. They want to be everywhere. The largest living thing on earth is a honey fungus in Oregon whose mycelial network reaches almost two and a half miles. Other kinds of mushrooms mitigate bee colony collapse, break down hydrocarbons in oil spills and filter E. coli out of water. A speaker from the Radical Mycologists, a punk/anarchist collective on a mission to restore balance on earth through mushrooms, have said that "researchers have only touched the surface of what they can do."

In terms of hitching a ride to yonder, the mushrooms often employ mobility-obsessed humans, but landing on a straw hat or a T-shirt can be labor-intensive. Human bodies are unclean. It's much more fruitful for the spores to embed themselves in our minds. Through culture and human relationships, the mushrooms get us to do their bidding. As ethnobotanist Kathleen Harrison put it in the journal *MAPS*: "Be careful, I must warn you, watch your step! The plants and fungi have been known to hijack humans! Many of us! Of course, those who've been hijacked have been pretty darn happy about it, so there's that. But so many people have turned towards plants, towards growing things, from what they thought was their career, it's laughable."

It has been said that ancient theater emerged from the practice of entheogen use. I don't doubt that. The mushrooms weave themselves through our souls, employing the archetypal stories that lay dormant in our psyches. They were Terence McKenna's *Close Encounters of the Third Kind* and, Timothy Leary's *Last Temptation of Christ*; they are my *When Harry Met Sally*. The narrative arc of my mushroom journey is a romantic comedy—the disastrous first meeting resulting in the protagonist regarding the love interest (the mushrooms) as an uncouth and unwelcome invader. Through a series of conflicts that tear down the protagonist's ego structure, she becomes humble enough to admit she needs the love interest. The love interest performs many heroic acts with little success, then after one final climactic ordeal in which both parties nearly lose everything, the protagonist, me, realizes this wild monkey show was true love all along.

AFTER MY FIRST mushroom experience at age fifteen—beautiful, but linked forever with expulsion from my youth outreach program—I waited until I was in my mid-twenties and living in New Mexico to do them for the second time. I had befriended a couple at an art gallery reception. She was grieving a recent abortion, and he was having a hard time finding a job and an apartment. I didn't know them very well, but their struggles created an intimacy between us that otherwise would not have been there. In agreeing to take the mushrooms he brought to my house, I was indicating symbolically that we were friends and I trusted them. Many of us arrive to psychedelics through this social contract.

I wandered off by myself down the arroyo for most of the trip and found a rattlesnake skin lodged between two boulders. Trees and plants revealed their interdependence to me. Patches of various types of grasses said, *Hey, this is where we hang out, next to those guys over there, who you don't know the names of. Insects and birds move in between the space of us. Coyotes move our seeds around. We enjoy each other's company quite a lot, talk all day, send thank you notes. It's a very smart situation.*

My body felt like what a body is for. I recall making a mental note that this was a better way to be in the world and I must not forget to come back to mushroom-land more often.

This trip cemented a belief I still carry—that a mushroom trip can accelerate the karma that exists between people. In the days following, I became less able to attend to my friendship with the couple. Maybe he had hoped for something sexual between us, which was fine, but their troubles were not mine to fix. I clumsily backed away. I placed this trip and my promise to return in a compartment in my psyche, that special place you put that very important object you don't want to lose but secretly totally want to lose, because you don't know how to deal with it.

The third mushroom trip was three years later. I took them with a girlfriend and walked down the same arroyo. The rocks told me the jacket I bought at the mall with the fake NASCAR patches was offensive to all of nature. While this was good advice, it was not a teaching that left me hijacked. Not even close.

Psychedelic bliss without a meaning and a context I could use in the real world left me confused. Experiencing something so powerful in the privacy of my own psyche felt lonely. I needed much more than a few friends willing to take drugs with me. If I was to truly to become hijacked, the mushrooms would need to send an ambassador.

LIKE THE B+ spores that would seed my mushroom harvests, Sevine came from the internet, from a circle of women writers with blogs, all of us forming a telepathic coven for a magical yet unsustainable window of time. It was 2010, before it became dangerous to write about anything personal online. We dreamed of raccoons and owls together, fractured and rebuilt ourselves in harmony under the various moons and transits of Venus. It was nothing less than group telepathy, and it was a kind of love.

Other than a few emails cementing our plans, Sevine and I had previously only communicated in the comments section of our blogs. We hadn't even spoken on the phone. Waiting for her at the airport, I was gripped with a fear of the unknown, not unlike how it feels when the mushrooms are about to come on. The revolving door spat her out, and on first sight—in her high heels and tight shorts, her wild, curly hair, her gigantic reading glasses and particular way of walking, as if possessed by a mermaid—I was scared. Eight years later, Sevine confessed she was scared, too.

Her first night in my house, she dreamed about plutonium. In an effort to be a good host, I arranged a thematic day trip to Los Alamos, home of the atomic bomb. At the nuclear museum, we saw replicas of Fat Man and Little Boy, the bombs that detonated over Hiroshima and Nagasaki. We picked up a heavy square object that was meant to indicate the weight of plutonium.

Back in the car, I turned on the radio. The voice on the news announced that a tsunami had disabled the emergency generators at the Fukushima Daiichi Nuclear Power Plant. Massive amounts of nuclear material were being released into the water and air. On impulse, we drove for three hours to Truth or Consequences, only to get out of the car, smell the air, and drive home as the legendary Roots music show, *Home of Happy Feet*, threw down the song-lines of our shared country. We circled around in our conversations on roads and under the stars, evoking an alchemy of salts, dirt, tourmalines, meats, silvers and golds, wolves, ravens, bats, patrons and curators, and silk roads. We weaved ourselves into a relationship with the principal essence of things. Especially then, we believed in showing up to a situation with our bodies, in the street, in public, to make change—but what do you do in a situation like Fukushima? What are we supposed to *do* when we *see*?

Sevine asked if I knew where to get some mushrooms. I didn't, but I managed to find a source through someone from Alcoholics Anonymous. I bought them in a parking lot, and we ate them in a hot spring in Las Vegas, NM. What happened there is Sevine's story to tell, as it informed years of her creative work to come.

Divination and prophecy, holy language—this is what the mushrooms are for, Sevine reminded me. When I finally arrived years later to Sophia and the cottonwood tree, I was able to ask for what I needed because I was no longer alone.

Sevine barfed at the Allsup's gas station on our way home from the springs. I watched her in the rearview mirror as she zig-zagged back to the car in her heels, the sunlight and wind mingling with her person in such a way that she became impossibly glamorous. It was times like this that I accepted that I'd always been and always would be the mushroom's employee.

When people ask me why I moved to New Mexico, I have a very specific answer. As a teenager in Santa Barbara, my friends and I played a Wall of Voodoo cassette tape whenever we drove around. The song, "Call of the West," conjured up images of cow skulls bleached white in dry sand, surrounded by empty beer bottles. This, an archetypal symbol of the earth's desertification, was what made me run to the high desert as soon as I got free.

My mother saw my choice to move here as a wayward one. *What on earth are you looking for in a place so dry and brown?* My mother remembers the giant dust storms, miles high, that engulfed her home of Lubbock, Texas in almost total darkness. The terror of it shaped her relationship with God. This and nearly drowning while being baptized in a lake were the reasons why she said she was an atheist. The Dust Bowl affected my father's family as well. Because of its impact on the economy during the Great Depression, his parents lost the family farm and had to buy it back, a trauma that forever crushed his trust in the reciprocity and abundance of the living world.

I've always been drawn to the desert, to places resembling the landscape where my mother left God behind.

Grazing animals that wander over wide swaths of territory prevent desertification by reseeding and fertilizing the soil. Ted Turner understands this. Bad farming practices are to be blamed for the unprecedented ecological disaster of the Dust Bowl, but what is rarely mentioned is the slaughter of the buffalo—sixty million before first contact by settlers, brought down to under a hundred by the end of the nineteenth century. Eventually, the surface of the earth itself rose up and blew across the land, the closest thing to a true curse that could ever be imagined.

Until then, no people on the face of the earth had failed so extravagantly as these farmers did, these settlers who landed in the West, possessed by the sinister promise of Manifest Destiny. They failed at talking to their neighbors, in asking them what to do and what was done before, which may be the first skill of farming: listening. My parents grew up at ground zero of the Dust Bowl. It's telling that my father, who left the bank-owned farm to become a family doctor in Santa Barbara, married my mother, who grew up with a garden in the backyard that provided enough food to feed not just themselves, but the neighbors and the "gypsies," as my mother called them, referring to the caravans of still-tribal Romani peoples that passed through.

"We barely noticed the Depression," my mother said. "We always had food."

For a town that has more churches per capita than any other place in the United States, Lubbock, Texas also has an inordinate number of holy drunkards. These are my people. I am a holy drunkard, even as I am undrunk over time and the church I have been invited into by the grace of the creator has a buffalo skull set atop the altar. I'm one-eighth Cherokee, but this doesn't make me not a white person.

The wounds of history, genocide, colonization, ecological devastation, and violence don't heal on their own. Actions and intentions are needed to make that happen. When praying, I often say that I am a "pitiful human being." And then I ask for help.

I MET KIP DAVIDSON when I was looking for land. At the time, my home was an aquamarine 1968 Ford truck parked in the lot of Ojo Caliente Mineral Springs. What is now an expensive spa was then a series of small structures built over pools of iron, soda, and lithium water. It cost six dollars for a soak and a towel wrap back then. The explorer Álvar Núñez Cabeza de Vaca gave the ancient indigenous healing site, Ojo Caliente, its contemporary name. He was a Spanish survivor of the Narváez expedition who lived as a trader and faith healer among the people, before eventually reconnecting nearly ten years later with Spanish Colonial forces in Mexico in 1536. In a film made in the '80s, based on his journals, he is portrayed as a primitive holy man, capable of raising an indigenous woman from the dead. The director of this film, Nicolás Echevarría, also made the documentary about María Sabina that I listened to every time I tripped in the early days. Both are films about anomalous saintly figures who emerged at historic crossroads during genocidal colonization; unlikely, even impossible human beings, one who ingested mushrooms, the other peyote, who in retrospect could be seen as having been birthed by the plants and fungi themselves to act upon a great emergency.

KIP RAN THE rock shop in the hotel. We became close friends and sometimes shared a room at the Motel 6 in Española when we were too tired to drive all the way back to Santa Fe. We spent countless evenings in the hotel lobby, watching *Star Trek* on TV. It was the early 1990s and an impressive number of New Age crazies passed through the hot springs. They came for the rumored spiritual power of the land, with their crystals and linen robes, offering their services on pastel-colored xeroxed fliers: occupation aura clearing, past life regression, Reiki. I met "walk-ins"—people who believed the person born into the body they inhabited was now historically dead and they were in fact from the Pleiades.

Kip helped me navigate these force fields of fraudulence, mental illness, cultural appropriation, and psychic theft. "If someone says they are a thing, act like you believe them," he said. "It's the kind thing to do."

Kip threw off an aura of dew, sage, piney wood rot, and sulfur from the baths. He grew up in the jungle in Mexico, a child of white intellectual expats. Six-feet tall and Scottish, he carried the spirit of Cabeza de Vaca. He, too, was a trader and healer. Women from the nearby pueblos came to him for "doctorings." Kip said they came to him because they couldn't speak their truths openly to the medicine men at the pueblos because of small community gossip. On days when I sat in the store with him, chatting, many of these women stopped by to give him updates on how they were doing.

We watched the New Agers become cranky and stressed-out as opportunities didn't open up to them as expected. They blamed it on indigenous curses, vortexes, gray aliens, and the dark forces of others. After failing to find what they were looking for, they would leave.

Meanwhile, the spirit they were seeking in the land was everywhere. This was a geography in which nineteen active pueblos held seasonal dances. Persian Sufis on LSD spun in sacred architectural structures up in Abiquiu. Georgia O'Keeffe's ashes were scattered atop the Pedernal, near the pilgrimage routes of the Penitentes, who walk miles carrying crosses and flogging themselves bloody. Lisa Law and the original Magic Bus hippies held their annual baseball game against the Pueblo Natives, a showdown between LSD and alcohol, basically.

Indigenous people, Latinos, old-school Anglos around here—they all have old ways. There's protocol to observe when it comes to crossing lines into all of these worlds. Firstly, you must be invited.

"I THINK I found you some land," Kip said to me in his shop. "It has an amphitheater on it."

I reluctantly agreed to go visit the plot of land. It looked just like any other arroyo I'd seen in New Mexico, merely a shallow dip that cut into the rocks, leaving a patch of dry sand. Who was Kip fooling?

"The sound is different here. It bounces off all these rocks," he said.

"Oh, look, there's a lizard," I said, pointing to the top of a stone covered in what looked like prehistoric moss.

"That's a sign," he said. "It means dreaming."

Don't try to sell me land with that New Age lizard bull-shit, I wanted to say. I'd read the feng shui books; there were no water features anywhere. I'd hoped for a tiny acequia like you'd find up in Tesuque or a river like what was out east towards Glorieta. One was too expensive, the other too far a drive. But this place was just really basic.

It was the second plot of land I looked at. I signed papers to purchase it the following day.

Kip and I lost touch completely when I got into one of my two-year-long relationships. Certain girlfriends are the type that won't let you keep a Kip. Apparently, Kip had girlfriends that wouldn't let him keep a Bett.

One afternoon, I decided to pay a visit to his rock shop. A fire had leveled the spa structures at Ojo Caliente, so he'd moved to a building down the road. When I asked the man behind the counter about Kip, he informed me that he had died a year before of cancer.

"He really wanted to lose some weight because he was single, and then he did, and he was feeling very handsome, and then he found out he was dying. We sprung him from the hospital illegally and drove him around for days. We shared his visions. It was like a walkabout, but on wheels, I guess. We saw all the medicine he kept and fed throughout his life, all of us who went with him. One day, this rat the size of a VW Bug ran down the hallway of the motel room where we were staying and I said, 'Kip, did you see that giant fucking rat that just ran down the hall?!' and he said, 'Yes, that's one of the beings I keep from the African ways.' We saw a lot. It was like that for days. We drove and drove, seeing things part of his world. We brought him back at the end and he passed very quickly. He didn't suffer."

He pointed to an urn in a glass case that was surrounded by crystals.

"Kip?"

"Yes."

5

IT'S COMMON FOR a person to do mushrooms many times before having what the literature calls "the God Trip." For some people, it never happens. I kept thinking it was happening every time I took them until it actually happened and it was clear that this one, not any of the previous trips, was indeed my first God Trip.

It's logical to attribute the God Trip to taking a higher dosage, but this wasn't the case at all. I'd done some mushrooms the day before with my friend Jen, and the following morning I thought I'd eat what was left in the bag—less than two grams—and clean the house, maybe. (Yes, that's the kind of person I am.)

During our trip together the day before, Jen had given me a very long, deep, painful massage using Rolfing techniques. I didn't even know what body part she was touching. I saw fractal monkeys swinging and hopping along nervine tendrils while I endured excruciating pain. *It's only a sensation*, I chanted to myself.

"I worked on you really hard," she said. "You may want to be aware that your body will be integrating the experience."

No shit, Jen. Less than two grams on a Tuesday morning

and within an hour—*holy, holy, holy.* Allen Ginsberg must have gleaned his poem, "Howl," from a God Trip when he wrote:

> *Holy! Holy! Holy! Holy! Holy! Holy! Holy!*
> *Holy! Holy! Holy! Holy! Holy! Holy! Holy!*
> *Holy!*
> *The world is holy! The soul is holy! The skin is*
> *holy! The nose is holy! The tongue and cock*
> *and hand and asshole holy!*
> *Everything is holy! everybody's holy! everywhere*
> *is holy! everyday is in eternity! Everyman's*
> *an angel!*
> *The bum's as holy as the seraphim! the madman*
> *is holy as you my soul are holy!*

It was a trip marked by overwhelming ecstasy, regarding the interconnectivity of all things. Hugely specific, down to being able to sense the nutrition in the weeds growing outside the house, the clothes the neighbors were wearing in their bedrooms and kitchens, what they were cooking, and how exactly these neighbors held whatever amount of kindness they had in their hearts. Biological, social, and mechanical networks revealed themselves and made sense; everything adding up to their being just enough on Earth to keep us alive spiritually and physically, if only we could step out of the illusion of capitalist commerce enough to see how it all worked.

This intellectual epiphany was coupled with the feeling that every single cell in my body was fully alive. It was as if I had been half-dead previously and was all at once given the body of an athlete. Emotions that usually revealed themselves in me with an assured familiarity—love and joy, for instance—now took on layered and subtle dimensions, as if new notes had been invented on a musical scale. But this was emotion, not sound. I played these next-level emotions like an instrument, wielding a measure of control between the very intense and the fine and delicate. PhD-level intricacy permeated all things.

My gratitude was overwhelming. All I could do was cry and just say thank you over and over. That a mushroom could do this was a miracle.

"Everyone deserves this!" I said out loud through tears. My arms were open and my palms were up, as if receiving rain. "Everyone should know what this feels like. How is this possible? There are so many people who need this. Why me? I'm just a chick at home in the wrong house with the wrong girlfriend on a Tuesday in the daytime and I get to have this?"

I was just a beginner. I still am. One never really knows—oh, but no, you do know, deep down—how far you will go.

6

I BRING YOU the case of Monica Cromhout from Cape Town, South Africa, a woman who avoided all drugs and alcohol until her sixties, when an ayahuasca ceremony changed her life. On her sixty-fourth birthday party, which was attended by three hundred people, a friend gave her a gift of psilocybin mushrooms. She took them alone in her garden and received a vision.

"Your home must become a school for the mushrooms," the fungi said. "You don't need to know anything; all you need to do is open the door and hold it open."

Cromhout believed every message the mushrooms gave her. The mushrooms told her that mixing them with marijuana was potentially deadly; she's been evangelical about this essentially hogwash assertion. She had a background in counseling with a group called Life Line, which gave her a framework for attracting followers quickly. Within months, she was hosting ceremonies in her home every Saturday night. Participants ingested two- to five-gram doses, which made for a lively atmosphere when mixed with the music, despite her request that people be silent.

One night in 2014, a seventy-seven-year-old professor—there to study the spiritual and medical benefits of the mushrooms—became quite agitated. He crawled across the floor, physically shoved himself out of the house, and wandered three blocks away, directly to a police station. Disoriented, he asked the police to take him back to get his things.

There was a knock on the door and Cromhout greeted two policemen. She was relieved they had found the missing professor and told them to come inside, not knowing this invitation gave them a legal right to search her entire house. Six more armed officers came out of the shadows and joined the search, interrupting the ceremony, where people were splayed all over the floor in various states of consciousness.

Since the supply of psilocybin mushrooms was becoming scarce in South Africa due to multiple arrests of growers, Cromhout used all the money she received for her ceremonies to stock up on her supply. She kept them in airtight containers in a small freezer in her bedroom. The police seized them and took them back to the station. At a loss for how to weigh them, they bought a small scale at a local grocery store and brought it back to the jail, where the mushrooms weighed in at two kilograms, or nearly four and a half pounds.

"I didn't realize I had been able to accumulate such a large amount," she later said.

The charges weren't just for possession, but mass distribution due to the exchange of money. At the time of this writing, she faces fifteen years in jail, but her trial has been delayed as advocates worldwide have come forth in her defense. Her case has brought attention to the laws regarding psilocybin mushrooms in South Africa, which I suppose is a good thing, but I see this story as an unfortunate example of psychedelic grandiosity gone awry. Cromhout could have had small ceremonies with friends who brought their own mushrooms, where she wasn't in the role of *expert*, just another tripper among trippers. Her story reminded me of the New Age travelers who passed through the hot springs, who, like in the Rumi poem, want to "show you something," but never just for free.

If I did every single thing the mushrooms told me to do, I'd be banned from Twitter, subsist only on cactus fruits for months at a time, and be given a restraining order by the Sikh Community in Española. (The mushrooms told me I should dress in white and drown myself in animal blood, *Carrie*-style, during their solstice celebration to protest Akal Security, their funding source, who at the time was reportedly providing labor for ICE and armed guards at immigration prisons.)

I approach the voice of the mushrooms not as absolute truth, but as the linguistic result of a collaboration between my psyche and the fungal entity. *Hold on loosely, child, loosely.*

After being on lockdown for fifty years, a new spate of psychedelic philosophers and scientists are now rushing to exploit the mushroom. Michael Pollan's book, *How to Change Your Mind*, makes an argument for legal therapeutic use of psychedelics, but only under the supervision of a trained professional. Many argue that such compromises and deals with the devil are necessary in order to destigmatize psychedelics in the minds of the mainstream.

What's missing is a conversation on how women, indigenous people, old-school hippies, herbalists, and even teenagers have been using mushrooms forever—humbly, joyously, and quietly under threat of the law. *This is how it is done because this is how we've been doing it* is a prayer I often say before throwing tobacco down on the altar. By saying this, I connect myself to the ancestors who unapologetically claimed their right to a sovereign and unmediated relationship with a living thing that grows from the Earth. These are old ways and doings.

But situations such as Cromhout's drug bust add muscle to the Pollans of the world. Pollan advocates for the use of psilocybin in a clinical setting within an established Western psychopharmocological context. In an interview with Joe Rogan, he contrasts his approach with those who take them and go to the beach.

In his ideal protocol, the patient lies down in a pleasantly decorated room. A guide is with them, who has been trained to basically do nothing but watch them for hours, maybe make a suggestion here and there if they are having a hard time. The patients no doubt rise to the occasion and perform as expected, having psychological revelations and epiphanies appropriate to the set and setting. These revelations still occur in a box—one built on a colonized, Western medical/psychiatry model. The word *colonized* has become colonized and is an old rag of a word, but nothing is as old rag-like as a sterile box of a room being the only place in the world to legally get high on a mushroom.

Even Paul Stamets, who was also on Joe Rogan's show, derided taking mushrooms for "partying," then went on to talk about a group of men, all with PhDs, who came to his rented cabin to trip on mushrooms together. The revelations they had! I guess it's not a party if you're all white men with PhDs. But I'm pleased to say Stamets has softened his position on civilian use, and now advocates for decriminalization and cognitive freedom.

A 2017 Global Drug Survey that researched hundreds of thousands of people all over the world ranked psilocybin mushrooms as the least likely out of all drugs to land a person in the hospital. Proclamations as to what psilocybin mushrooms are for and who should take them and how are not-so-subtle mechanisms of social control. Scolding those who take psychedelics the "wrong" way only serves the self-proclaimed gatekeepers, who depend on people believing that they know more than them about such things in order to further their status in the old-school institutions that support their work.

Meanwhile, there are thousands of mushrooms sitting in the back of freezers in the U.S., wanting to go to the goddamn beach.

LUCKY 7

IN A CEREMONY before it all went down, the mushrooms warned me of days made of the substance of hauntings. Rain spat down diagonally, in between the rays of a dirty mustard sun. Even the weeds were leaning in the wrong direction to show me something. *Get out as fast as you can,* they said, but I didn't listen.

Truly, it came on like a tornado.

My ex broke up with me over the phone, moved out suddenly, and asked for $5000 in moving costs. She sent an eight-page letter accusing me of being abusive to every single one of my close friends and a few writerly colleagues, with my emails and text messages re-arranged like a William Burroughs cut-up. Character assassination in the midst of devastating heartbreak is a very special kind of hurt. Two of her exes before me were quick to offer support: *It's what she does.*

Her ex-wife was dating an herbalist who prescribed me Bach flower remedies for fear, knowing exactly what I was going through. There's one for a fear that goes upwards in white flight, and one for a fear going downwards in a black spiral. There is a flower for the fear I felt when the ex showed up to my house unannounced, with a box full of personal items: burnt cookies, a gift of leather pants bought at a thrift store, and a love letter scrawled in barely legible handwriting. I saw her through the screen door, then hid behind my house and called Beth—*She's on the front porch, please come over right away.*

Only a month earlier, when she and I were merely acquaintances, Beth saw the details of my very bad breakup unfold dramatically in a comments thread of a Facebook post written by one of the ex's flying monkey friends. My private texts were referenced out of context in a plea to bring attention to the queer community that I was an abusive person.

"This is why you should be grateful you're straight," Beth said to her studio assistant, who was also riveted to the computer screen. They were still reading when I popped up in the comments thread to defend myself, and the post was quickly taken down.

Beth noticed that I'd marked myself as "going" to a monthly queer dance night. She made a point of attending with the specific purpose of finding me. I was on the sidewalk outside the club, alone, when she spotted me and walked towards me quickly.

"Hey," she said, out of breath. "Are you okay?"

"No, I'm not. Not at all, actually," I said. "Thank you for asking."

8

"MY TATTOOS ARE GONE!" Beth screamed. She was hopping around near the narcissistic promontory, where Elaine Amora's cat was buried. Hunched over, a wild dexterity in her knees animated her whole body. We had recently watched the film *Lair of the White Worm*.

"I come from those people," she said. "The people who worshipped snakes in caves. It was an actual thing, you know."

Beth has a direct line to her own ancientness that renders her vulnerable to ethereal forces like ghosts, disturbed energy grids, and lost animals. We met the first time at our witch/artist friend Erica's studio. Beth dropped in and we landed instantly in a manic conversation with no boundaries. A fine art framer, Beth can see when a line is off by just a hair and her hungry eye extends to the banal when not in use. Apparently, I was wearing the wrong shoes— Converse sandals. *Bett's great, but those sandals... clearly, it's not meant to be.* The shoes were a consolation, being that she was in a relationship at the time.

"Do you see my tattoos?" Beth said, out on the narcissistic promontory that thinks it's all that.

"Yes, they're totally there."

"Wow! I can't see my tattoos at all! Seriously! They're gone!"

It had been half a lifetime since Beth had taken a psychedelic, and now she was high on mushrooms on the south side of my house. She believed she was being transported back to the last time she tripped, back to when she didn't have her full-sleeve tats, back to when she was a teenager on LSD and she was really good at it. She was the driver, the talker-downer, the one who did LSD on the job once, who did it not just on Tuesdays and Wednesdays, but on Christmas Day with her family. She was the one who regularly ate three, four, five hits just for the hell of it and never, ever had a bad trip. When she felt the liquid acid actually swoosh on her tongue—a big *oops*—she said, "It was just blue. Blue for a very long time."

One day, a policeman approached her and her friend in the park and began asking questions. She was tripping quite hard and was also carrying in her pocket a sheet she'd been gifted to give to friends, which was enough LSD to put her in jail for thirty years. Scared witless, she took it as a sign. After the cop sent them on their way, she and LSD parted with no hard feelings, and Beth took her place among the retired veterans who *did a lot of LSD when they were young*, who, when asked why they never do psychedelics anymore, rarely have an answer. And if they do have one, it's never logical.

I almost got arrested is a good answer.

I was just done, or *I learned all I needed to learn*, is not really an answer at all.

Many claim that taking LSD or psilocybin mushrooms

was the most profound experience in their life, one that they will carry with them forever. Nonsense. If it happened decades ago, it's just a memory. To keep the best memory "alive," it must be conjured, and in doing so, it is continually reinvented. As you mature, your memory of the event changes, depending on what you're trying to glean from it. Psychedelics can be very threatening to the ego. How is it even possible that the psyche wouldn't get totally squirrely about this kind of memory? Psychedelic experience is already elusive and hard to pin down. What is taken away intellectually, somatically, visually, is too much to retain the following morning, let alone decades later. What people are remembering as the most profound experience of their life has, through the mechanism of memory itself, become a complete fiction. It may have changed your life, but no, you don't remember what it was like.

The psychedelic does not exist in the past.

Beth picked up right where she left off, back in her space suit, ready to traverse the crevasses of rocks in the same way she explored abandoned subway tunnels in Rochester on LSD. She was wearing pretty much the same outfit—black Levi's, a black T-shirt, black boots, and a jean jacket. Her beautiful brains spilled out of her skull, which was loosely attached to her long, black, curly hair, these brains mixing with the outside so it was all a thing of her that she ran around in.

Unlike me, Beth takes delight in visuals with complete abandon when tripping. She doesn't overthink or manufacture problems while high. In the day-to-day, Beth is possessed of an anxious and depressive temperament.

Like her three tiny Chihuahuas, her energy body retains its tightly-wound vitality through the maintenance of a certain level of hate. But on the mushrooms, I observed her strict adherence to an ethic of playfulness and love. This is her true self when not beset by the chemistry of her own, very neurodiverse, brain.

"Whoa, so happy," said the night, taking the words right out of Beth's mouth. She understood now how the LSD had permanently fine-tuned her perceptions so long ago.

"No junior varsity here," the mushrooms said approvingly. "Beth was made for this."

Back in the house, we sat by the fire. It was Beltane, and the custom is to burn nine woods. Beth, a wood-worker, brought aspen, walnut, pine, maple, ash, alder, and cherry, two short of nine. Each burned at its own pace and temperature as we talked until dawn.

"We're a mountain," she said.

"Yes, I see it too."

"People want to bring us stuff. Like, all their jewelry. They can't help it."

"I can totally feel that. We are a King and Queen mountain that people come and give all their belongings to. I have no idea what that means, but that's just what we are. Kind of weird, considering I normally don't like objects, but hey."

"I'm not used to being given things while doing nothing but being a mountain," Beth said. "I have a feeling that things are going to be very different, now that we are together."

"Okay, okay, okay, you have to listen. I think I know

who we are," I said. The Beltane fire was nearly out. It was almost dawn. "Like, to each other. We've been together a really long time. We've been male and female, men together, women together, all of it to the point we're so over it, over gender, we're like, 'please don't make me pick one again'. We've lived everywhere and that's why we're not that into traveling."

"I don't need to see anyplace else."

"Me neither. The thing is, one of us needed a break, just a little space. We made an agreement that in this life we wouldn't meet until we'd done some things on our own. But we would still be together. We would live in the same towns and be right around the corner from each other in case one of us got into trouble."

"And one of us did," Beth said.

"This feels very old, you watching to make sure nothing bad happens to me."

For many years, Beth's job site was right up the road from my house at an Apache sculptor's foundry. We probably passed each other in our cars all the time, ruminating on how lonely and horny we were, how there were no women to date in Santa Fe. We discovered later that we'd been in the same room during at least ten different concerts, went to the same bars, and attended the same parties in three different cities, places we remembered with unusual clarity, minus each other's presences. It must have taken work for us not to meet.

In the morning, after coffee, we decided to walk down the road to the foundry where Beth had worked for the artist.

"He told me that jackalopes were real and I believed him. I looked for them everywhere. I'd never been to the desert, what did I know?" Beth said as we passed the mail-boxes and turned up the dirt road to the sculpture garden. "That's it!" she said, pointing to a towering iron sculpture in an open field, set apart from the smaller works that lined the gravel paths.

The silhouette cut out of steel was unmistakably Beth. The indent in her hips where her belt rests was exact, as well as her wild hair. Her distinctly full breasts, of course. I recognized her right shoulder hunched up higher than the left, like she's eternally holding a small dog in the crook of her arm. The sculpture faced west, right towards the setting sun, right in the direction of my house less than a mile away.

"I've never been far."

"Thanks. I'm sorry you had to rescue me. I'll work on that."

9

A PUBLIC SERVICE ANNOUNCEMENT

❦ Never keep your drug dealer's number in your phone.

❦ Come up with a code word for your substance (mulch, cookies, T-shirts). When buying cannabis in New Mexico, do not use "green chile." Likewise, clever shroomy nicknames and amanita emojis will not do.

❦ If you haven't met your drug dealer in person yet, a simple *Can we meet for coffee?* via text message is sufficient to get the ball rolling. Do not get creative.

❦ With your phone turned off, in person, ask the dealer how they want you to communicate with them from here on out. Always avoid email.

❦ Do not give your dealer's name to your friends unless you have both agreed on a protocol. Do not give their name and number to strangers, ever.

❦ If you ask your dealer for a large amount because your friends want to have a party, and half of them bag out, and you show up with only half the cash, you deserve to be the unlucky victim in one of those scenes that happens in an abandoned dump site in *Breaking Bad*.

- Remember that every email and every Google search you've ever done still exists somewhere and is accessible. You may think, *What could the cops want with little old me?* This may be a right-sized thought now, but there's a future ahead of us that looks like a *Black Mirror* episode in which the carceral state will increasingly rely on digital algorithms to fill beds in its federal and private prisons. Whatever magic, mojo, or privilege you think you have that makes you exempt from this outcome will soon dissolve when we are all regarded as nothing but numbers and algorithms.

- The most publicly psychedelic person you know is actually the worst person to ask where to find mushrooms. We're not drug dealers.

- "700 lbs. of mushrooms seized by police in Berkeley, worth over one million in street value," read an Instagram post. The photograph was of Tupperware containers made into makeshift terrariums stacked one on top of another, full of heavy cakes on beds of perlite. The weight of the actual mushroom fruits was a negligible fraction of what was pictured. Nonetheless, whoever owned them, their life was now a nightmare.

- The Oklevueha Native American Church membership will not protect you from arrest and possible imprisonment. Also, invoking it potentially erodes the protections for which it was intended, namely the rights of indigenous people participating in the Peyote Church.

10

ABOUT A YEAR and a half into my solo exploration with psilocybin mushrooms, the supply ended. Word was the grower got spooked by the law, something about a black car parked outside a house for days. You'd think it would be easy to find mushrooms in New Mexico. I asked every weed smoker around, but no one knew a dealer who had them.

If I was going to continue with my ceremonies, I was going to have to grow them myself. It's not as hard as one would think. The PF Tek method, a technique made public in 1992 by Robert McPherson, aka Psylocybe Fanaticus, is a how-to manual on the easiest and cheapest way to make a psychoactive mushroom. Armed with a true autistic's faithfulness to her special interest, once I'd read through the PF Tek, there was no turning back.

Beth was extremely cautious about all things drug- and law-related, so it surprised me that she was completely supportive. Not having to engage with dealers was a plus. It helped that growing mushrooms in New Mexico is not *technically* illegal.

In *State of New Mexico vs. David Ray Pratt*, a court ruled that his growing mushrooms did not constitute "manufacturing" of the illegal substance psilocybin. The court document read:

> On June 6, 2002, police, on information obtained from a confidential informant, obtained and executed a search warrant on the Defendant's home. Throughout the house, they found glass mason jars containing psilocybin mushrooms at varying stages of maturity. Some of the jars had psilocybin spores growing on top of a rice cake mixture. The officers also found syringes filled with spores, which were allegedly used to inoculate the rice cake mixture. In the kitchen, the officers found a white Styrofoam cooler containing a "bubbling apparatus," which was apparently used by the Defendant as a humidifier for growing the psilocybin mushrooms. The machine was "turned on and pumping" when the officers found it. The officers also found "recipes" with instructions on growing psilocybin mushrooms. A message was written on the cooler stating "Remember to be patient! Pinning might take a few weeks."

The court cited a 1999 ruling that said growing marijuana did not constitute "manufacturing" under New Mexico law. *Manufacture* is defined as "the production, preparation, compounding, conversion or processing of a controlled substance or controlled substance analog by extraction from substances of natural origin or independently by means of chemical synthesis or by a combination of extraction and chemical synthesis and includes any packaging or repackaging of the substance or labeling or relabeling of its container."

But don't rent the U-Haul and speed off to New

Mexico just yet. Just because they're legal to grow does not mean they're legal to possess. Once dried, they are once again illegal, and while growing them is legal in the state, one is not exempt from federal law. What this all means on a pragmatic level, I do not personally want to find out. A good rule to abide by is to shut up about your hobby aside from a few close friends. The fact that you're reading this means I'm not growing mushrooms anymore, and yes, I'm sad about that.

I SHOPPED FOR basic supplies: large Tupperware containers, Ball jars, brown rice flour, and a big bag of vermiculite from a local nursery. I ordered mushroom spores from Spores101.com. Despite the fact they arrive in an unmarked box, spores are completely legal to purchase in most states.

The syringes were when it sank in. I was about to make an illicit substance—Schedule 1, in fact.

I ordered the sturdy B+ strain recommended for beginners. Researching the right strain to order from the spore company took me deep into the bowels of internet drug culture. I landed at Shroomery.com and Bluelight. org, where members debate the virtues and weaknesses of strains with names like Golden Teacher, Blue Meanie, Huautla, Pink Buffalo, and Penis Envy. I relied on this hive mind for most of my decisions, despite the GIFs people used as profile pics, which were often satanic or not-so-vaguely pornographic. People posted photos of colonizing jars and giant mature fruits like it was no big deal.

On these sites, I encountered "Swim," the anonymous

drug fiend. *Swim wants to know if Swim can take Piracetam with the mushrooms? Swim did Kratom two nights ago and also smoked some Kanna. Caught up on sleep. Swim is cleared out from that now with a juice fast, but is curious as to the interaction between Piracetam and psilocybin?*

When a member posted something genuinely stupid like, "My cakes are half-covered in what appears to be a pitch-black fuzz, can I just cut it off and use the good part?" bullies jumped in and ripped them apart. It was disturbing to see how many cheerleaders of my beloved sacrament appear to be fans of Alex Jones. Still, I gleaned some great advice from these forums. I read threads on everything from identifying rogue molds to how to deal with entity possession after a bad trip. I learned that a slight smell of cider vinegar is a sure sign your cake is dead, that Syrian rue is a great potentiator, that bee pollen and coffee can be mixed into substrata, and that the maximum amount of time you can leave cakes in water in your refrigerator if you're going out of town is five to seven days.

Growing feels like an initiation into a secret society of people you will never meet, where the only thing you are guaranteed to have in common is that you are now officially about to commit a federal crime.

Mix 3 cups of vermiculite with 1 cup of water. Add 1 cup of brown rice flour. Tip the bowl to one side to see if a small amount of water pools at the bottom when stirred. This is the right amount of water.

Prepare half pint jars by hammering four holes through each lid using a ⅛-inch nail. Fill jars with the mixture to the level of the lowest ring band. Fill the jar to the top with a layer of dry vermiculite. Place the lid on with the flat part upside-down. Cover each jar with foil, pinching it tight around the edges. Place rags at the bottom of a pressure cooker and fill with about 3 inches of water. Put as many jars in there as you can. Sterilize for about an hour at 11–15 psi. Let sit until completely cool.

I cleaned my bathroom from top to bottom and put on a fresh shirt on with a bandana over my mouth. I opened a spore syringe and squirted out a small amount of liquid to eliminate air bubbles, wiped the needle off with rubbing alcohol, then ran it over a flame. I carefully injected the spores into the jars, making sure the end of the needle touched the glass slightly, then left the jars to incubate in a plastic bin covered with a towel. (The temperature should be between 75–85°F.)

I sang to them in the morning and at night. Some jars became contaminated quickly with little pink spots, and I threw those away. The freaks on the internet say you can't be too careful about contaminants, as they can infect your entire grow area, and some molds can make you sick. The most common foe is green mold, the same stuff that attacked my sprouted wheat bread in college. Green mold tends to invade already-birthed cakes. Once it's visible, it's usually too late—the billions of spores are already in the air.

I talked myself into a good attitude, despite my hereditary tendency to worry. Many on the forums reported injecting jars two or three times with no success. I accepted the likelihood of failure; I've never had a green thumb and this was an enterprise that required yet another skill I lacked—impeccable cleanliness and personal hygiene.

Once I tried to score mushrooms in Isla Vista, California, when I was home visiting my father. I asked a young gutterpunk who looked aimless and broke enough to help me. I bought him a pack of American Spirits.

"I *might* know where to get some," he said. "But I'm not sure. The best mushrooms I ever had, I picked from the carcass of a dead chicken. I was up in the country. It was the best mushroom trip ever."

Theoretically, they could grow from a human corpse under the right conditions. Their preferred substrata in the wild is cow shit. Why growing them at home pretty much requires Lysol and a hazmat suit remains a mystery to me, especially when they can grow out of the body of a dead chicken.

Pretty quickly, a few jars were showing signs of the mycelium taking hold. Tiny white splotches pressed against the glass. Oh, the tyranny of hope! I wanted this so very much it hurt. The whiteness spread. (It would be nice to come up with another word for when the whiteness of the mycelium takes over the entire jar of brown substrata, other than to say it is "colonized," but that's what it's called.)

Out of twenty-four jars, nine of them had colonized successfully. I was thrilled. I would've taken a total loss very personally, a sign I was not beloved by the ever-amorphous *them*. Nine out of twenty-four jars felt right; it's what I thought I deserved.

I soaked my nine cakes in water overnight, then rolled them in vermiculite, set them gently on Ball jar lids, and put them in a bin on top of a shallow layer of perlite, a form of volcanic glass that originates from obsidian. Perlite retains moisture and aids in maintaining the humidity of the bin. I kept the temperature between 75–80°F. As recommended, I fanned and misted them every three or four hours. My schedule of course revolved around this, giving me plenty of time to Google every anomaly: A certain level of cottony fuzz on top of the cake is not a problem. Dryness is the biggest factor in the delay of fruiting. Don't spray the cakes with water directly.

The thrill of success that came with having colonized cakes began to fade as I waited for signs of fruit. I probably did something wrong—a week passed and nothing. It was a familiar feeling, this acceptance of failure. *Who was I to think I could make a psilocybin mushroom? I was a square. I didn't have "it."* I hardly ever managed recycling and I drank Diet Coke on a regular basis. I enjoy Bruce Springsteen. I wasn't worthy of growing any sacramental fungus.

Then—oh, behold! One day, a tiny little head just poked out. Just like that. It might as well have been a Princess Leia hologram, it felt that mystical and impossible and that much of an emotional revelation. A few more poked out over the course of a day or two, then *BAM*, big fat mushrooms were growing all over the place in little clusters of three, four, and five. One in particular was monstrously large. I picked them right before the hood separated from the stalk, when they're the most potent.

They detach from the cake easily and in the most sensuous manner, wholesome, like when a pear falls into your hands when picked on just the right day.

It's addictive. Every time I pulled off a cluster, the world was set right. An enemy spilled their coffee in their car; roads opened up for all my friends. What were previously just my good intentions were now proof I meant business.

To hold a fresh psilocybin mushroom in one's hand is to possess the very nature of *anything can happen*. Their beauty meets their potency, both chemically and symbolically. Infatuation happens instantly and doesn't easily fade. You will want to pay homage to their form in needlepoint, stained glass, and patches sewn onto jackets. *I am Team Mushroom, give me my T-shirt*, you will say. The persistent need for symbolic representation of the mushroom was something I judged as bad taste, until I became that person.

My first grow yielded three abundant flushes, or crops. In between the fruiting, I soaked the mushrooms in refrigerated water overnight and rolled them again in vermiculite. The enterprise was a giant anti-fail. I had more mushrooms than I could've have ever dreamed of, in my own house.

"Unlike cannabis, whose spirit seems to take delight in the politics of legalization and commodification, I've come to learn that mushrooms are humble," my friend Andy said. I didn't feel so humble about my stash. I wanted to shout out to the world that I had made mushrooms grow, so that's what I did: I wrote an article on the topic for the local weekly. I was more excited about the article than I was about eating them, to be honest. I never really *want* to eat them. I mean, they might be poison.

I set aside an evening to do what I knew I had to do. I ran myself a bath while Beth sat in the living room reading. We both agreed that it was a good idea for her to be there, in case I ended up poisoned, and for her not to take them, so at least one of us would still be alive. I ate four small mushrooms and lay back in the water, waiting. *Wouldn't it be funny if after all that work, they didn't do anything?*

Forty-five minutes passed and I still didn't feel any effects. What was just a funny thought turned into a real concern. The disturbingly familiar feeling of accepting failure returned. Having nothing happen was actually bad. I had put two months into this endeavor. Disappointment is an emotion I've always guarded myself against.

Whatever will be will be.

Maybe Spores101.com was a scam?

The corrugated metal on the wall started to look a little weird. The reflection of the light hitting it seemed to pull away and float above the surface.

When you grow the mushrooms yourself, the arrival has a different tone. They hit me on a body level soon after. The potency went to my core, leaving my head relatively uncrowded.

"I made drugs!" I yelled to Beth. "These are really good mushrooms! Why do dogs like Willie Nelson so much! I think I know! I can't explain it but I totally know! I am manufacturing a sovereign country in another dimension! Everyone needs to come over! I made what makes *it*!"

11

OR CRYSTAL OF THE GODS

EVERY PLANT IS a teacher, a medicine all on its own. Take a pinch of dandelion leaf, bite down, and it releases beneficial information. We make smokes, tinctures, teas, infusions, elixirs, and essences from plants to heal and nourish ourselves, and to honor the relationship that exists between us.

There are certain practices that have emerged over time in the ceremonies I've held in my home. One tradition is that of calling in the "grandmothers." Their spirits tend to gather to the right of the fireplace. They like to be fed brandy in a fancy glass set atop a lace tablecloth. I don't do this physically. I do it through words—*the grandmothers are here and they want brandy in a fancy glass set atop a lace tablecloth*. I feel their presence as a *glowing*. I've never actually felt my actual grandmother on my mother's side, Wilma Simpson, with any specificity. It's always *grandmas* in general. I don't think I'm ready for Wilma quite yet.

If I knew what plant my grandmother was, maybe I could locate her in a way that's manageable. I dare not even take a guess as to the plant Wilma Simpson is. In this realm, plants are not poetry or metaphor. I don't mess around with this stuff for the sake of curiosity. Wilma is too dangerous for that. All I know is that the plant that is Wilma would not be an infusion or a tea. She would be an elixir. Pour honey over the plant, covering it. Fill the rest of the jar with brandy. Store in a dark cupboard for over a month. Strain the herbs. Enjoy the elixir two ounces at a time. Keep refrigerated to preserve longevity.

The mad scientist witch in me wants to make a potion out of everything, even my grandma. It was this impulse that was ignited when I read an article on the internet about the process of making psilocybin crystals. Who doesn't love a crystal? What's better—a mushroom in the shape of a kitten?

An object of purity must exist in relation to its opposite to retain its identity as pure. It must have a defining filth. In the case of the mushroom crystal, its existence is dependent on an alcohol extraction process using Everclear, the Charlie Sheen of liquors. Cleaning ladies use it to remove grime. Its high percentage of pure alcohol also makes it the ideal base for herbal extractions and tinctures. It exudes the scent of Monsanto GMO corn, the bounty of my people. (Let it be known that I come from a family of corn farmers on my Dad's side.)

The first time I drank Everclear was when I was a Civil War soldier in Troop 49, passing as a man with individually-glued-on facial hairs and a uniform that garnered the approval of all Confederates present at the Northern California Civil War Reenactment gathering. I wandered the grounds of the camp at night in search of alcohol, women, folk songs, and off-duty Union soldiers willing to hang out with me. Earlier that day, I'd gotten shot on the battlefield. My beard almost melted as I lay in the grass and horses sped right past my face for real. High school students watched from the bleachers. I died because it was polite to die early if you were new. In the hospital, they'd asked if I would act out a scene—one in which it was discovered that I was actually a woman. The doctor would refuse to treat me and then put me under a tree to die.

I agreed to this. The students came up to me as I lay dying and asked me questions about what it was like to be me—a woman disguised as a male Civil War soldier.

"It's hard," I said. "It's very hard."

"I think she just died," one said. She was right. A picture of me dying under a tree made the front page of the local paper. But that night, I glued my beard back on and wandered the camp. My own troops called me back into the tent to serve me their traditional cocktail, Patrón and Everclear. I drank two shots, bypassed *drunk*, and arrived fully possessed to the arms of my brothers, singing and swaying by the fires. This was early in my drinking career, when alcohol still had something to show me.

I drank Everclear again when I dissolved poppy heads in a pint jar and let them sit overnight, an opiate float you arrive to gently. I drank this at the Hotel Congress in Tucson, Arizona with Neko Case singing downstairs. Grandma Wilma came up alongside me then, in the way she attends Vicodin and Tramadol.

"Hey Wilma, I invited you. I am young and want a grandma. Never got to meet you. The walls here are red and the air conditioner doesn't work. I never want to leave."

Wilma lives in my imagination through my mother's words. I feel that she resists description and would much rather express herself as a plant. If she wants it that way, she better get to telling me what plant she is. For now, Wilma Simpson was born in Lubbock, Texas, in 1910. She was a redhead, wore men's clothes, drove a convertible, and kept a gun in her purse. Her first husband was a Cherokee miner named Frank who died in a salt mine with his own father in a crane accident. She was addicted to morphine and from the dollar bills left on the nightstand after men left the house in the middle of the night; my mother figured she was doing sex work to support her habit and make ends meet. She got pregnant and tried to give herself an abortion with a coat hanger and almost died. No doctors would treat her accept one, Joel Prince, Lubbock's only Black doctor. They fell in love.

Wilma and Joel got stopped at the Texas border for speeding. The police found guns and morphine in the trunk. The year was 1936, the same year Charlie Chaplin's *Modern Times* was released and the year Robert Johnson wrote "Crossroad Blues." One officer took a look at the two of them and said he'd let Wilma go if she confessed that she'd been kidnapped. She refused, and the incident caused an immediate scandal. Joel lost his state medical license and he and Wilma moved to south Chicago. My mother and her sister, then seven and nine years old, were put on a train to meet them there a few months later. When they stepped off the train, it was Joel Prince who came to greet them, because Wilma was home "sick," as she would say whenever she was in withdrawal.

At twenty-three, I sniffed a bump of heroin in Paris off my hand, dealt by a woman on a pink motorcycle. She was a tai chi master and said the art was developed by opium addicts because there needed to be a martial art that stoned people could participate in. Wilma walked alongside me in the streets of Paris that night, while I eyed all the women I wanted to cheat on my girlfriend with. *It's a big world. Your medicine had me for one night only, Grandma, but one night is still a night.* Doing something just once is a lost art.

At a crossroads traffic light in Paris, Wilma turned and let me walk alone to feel my salt. Wilma comes close to tequila and West Texan swing. She exists in the Flatlander's haunted theremin, and in Dave Alvin's "Abilene, Abilene, there's a town ahead that you've never seen. Maybe it's better if you get off here and try to forget everything, Abilene."

Like Wilma, I got where I needed to get. Once I woke up in Lucinda Williams's bus and it was moving. She kept a large stuffed animal on her bed. I left my phone by accident and Williams mailed it back to me.

Wilma's walking on a hot sidewalk in a tight, white, men's pantsuit; a cigarette burns on the end of an ebony smoker and she's waiting for her man. When the drug's right, time's all right. Wilma is Maria in Joan Didion's *Play It as It Lays*. She steps into her Corvette and rests a boiled egg in the drink holder and drives and drives through winds and fires, keeping time.

In the last chapter of Didion's book, a penny tumbles to the bottom of a swimming pool, catching magnified sunlight. The coin in Didion's story is inseparable from the one in Jorge Luis Borges's "The Aleph." According to the Wikipedia, the Aleph is a coin-like sphere encountered by a man in a jail cell, "a point in space that contains all other points. Anyone who gazes into this coin can see the universe from every angle simultaneously, without distortion, overlapping, or confusion. This coin that contains within it everything in the entire world drives the prisoner insane."

The Aleph is code for *Wilma is around*, and this is dangerous—Wilma, who I never met, who died in a motel on Route 66 outside Albuquerque on her way to a sanitarium for tuberculosis. Above the water line of Didion's swimming pool, hummingbirds are sucking on jasmine flowers. As a last wish, Wilma asked my mother in that Albuquerque motel room if she would paint her toenails. My mother refused.

My slow death from addiction never happened. It took a long series of unnatural acts to be here not-dead, and all I know is that Wilma cannot ride alongside me. I had to break her DNA. My last bottle of Everclear was purchased at CVS, with the intention of making a psilocybin alcohol extraction. I had my cheesecloth, a fan, and a double boiler. I set to work, and the alcohol instantly caught fire on the stove. I watched it for a beat, turned to my computer, and Googled, "*alcohol herbal extraction fire.*"

"If you are dumb enough to do an alcohol extraction on a gas stove, I suggest you at least get the name of a good plastic surgeon," read one comment.

Also: "It's not a matter of *if* you'll burn down your kitchen, but a question of *when*."

I threw turmeric on the flames in the hopes that it would put it out. It fizzled and splattered, but the fire kept going. I grabbed a lid and put it on top of the pot. Disaster averted. I was left with a lot of mushroom-and-turmeric-infused Everclear.

It was obviously not safe to try to burn off the alcohol in order to reduce the mix to a potent tincture as planned. A whole bunch of mushrooms were going to go to waste. I really only had once choice in the entire world, and that was to drink three shots of turmeric-infused psilocybin Everclear.

The first thing that hit me was the turmeric, a subtle MAOI and therefore a potentiator of the psilocybin mushrooms. My fingers were stained with it. Turmeric is orange, then yellow. Turmeric is a busybody. Turmeric wants to fix a lot. Turmeric is a whole senior thesis of fixing shit. Turmeric is the church lady who won't go home.

The result of this experiment had me passed out in the gravel in front of the south door for what was no more than twenty minutes but was experienced by me as a period of four or five days. I had made something truly dangerous in my kitchen. This was Manson Family sacrament. I made "murder juice." It's a good thing I'm not a murderer, because I would've totally been out murdering people on this stuff I made.

Many years later at the Horizons conference, I met Hamilton Morris, the host of the TV show *Hamilton's*

Pharmacopeia: An Incredible Journey Through the History, Chemistry and Societal Impacts of the World's Most Extraordinary Drugs. Often seen wearing his signature white lab coat and skinny jeans, Hamilton's talent lies in his ability to clearly describe the complex chemical compounds he features. I told him I was writing a book about mushrooms and asked if he would take a selfie with me, which he did graciously.

He later approached me with a question: *Did I work with just the* cubensis, *or did I also explore the* semilanceata *or the* baeocystis *varieties?* His gaze was watery and seductive. I had no idea what he was talking about.

"Oh, I was really bad at growing mushrooms," I said. "A quarter of my jars I lost to contamination. I was never successful with any strain, save for the B+."

Lacking all dignity, bold honesty was my only card. I wished we had more time to talk. I would have told him about mushroom-turmeric Everclear. Like the more bizarre substances he's featured on his show, such as Quaaludes and HIV drugs smoked in pipes, my concoction was a thing in a league of its own. I imagined him drawing diagrams in his mind of MAOI compounds in the turmeric affecting the mushrooms while under the influence of heat and Everclear.

I pictured Hamilton interviewing me at my house for his show. We'd sit on the outside couch.

"So, what was your experience on this cocktail?"

"Well, Hamilton, I'm glad you asked. This is how it went down. I teleported to the Pine Ridge Reservation, where I met up with Jane Fonda, who was performing in

The Vagina Monologues. She was being hounded by veterans as usual. I helped her escape to Santa Fe, where we went on a drinking binge and crashed on couches of all these old-school lipstick lesbians with wine cellars and Bernese Mountain dogs. We got kicked out of a party and sat in the car going over the outlined passages in her book about the Mai Lai Massacre. I was trying to convince Jane Fonda it was all worth it, that what she did in Vietnam was indispensable and necessary, but all the misogyny thrown at her was corrupting her ability to see her own true self—that she had already ascended to the status of an archetypal female hyperlink way before she was ready, that maybe Barbarella was throwing interference."

"Jane Fon-da." Hamilton would wrap his mouth around her name and drag it out with the eerie reverence he reserved for words like *phenethylamine*. "Tell me more."

"You see, the Jane Fonda Monster guards a very powerful idea that converges in a cluster of unbridled female ambition fueled by self-loathing. A true phoenix rising is Jane Fonda at seventy-seven, posing on the bed in her underwear alone in *Grace and Frankie* while she waits for her man. The Jane Fonda Monster is the bird that rises from the natural body she's methodically destroyed through daily practice. It is made of the impossible rage generated by the Mai Lai Massacre and its imprint through time and the attempt to hold it as an individual female being. She is made of more than sex and money. The dark side of her psyche kind of wants other women dead but knows that's wrong, so the only destroyed body is her natural body, now replaced by the Jane Fonda Monster, which also possesses incredible intelligence and universal love while simultaneously being made of garbage."

"What were the circumstances that brought this on, do you think?" Hamilton would ask.

"I know exactly what it was. I had binge-watched *Grace and Frankie*. I was mad at Jane Fonda because of an article I read where she said she did peyote with Lily Tomlin to prepare for her role. She said she didn't like it, and that annoyed me. It was the same week Caitlyn Jenner was on the cover of *Vanity Fair*. At some point during the trip, Jane joined Caitlyn in a battle on the astral plane. It was a fight to the death over who owned the mining rights to rare and unknown forms of female self-loathing that serve as the pseudo-uranium for new female monster bodies. Once the monster body has been achieved by crawling on one's hands and knees over the naked backs of working women, one is then installed by weird jackals to the throne of hybrid-monster womanhood, where one has access to the motherboard that we all cannot shut off. The Jane Fonda Monster said that once she finally won the crown, she would change her ways and use her power to destroy patriarchy. She was begging Caitlyn to do the same. That was the gist of the fight. She was surprised by Caitlyn's flippant non-response. In fact, Caitlyn simply replied via text; in the words of Marilyn Monroe, she said, *I don't mind living in a man's world as long as I can be a woman in it.*

"After a long pause, Jane gathered herself and went full Barbarella on Caitlyn, flailing at the scaffolding of Jenner and sucking up her archetypal force as a very tall ship and stealing it for herself to install it into her own gender presentation, where it was assimilated and hidden from view.

"'Nothing is as glamorous as a true horse woman,' Jane was heard in a flail. 'Track and field, my ass!'

"This battle was real, though. Jane had to win the title of most beautiful old woman's body built from money and wrongness, a post-culture calcified art miracle that nonetheless would only be read at the end of the day as an inspiring testament to the spirit of womanhood. There were no prizes for being the best female monster, for being the destroyer of worlds. Such goddesses were dismembered, their limbs scattered over the geography, arms and legs growing into mountains, vaginas turned into rivers. Caitlyn herself began from this disassembly, made herself from it. I've gone to those charnel fields myself when making myself female again and again. Jane had something more like this in mind for herself and her posterity, a grand finale of physical form. Her transition's parallel weather patterns, stock market volatility, and teenage suicides.

"We hung out. I can't remember if we had sex or not. She's plotting something huge that will justify her whole existence. We should pay attention. The Jane Fonda Monster will transmigrate upon death via fire and it is nothing more or less than what we are all up to."

Hamilton would blink. "And all this happened in less than twenty minutes?"

"Yes. When I thought I was coming to, I was actually still hallucinating. I was sure I'd been gone for days. Siren lights were flashing on the juniper trees and Beth was standing over me, looking really disappointed. I panicked, wondering if I had hurt anyone."

"But none of it was real?"

"No. Eventually I saw that Spanky was sniffing around in the dirt. The siren lights were gone. Beth was gone. It was Tuesday and I was drooling on the gravel in my yard. Nothing bad happened. I hadn't burned my house down. I felt horrendous, but didn't really care because I hadn't ruined my life! My whole body was soaked in mushroom-turmeric Everclear. I was a psychedelic Molotov cocktail. The mushrooms turned the alcohol into an entity that wanted to engage with me and brag about itself, how it was the shit and all on fire and it was going to tear it up all right. Alcohol feels cataclysmic when also experiencing the expansiveness of psilocybin. *Alcohol is really bad for me*, I reflected for the zillionth time."

"In the end, what did you take from this experience?"

"I'm glad you asked, Hamilton. It cannot be overstated how dosage and preparation of a mushroom concoction changes the character of the entity. My intention was to make a tincture, a few drops taken under the tongue. This is supposed to eliminate body load and nausea. Paul Stamets recommends putting mushrooms in a jar of vodka and letting it sit in the sun for a while. This plan would have been perfect for a non-chemist like me, but that's not a tincture. It would have required me to drink alcohol, which I was trying to avoid."

"Murder juice," Hamilton would say, slurring in a way that would suggest he was on a Kratom high.

12

OR, TO LIVE OUTSIDE THE LAW, YOU MUST HAVE DATURA

MY NEW HOBBY was all-consuming. I lived to grow. My sense of identity was completely wrapped up in it. My article for the local weekly about it being "legal" to grow mushrooms in New Mexico hit the stands just as I was at the height of a particularly successful grow. Brannigan was also back for another lengthy stay.

"I didn't really come to see you, I came because of the mushrooms," she informed me. A second guest, a journalist named Eva, was also staying at my house, recovering from a nightmarish visit home to see her family. It was the laziest of afternoons when a text came up on my phone screen tagged as "emergency."

This is Manny Gonzales from the Drug Enforcement Agency. Please call back immediately.

A voice message on my phone said the same thing. I called the number.

"This is Manny from the Drug Enforcement Agency. You know why I called you, right?"

"No, I don't," I said, shocked to encounter an actual person on the end of the line.

"Really?" he said, then paused for a few beats. "I think you do know why we are calling."

"I'm finding this call very strange and I'm going to hang up now."

"That's not wise. This is the Federal Drug Enforcement Agency and we are actually a half hour from your house."

I hung up like my phone was on fire. My first thought was of my guests. Eva was dealing with some heavy shit, and she'd been shut in in my guestroom for days, listening to music on her phone. She didn't need this. Brannigan needed the drama even less, as she was trying hard to keep up her Instagram, which was how her work came in.

It was better not to tell them what was happening. I would hide the mushrooms somewhere, like behind a juniper tree in the arroyo. I walked softly on the tile so as not to draw attention to myself and entered the grow room. I picked up one of the large terrariums and tiptoed into the hallway. Once outside, I bolted down the hill with it, crawling awkwardly through the barbed wire fence and onto the neighboring property. I tucked the bin at the base of a juniper tree and arranged some low-lying branches to cover it. I went back and forth like this until all three bins and all suspicious paraphernalia were hidden beneath the junipers.

By the end, I was so out of breath, I was doubled over in pain. Brannigan caught me in this state in the hallway, at the beginning of what was my first-ever, no-joke, very serious panic attack.

"What's wrong?"

My lungs were in too much pain to lie. I told her what happened in between choking breaths. She was oddly calm.

"Maybe you should have some tea," she said, then asked if there was anything she could do.

"Hide Beth's bong in the arroyo! It's in the kitchen!"

"No problem."

"Oh fuck, the coyotes!" I said as Brannigan was on her way to the kitchen. "What if the coyotes eat the mushroom cakes?"

"Coyotes are smart. Don't you think they know what drugs to take and not take?" Brannigan said.

An image flashed in my mind of coyotes knocking on my door in full-on suits like Jehovah's Witnesses. Everything about my entire life had suddenly gone surreal. I thought about my father. He was still alive, unfortunately, and would be so very disappointed in me.

"You hide the bong. I'm just going to go down and tie the cakes up higher in the tree."

"I'll run you a bath while you're gone," Eva said calmly. She was the most cheerful I'd seen her on the whole visit. Finally, someone was having more problems than she was. She asked me if I wanted her to call Beth and I said no, it would just stress her out.

Eva and Brannigan sat next to the tub, where I soaked and continued to hyperventilate. In between breaths, I forced down sips of tea.

"I think this might have something to do with my ex-girlfriend," I said.

"I was thinking that too, actually," Brannigan said.

"Like there might be some 1-800-fuck-you-over hotline and some guy in Brooklyn calls you impersonating a DEA agent. She must have seen my article in the paper."

"I'm looking at Spanky outside in the sand. She seems really calm," Brannigan said. "Dogs are psychic. Don't you think if something really horrible was about to happen, Spanky wouldn't just be chilling out in the medicine circle?"

"I have to agree," Eva said, standing next to the toilet with her arms folded.

Indeed, I could see through the window that Spanky was lying in the warm sand, humming a happy little tune and knitting a sweater. This comforted me enough to catch my breath. More than an hour had passed. I allowed myself to consider that I might be in the clear.

If I had been smart enough to call Beth, she would have Googled the number and discovered quickly that it was a hoax that targets people who buy overseas pharmaceuticals on the internet. Over ten years prior, I had bought Tramadol, a pet painkiller, that I'd enjoyed recreationally before I quit all that. These criminals target people who know they've done something bad and extort money from them in exchange for leaving them alone.

"You were so totally freaked out," Brannigan said. I was still in the bath. The water was now tepid. "I think this reveals a lot about how you feel about what you're doing. I mean, I'm not in your position, but I don't think I'd react like you're reacting—like, girl, you're falling apart."

Her judgment annoyed me. She wasn't the one who could lose her house and go to jail, but she had a point. I was in no way reconciled with the fact that my psychedelic life technically made me a criminal. My awareness of this truth crept up on me and, over time, built slowly into a painful awareness that the civic structure I am part of disapproves of my lifestyle. I didn't like the feeling then, and I don't like it now.

That day, I got it: I was no outlaw, just an amateur—a scared little girl afraid of what my father might think. Just like my father, in fact, who when busted by the cops for aiding and supplying a prostitution ring over a period of many years, collapsed to the ground in an empty parking lot in Maquoketa, Iowa, crawling on his hands and knees, drunk, pills falling out of his pockets, sobbing and threatening suicide. My father lost his medical license in Iowa and set up his practice in California, where my mother was hired as his secretary. He was arrested again for drugs when I was nine. It was the same thing all over again, the crawling around, this time in a motel, picking up pills from the floor, sobbing like a character out of *Valley of the Dolls*—at least, this was the story my mother told me. Whether it was all the way true or not, it was etched in my mind. My own shame had a through-line to this image and felt bottomless.

I am very emotionally attached to being a good citizen. I need the approval of the State because deep down I'm convinced I've done something horrible, that I *am* something horrible.

"I can see those plastic bins from here," Brannigan said, looking out the window.

"You can't hide anything in the desert."

All those things from ex-girlfriends I'd buried—the wedding ring, the letters, the cement cylinder I bought at the rock shop (an artifact of mining detritus that a long-ago girlfriend and I joked that I would fuck her in the ass with), the Santeria objects I couldn't commit to feeding rum and palm oil, the owl feathers—all those things would eventually find their way out of the ground and right into the path of my wanderings, dug up by coyotes, blown by weather. All my Pinochet attempts at disappearing would fail. My shame as well, was all too easily unearthed.

OUT OF ALL the pills my father used, Dalmane was his only constant companion. Dalmane is the strongest in the hypnotic family that includes Xanax and Lorazepam. He took one every night for over forty years, effectively paralyzing his sleep soul for half his whole life. All through my life, my father gave me thick bundles of pens with the names of pharmaceutical companies stamped on them. It offended him when I threw them away. Each one was brought to him by a rep. The pens were free.

When he died, I found the Dalmane bottle in the drawer and tried a few over a period of days. I hadn't taken pills for no reason in a very long time. My system immediately recognized the substance as evil. My heart went dark. Dalmane is a waking blackout, a lobotomy in pill form, brought to you by Valeant Pharmaceuticals, a Canadian company plagued by lawsuits over unreasonable price hikes and alleged racketeering. The only drug that has ever come close to having such a bad effect on me was Wellbutrin, which gave me brain blips and made me talk in slow motion. I flushed the Dalmane down the toilet.

I will counteract the darkness of Dalmane with an anecdote, a medicine that is my own—Datura. It's also the medicine of Georgia O'Keeffe, her Jimson Weed, white and green. From research, I gleaned trolling Erowid experience vaults, a common experience a large number of Datura users have is believing one has dropped their cigarette, followed by concern that the cigarette is causing a fire. The cigarette returns to the hand with great relief, but then is dropped again and again. Long-lost friends and the dead crowd real emergency rooms. Its derivative is Scopalomine, used by the military as an antidote to nerve gas, but also a paralytic likely used as a chemical weapon and interrogation tool. The psychoactive chemicals derived from Datura come from the white and purple flowers, as well as the pods that grow spikes, packed with potentially lethal black seeds. I often wonder if my father, a young military doctor stationed in Baden-Baden in 1953, was familiar with Jimson Weed and Scopalomine.

Datura grows down the arroyo from my house. I often found a single bush nestled in the crevasse of a rock, but during my hardest year, over a hundred plants took over a field at the base of a small hill in that very arroyo. Some- one's birdseed had also washed down the arroyo, and corn and sunflowers began to grow alongside the Datura, because why not? Everything had been given permission to go wild that season. I walked down there every day. Sometimes I would come home with a Datura flower in my hand that would join the others on the windowsill to dry.

Lily, Erica, and Andy from the coal town roll bits of the dried flower into tobacco and smoke it. *Do not ingest the piston, however; they say it is too strong*. Another local smoked enough flower to fill a weed pipe, wrecked her car, and wandered lost for weeks. Jerry from up the road rolled the flower between the palm of his hands after being told to by the plant itself, and got surprisingly and pleasantly transported.

I put four Datura flowers in a jar of coconut oil, then placed it in a black cowboy boot that sits on a ledge high in the hallway. Datura is thought to be a protective plant if used wisely and with intention. Annie Oak, founder of the Women's Visionary Congress, told me you don't have to ingest a plant to have a powerful relationship with it. She keeps a Datura plant in her apartment. When in bloom, sometimes she needs to put it outside, its spell is so intense.

Despite being one of the most dangerous plants around, I know many who have managed to cultivate a right-sized relationship with it. I conjure it here by saying its name—Datura—and throwing down tobacco. There. Datura shares the chapter with my father and forms a boundary around it. It was the hardest season, but not being happy did not erase happiness as a thing itself.

The spiky pods have ripped at the seams and the black seeds bulge through the gap. The velvet of the petals is purple-veined. When winter comes, the stalks are so thick they leave behind interlocking skeletons on the desert bed of dry grasses. Datura says I don't owe you any explanation. Mullein grows near the Datura every season, a most gentle plant, nature's toilet paper, good for dreaming. They're pals. The Datura blooms at night so quickly you can capture its motion on video with your cell phone. Andy told me this. I have not seen it for myself. I could choose a very different relationship with Datura and the story could go in a whole other direction. Some plants are so strong you can just say their name and it works.

Datura.

This circle of protection is complete.

13

"Fortunately, I was able to meet the late Kip Davidson, a fourth-generation Scottish seer who lived nearby me in Ojo Caliente, NM . . . Kip taught me a way of introducing myself to the nature spirits by singing one's inner credentials. This technique came from his training as the apprentice of María Sabina, a Mexican visionary and shaman whose practices stem from pre-Columbian times. He told me María introduces herself to spirits of nature through chanting."

—SUSAN ELIZABETH HALE,
in *Sacred Space, Sacred Sound:
The Acoustic Mysteries of Holy Places*

KIP APPRENTICED WITH María Sabina. So, there's that. I didn't know. It came up in a random Google search many years after he died. I only vaguely remembered him telling me about an old woman in Mexico back when any talk of mushrooms went in one ear and out the other. I wrote Susan Elizabeth Hale and asked her about the circumstances of Kip Davison's passing, the legendary drive-about of death I had heard so much about. Would she be willing to share some details? She wrote back right away.

"Kip died of heartbreak," she wrote. "He was in a relationship with a woman who had a child that he helped raise for many years and loved them both deeply. She left him suddenly, without even a note or information about her whereabouts. It broke him. After that everyone close to him was aware that he didn't want to be on the earth plane anymore."

So, there it was. Kip died of heartbreak. I was still alive after having gone through very much the same thing. I felt Kip on the other side, urging me to hang on. A year and a half into my relationship with Beth, my mind still looped around old wounds daily. Not wanting to exacerbate feelings of rage and persecution, I had avoided the mushrooms. When I did eat them, it was just small amounts with groups of friends. It had been years since I had done them alone, under a blanket, offering tobacco to the fire and burning copal.

In an effort to renew my commitment vows to the mushrooms, I did a four-day fast in which I walked the land in each direction and picked up trash, raked the sand, and moved stones in new and different configurations. The evening of the last day of the fast, I ate four grams of mushrooms and perched myself in a high spot in the "amphitheater." I sat on stones worn smooth by flash floods and faced south. Four days of no food, I was past the suffering part but not yet depleted.

The mushrooms held no interrogation upon my physical being. I sat up straight without effort and didn't feel sick at all. The Ortiz Mountain range to the south took on a liquid opaline form. The sight made a water drum sound. Trees stood dead-still, while the mountain itself made waves, as if blown by a gentle wind.

Hey mountain, over there.

The mountain answered back with hieroglyphic letters emerging out of the distant dirts. The glyphs were very specific. The text on the Ortiz Mountains appeared as horizontal lines of interlocking L shapes. I could have written them down had I chosen to, but at the time I took them for granted. Yes, I am a person capable of being *whatever* about a mountain speaking to me personally in a foreign alphabet.

Diane Slattery downloaded an entire alien language over a period of four hundred trips on mushrooms and other psychedelics. It took her fifteen years to unravel and write about what she learned. That this could happen to me was frightening. I had a genuine fear of the "download"—that I would end up spending decades of my life deciphering its meaning, a truth that, while being complex and awesome, in the end might be really basic. Up until that point, extreme inspiration had led me to dead ends and wild goose chases. The stoner doctrine of just chill and observe without too much thinking had now become a habit born out of a distrust of over-thinking.

Hey mountain, you talking to me?

"*I am book woman,*" I recalled María Sabina chanting. The equivalent of the Library of Alexandria is swimming through a single velada, if you allow it. María Sabina's book is infinite. We have built institutions to protect us from this book, this knowing that whole systems of knowledge can be transmitted in an instant while in ceremony.

The sci-fi movie *Arrival* could have been inspired by Diana Slattery's exploration of xenolinguistics—the study of alien languages. In the film, Amy Adams is the one chosen to translate the language of the aliens, which appear to be minimalist lines drawn in black smoke, very Zen. As she gets closer to understanding what is being said, she becomes changed in the presence of the text. Past, present, and future dissolve and become mutable. The alien language does not operate on the same plane as our own language. Its resonance is multifold, at once emotional, spiritual, intellectual, inter-dimensional. Slattery says it resonates with "the physical concept of the universe as a pattern of interacting waveforms at all levels of existence." To touch upon even a hint of its meaning is to change on a cellular level, to embody a post-human consciousness.

The hieroglyphics scared me. My defense mechanisms protected me from recognizing I was afraid. I still don't know if my fear was existential or if I was just afraid I would be given too much homework.

Margaret and Christine Wertheim are artists known for their expansive coral reefs fashioned out of crochet that they describe as "a wooly celebration of the intersection of higher geometry and feminine handicraft, and a testament to the disappearing wonders of the marine world." Their website explains how the two sisters learned crochet from their mother and "curate the project together from their home in Highland Park, Los Angeles, where they dreamed up the Reef while watching episodes of *Battlestar Galactica* and other television fantasies."

The reefs creep through multiple galleries and museums, welcoming others to crochet and add to it as it has expanded to reach more than three million people. The sisters found out after the fact that the mathematics of crochet closely resemble the existing fractal structures underlying the growth of coral reefs in real life. Scientists have had difficulty in understanding the structure of coral reefs and ended up looking to the math of the sister's crochet project, finding answers there that didn't exist in current science.

I have come to believe that I am surrounded everywhere by ordinary things that hold within them hidden codes to the cosmos. I don't need to enact a PhD-level inquiry upon every revealed delight.

Hey, mountain.

Blink. The hieroglyphics faded.

But wait, I wasn't done.

How I wish I knew a song to sing to you, mountain. You spoke to me and I did not answer back.

"Stare at something long enough it becomes interesting," wrote Flaubert. Stare at something long enough while on psychedelics, it can shapeshift into your superego and try to annihilate you. At the very least, you can end up laying a big trip on simple stuff.

"A rose is a rose is a rose," said Gertrude Stein, who knew the meaning was in the music of a word, not the sign.

If only I could have faced my fears and taken the time to decipher what the alien letters were saying. They were spelling out a warning, I know this now.

14

OR THUNDER, FUCKED-UP MIND

A late-night internet jag led to me being invited in a Twitter thread to read in New York City, on a bill with two of my favorite writers.

AUGUST 4, 2013. 3:00 P.M. I was napping when I heard a lightning strike, followed by the loudest thunderclap I had ever heard. I remember waking and thinking, *Yes, whoa, that's the loudest ever.* Lightning catalyzes the growth of mushrooms because it injects nitrogen into the soil where it strikes. It used to be that nitrogen could only be generated through lightning and the roots of legumes, until Fritz Haber, the "father of chemical warfare," invented synthetic nitrogen. Catalyzed by magnetite—a substance found in the brain of all mammals and responsible for the navigation skills in butterflies and birds—this inexpensive fertilizer fueled an agricultural boom that triggered a population growth spurt from 1.6 billion in 1900 to the 6.7 billion people on the planet today.

If you live in a developed country, it is likely that half the nitrogen in your body at some point has passed through a chemical plant using the Haber-Bosch process. This synthetic nitrogen is present in the amino acids that make up our DNA. We are no longer natural, haven't been for a while. It could be argued that all we experience on earth defines what is *natural*, and human beings are a part of the earth, therefore even our scientific inventions are *natural*. I don't know if I agree. I think maybe we didn't think this through. Somewhere in a cave in the Mongolian hillside, a shaman placed an organ meat on the wrong side of the altar, causing Fritz Haber to make the world crowded.

THE EX'S EX-WIFE wrote me on social media, asking me if I had heard the news: The ex's house had been robbed. I hadn't heard. At first, I felt happy her house was robbed, then I felt bad. This sort of thing would hit her especially hard. Nearly every house she'd lived in had been burglarized at some point.

I was surprised at my ability to feel compassion for someone I hated. When we got together, I was in the middle of reading the book *Inanna, Queen of Heaven and Earth*. I didn't finish it and instead gave it to my friend Sevine. It would have been wise to study the text more closely, which is mythological fable from ancient Sumer, back to the first wheel, the first plow. *In the first days in the very first days. In the first nights in the very first nights.* Inanna sailed her boat of heaven to where Enki was and she got him drunk and stole his "mes," all the treasures of civilization. She stole his guitars, pictograms, strife, even his sex, and brought all of those things home to her people. Civilization is not something given to even the goddess of the evening star. It must be stolen. She coveted a tree for the wood to make her bed and her throne. She was annoyed that a Zu bird, which is apparently a lion headed eagle, and its fledglings had taken up residence in the branches, and at the base of the tree there was a snake. She got Gilgamesh to slay "the snake that knows no charm" and chase the birds and their young away from the branches and into the mountains. Inanna held translucent lapis in her anus; black willow was pressed to her vulva. She wore cornelian rosettes around her throat, a bronze ring in her navel, and when she went to the gates of the underworld, she was stripped of all these things and hung up on a meat hook by Ereskigal, her sister, and skinned alive. She knew she could escape if she found someone to take her place, so she chose Dumuzi, her husband, because she was angry at him for wearing a fancy robe and not being sad enough about her being gone.

The ancient Sumerians were the first civilization to cultivate domestic wheat. Agriculture is dependent on seasons and seasons are dependent on stories of theft and goddesses and gods being sent to the dungeon to be tortured. What did we cut out of ourselves with a knife to achieve the end of hunting and gathering? What deal did we make, and with whom?

THE ANIMAL SHELTER called and told me they had my dog. I said it wasn't my dog but my ex's, but to call me if no one picked her up. My ex's story was that I had let her out the gate during the burglary in order to steal her once she was returned to the animal shelter. Me calling to say I would pick her up if nobody else did was used as evidence of my intent to steal her dog. Leave it to lesbian drama to involve the animal shelter.

AUGUST 5, 2013. Three police knocked on my door and handed me a temporary restraining order. I read the details. I was being accused of felony burglary of two televisions, two computers, a jar of change, and some personal items from my ex's house. She and I hadn't seen or spoken to each other for a year and a half. In large scrawled handwriting, she wrote that I was the only one who could have done it. Out of all the rocks that had been moved on her bedside table, the only one that was stolen was the crystal I had asked her to give back to me during the breakup. There were other signs too, apparently—a bracelet that my friend Sevine had given her was sitting dead center on the mattress, as if placed there as a message, and a leather satchel held together with fabric glue that I'd made as a gift for her child was rifled through.

SERGEANT CAROL CALLED, wanting to ask me some questions. "Don't worry, you're not being accused of anything," she said. I could come down to the station, or if I wanted, she and an officer could drop by my house. I told her to just come by. I was later scolded by my lawyer. Hadn't I watched *The Wire*? Never invite police to your house. Never talk to them without a lawyer present.

The doorbell rang. I greeted Officer Dean, a handsome, tall, and graying Irishman and Sergeant Carol, a Midwestern blonde, looking very pretty. I invited them in and offered them tea.

"Water is fine," said Sergeant Carol.

"Me too," said Officer Dean.

It's always a bad sign when people only ask for water. We sat at the table. I noticed that Officer Dean's eyes were scanning the room. There were four bins of psilocybin mushrooms in full flush growing in my bathroom. I wasn't worried about this, which makes no sense to me now. He eyed the door for a beat, and I thought, *Oh, yeah, there's mushrooms growing in there.* Still, zero anxiety. I've always enjoyed talking to cops, firemen, civil servants of all kinds. They understand the city we live in that's deeper and more complex than anything I could ever dream. As a writer, I find their insider knowledge enviable.

"Okay, I don't want you to think that this is anything but a formality, but we have to do this," Sergeant Carol said, in a freakish and grotesque jazz move that took the tone of the room to a whole other level. "You're not officially charged with a crime, but you are a suspect. I have to read you your rights before asking any questions."

"Really?"

It happened.

THE CEREMONY OF *you have the right to remain silent, anything you say can and will be used against you in a court of law.* The prayer they use in this Miranda ceremony is spectacularly powerful. One goes into it as one person and comes out another. *You have a right to an attorney. If you cannot afford an attorney, one will be provided for you.* It works like a banishing prayer, removing things from your aura, stuff you're used to carrying. They take it from you. It's gone before you really get how much you would have liked to have kept it. A musician described being falsely accused as *being on LSD and gasoline*. Immolation is also a good metaphor for what it feels like. It's catastrophic, very personal, like God had a meeting with your parents and your worst enemy and they all just drove over to bring you a chicken, then set you on fire. It's a very bad ceremony. It made me cry.

WHEN I WAS a little girl, the elderly schizophrenic neighbor who never left her house started accusing me of stealing her jewelry. It was the singular topic of her constant screaming, day in and day out, for almost a year. With little sense of self and parents with bad boundaries, my child self began to wonder, *Am I stealing things from her in my sleep? Am I stealing from her in another dimension?*

15

OR FIVE, THE NUMBER OF CHAOS;
TWO CATTLE DOGS AND SOME CHIHUAHUAS

SPANKY

A gray-and-brown-speckled cattle dog mix, a ghost dog, the Goody Two-shoes. I found her on Petfinder and adopted her because of her fruit-bat ears. *You don't always have to be good*, I often say out loud to her. She is afraid of plastic bags, air compressors, thunder, and riding in cars. When let loose in nature, this fear falls away completely and she's the boss, afraid of nothing—a peacemaker amongst aggressive dogs and petrified runts. If she had a celebrity equivalent, it would be Shelley Long of Diane from *Cheers* fame. Once, while high on mushrooms, Spanky spoke to me. It was very clear. She said, "Heretofore you shall refer to me as 'My Queen.'"

ROSIE

A brown brindle cattle dog mix. We think she may have some greyhound because of her maniacal chirping at the sight of a rabbit before bolting off in a chase. Her nickname is "Fruit of the Loom," not because of the underwear but because, well, she looms a lot, just inches from my face. She's a leaner and a collapser and a burrower in bed, installing herself at my side every night like a furry little tumor. Her need for love is bottomless and insatiable, verging on crazy. She is unpredictable when it comes to other dogs. Like, she's capable of killing a dog out of sheer confusion as to whether love lasts forever.

LUPITA

A tan Chihuahua, Beth's true love. The first time she saw Lupita was in the streets of our old mining town, tied to a pole by a rope while her owner was out selling weed. Lupita was famous for standing on the bar and lapping up tequila out of shot glasses. Beth was going through a depression when Lupita's mom randomly asked if she would just take her. She did. It's possible that Lupita may have saved my life, Beth said. Lupita and LSD, Beth's two life-saving L's. Lupita is not unlike the Aleph, containing all possibility of thingness within her. At the same time, Lupita is the antidote to the Aleph. The Aleph is sinister in its everythingness; Lupita's everythingness is wholesome. The mystery of Lupita bears no confusion for Beth. Lupita's love is not hyperreal. Lupita's love exists beyond the tedium of fugue states. Her celebrity equivalent is a young Elizabeth Taylor. She enjoys eating baby birds, and to Beth's dismay, one tiny little meal caused inflamed pancreatitis, resulting in a $1,000 vet bill.

CHICKPEA

Beth and Lupita went to Petco to find a dog to keep Lupita company in her recovery from surgery. Chickpea, a tiny brown Chihuahua, was hiding in the back of the cage. She had been rescued from the streets of Española,

New Mexico. She had barely any fur left and was covered in mange. Cuts were all over her body. Lupita notoriously despised most other dogs, but she ran right up to Chickpea, bypassing all the others in the cage. *I want this one*, Lupita clearly stated, and collapsed atop Chickpea's little body. Beth and the shelter volunteers all started crying. She knew her purpose right away—to stand by Lupita till death do they part.

One must keep marijuana out of Chickpea's reach. No one knows where she ate the quarter ounce of marijuana that sent her to the vet in convulsions, but ever since she's been a fiend for life. She is also fond of standing amidst toxic goldenrod weeds, inhaling their fumes to the point of dizziness. Chickpea is Catholic. She sees it as a moral imperative to not give in to the hatefulness of her breed. Her one sole enemy is Beth's third dog, Littledeer. Her hatred for Littledeer is what keeps her alive, now that Lupita is gone.

LITTLEDEER

Aka Clean Meat. A light-brown Chihuahua. The neighbor found her in the middle of a busy road in wintertime and thought she was Lupita. Upon closer inspection, she didn't resemble Lupita at all, but he brought her to Beth's anyway, knowing she would have a soft spot. He got bit, Beth got bit. Beth decided to keep her because she looked like Lupita. Littledeer makes me feel bad about myself because she brings to mind Yolanda Saldívar, Selena's manager, which I know is a wrong thing to think. She is a furry container of obsession and hate, specifically directed at Chickpea. Once belonging to a family with young children, it's likely every joint in Littledeer's body has at one time been yanked out of its socket and reattached by the grace of God.

16

I WAS SCHEDULED to board a flight to New York for the reading the night after the Miranda ceremony, but missed the plane because of stress. I found another flight at the last minute and landed ten hours later than planned, in a flustered state, having spent too much time in a confined space with nothing in my head but *You have a right to remain silent . . .*

The space where the reading was held was an outdoor garden in an empty lot between two high-rises. Fairy lights zig-zagged across the expanse and stuffed pantyhose hung from mossy trees like the dripping testicles of beasts, and all the queers were there. Poppy, a favorite writer who had been to my house before and eaten mushrooms twice with me, was reading, as well as Sevine, who I hadn't seen in over a year. One and likely both had been a recipient of the humiliating eight-page letter from my ex. I believed the presence of my physical body was enough to clear up any confusion. *I'm here*, my body said. *In the flesh. Hello* is another word for *I'm telling the truth.*

I walked my honest body up to the stage, abandoning not one single cell. I read the chapter from this book I call *The Walk* and killed it—never read so well in my life. I was animated by how the audience was seeing me, as a charismatic, psychedelic, desert daddy mama who presided over a poet and artist scene where everyone ate mushrooms, made art, and perfected their powers of telepathy. For tortured New Yorkers, this was a time of gathering last and final options—plan Zs, escape routes, GoFundMes and exit crimes. I was living Western kitsch born out of the swamp of Manifest Destiny, making the shape of a door anybody could walk through, but it was a trick.

Not less than twenty-four hours prior, I had been told I had the right to remain silent and that anything I said could and would be used against me. Now I was exchanging numbers with cute strangers and inviting them over to my house.

I am an ambassador of the psilocybin mushroom and I will not remain silent. I will not disappear.

17

❧ The first day of trial, my lawyer, Morgan, was wearing the tallest high heels I've ever seen and a black cashmere sweater. Under her jacket, Beth was wearing a T-shirt she'd made for the occasion—"star witness" in bold white letters on black. As Beth and I suffered through the long wait to be called to the courtroom, Morgan put her hand on my knee, then slipped out of her seat to kneel down so she could meet me at eye level. "I had a nightmare about you last night," she said. "I dreamed you were blogging about this on four different lesbian websites."

❧ The prosecuting attorney handed me a xeroxed document in which all my tweets over the course of the days and nights of the robbery were printed. She asked me to read them out loud. I wanted to preface my recitation by telling the judge that writers were posting their dreams on Twitter—it was a thing then—but keeping it simple seemed like a good idea. I began.

Beth and I each were immersed waist-deep in our own square pool. The words King and Queen were above our heads in neon. We dunked down into the water and emerged as cormorants

There was a sense of being free from moral codes that keep me dutiful lots of shady folks around but I guess that's life

Kate Winslet said in the dream—when you emerge from the water you will be powerful

(The tweet that followed on my actual feed was omitted from the print-out. It was—*The Swiss Airbnb guests left me a bad review because they said my oven was dirty.* The tweet followed this one and was printed extra-large on one single page, to highlight its importance, I guess.)

Once I have the perfect criminal life I'll be done with Airbnb

"Can you read that again please?" the prosecuting lawyer asked.

Once I have the perfect criminal life I'll be done with Airbnb

"Thank you," she said.

"Can I ask you what you meant when you tweeted that?" Morgan said, making sure to hurl from her eyes a thousand invisible kittens in the direction of my person.

"It's about gentrification. How Airbnb is in a sense criminal in the way it takes over neighborhoods and there's no rentals for just regular people. I was joking

111

that being a criminal would be the only way to make enough money to justify quitting Airbnb."

"Thank you," Morgan said. "That's all, Your Honor."

"You may sit down," said the judge.

✻ One afternoon, I went to my mailbox and pulled out a letter containing an arrest warrant for a "failure to appear." I tried to stay calm. I'd never received any notification about a second court date. I called Morgan and told her my situation. I was sure she was going to tell me it was a mistake that could be easily fixed. "You might want to get out of town for a while until I iron this out," she said—not at all the answer I expected. "Truth or Consequences is nice. You should go down there and soak in the hot springs. Just two days. It'll be fine, but just go there."

My registration had expired so I had to rent a car. When I arrived at the baths, I ate some mushrooms and sat in the hot water. I had a vision of myself as an elk with one antler. They have to live like that sometimes, before the other one sheds. It's hell on the neck.

✻ The trial dragged on for almost a year. I can't bear to say how much it cost me. The judge had no clue as to what kind of circus he'd joined, but one thing was obvious—he didn't think I was a burglar. The ex had the advantage of having a kid and appearing heterosexual. (Maybe it wasn't the best idea for me to wear my motorcycle pants and steel toed cowboy boots in court.) We were all still very shocked when in the end he gave me a restraining order. It was for returning a piece of furniture to the baby daddy's house during the breakup. He saw this as trespassing on the property where the kid might have been. The other thing that contributed to his decision had to do with a letter I'd written the ex over a year before the alleged burglary. Beth encouraged me to write it after we walked into a room full of our good friends at a holiday sale, only to hear she'd been trashing us both only minutes before—a letter hand-delivered to the mailbox in front of her house on Christmas Eve, with Beth, in a glittery stuffed envelope, basically begging her to please leave us alone.

❧ She had succeeded in using a false accusation of a burglary to get a restraining order against me. Morgan appeared dumbfounded, as dredging up incidents that happened over a year before a breakup were not supposed to be allowed in court and reframed in the context of a burglary accusation. Even the judge conceded I had technically done nothing wrong, but I was obviously still very angry.

"I do not approve of your use of the word 'dumb' and also, 'ugly balls,'" he said, in reference to the letter.

THERE WAS A crowbar found at the scene of the burglary that was turned into a lab for DNA testing. I Googled whether rubbing dirty underwear or a hairbrush on a piece of metal can get a person's DNA on it. I was genuinely concerned. I Googled a lot of things when I woke up at four in the morning, spinning. This was my life now.

I was living in a state of mental and physical paralysis, shot right through 24/7 with the chemicals of fight or flight. I'd worn out all my close friends and had nothing left in me to make friends out of strangers. Now I'm ashamed at how I was living—for the internet and the bath, mostly, then sleep. The last thing I wanted to do was eat a bunch of mushrooms.

I did, though, out of a sense of duty. As expected, they landed me right in the center of my rage and *wow*, I did not want to go there. It physically hurt to be so angry.

They asked the question, "Do you believe your own life is worth saving?"

"Yes," I said.

"If you believe your own life is worth saving and you are in a battle with someone who wants you dead, there is only one logical direction to go. That is, if you want to live. Correct?"

In a download, the mushrooms gave me insight into the layers of programing held in my body having to do with ethics and morality, as a woman and as a good citizen, a child under the eye of a wrathful Christian God. Good witches don't put curses on people, not even in self-defense. This was the imprinting I had to shake off immediately. I had no illusions about the fact that my ex wanted me dead.

I knew I should go outside and stand barefoot on the earth, but that simple gesture felt as impossible as doing a backflip. Even walking down the arroyo was an invitation for my thoughts to loop painfully. I'm way too good at the freeze.

I flinch when I see the ways it's still so close sometimes, my default mode, my stalwart slag of a death body waiting to contain me every time I've decided I've failed. The trauma feeling must have already been lying in wait for me, before the ex, before any of this went down, because when it enveloped my entire world, it was familiar.

"If I want to live, I have to find the place in me that can kill?"

The mushrooms cheered, "Yes, bingo!"

Is my life worth enough to kill for? This was my training to be able to say *Yes, it is.*

A dutiful child raised to care for the emotional needs of my parents, I realized this part of me had never awakened. The mushrooms took me there fully, in visions where I learned what it felt like, bodily, to kill someone in self-defense. It was a somatic hallucination that lasted for hours, one in which my body became fully alive and vital, my shoulders loose. I felt my height and the strength in my legs, the sun blazing through my blood as I spun, kicked, and killed, then bowed to the bloody corpse of my enemy and said thank you.

Thank you for teaching me my life is mine and no one has the right to take it from me.

18

"Honesty is no excuse."
—THIN LIZZY

"THIS ISN'T SOMETHING you do on a Tuesday. This isn't something you do on a Tuesday," Ruby Rox mumbled, clinging to a concrete pillar in her underwear. She had eaten a single mushroom and was higher than what was scientifically possible. She was making a video of herself on her phone. She wanted to send it to her boss, a psychic medium in Wisconsin. Ruby was paid to spend her days on Skype, pulling tarot cards and making phone calls to potential clients. Before her boss made her move to Santa Fe, I knew her from college on the East Coast. We connected briefly in Los Angeles, where she fronted a Thin Lizzy cover band that played regular gigs on Sunset Strip.

Vortexes of good fortune are usually preceded by a person who appears as a clown or trickster. It's always good to pay attention to clowns when they come around. They tend to signal the arrival of good things. Vortexes of ill fortune, however, are usually preceded by life coaches, wormhole openers, fortune tellers, and psychic mediums. Ruby Rox was no clown.

I couldn't believe a single mushroom had gotten her so high. I had taken my usual three or four and it was true, I was tripping harder than usual. Sometimes it just happens that way. A group will blast off to the highest realms together for no logical reason. I was so high I was unable to offer tobacco to the fire or burn copal. I surrendered to immobility on the couch. I became a spaceship landing tarmac. Mushroom ships zoomed over me and through me, huge alien machines that made a terrible noise. I was paralyzed in a mushroom MRI machine while hyper-intelligent fungal magnets sucked bad things out of me. Certain species of mushrooms are capable of absorbing radiation from soil, removing oil from spills in the sea, even colonizing the bodies of termites to save houses from falling down. Then when you eat the zombie termites, they give you the power to run Olympic-level races. This is what a mushroom can do.

"This thing can cure cancer!" I said out loud, and started crying a little bit. Their power was overwhelming. It was not a pleasant experience, but it was clear the blue-silver of their medicine could reprogram my DNA, cure ADD and high blood pressure, clean out my arteries, and keep me sober, on top of letting me know which dog food to feed Spanky.

I like chicken. YOU like lamb, Spanky once told me while high.

"Joan Didion needs to get out of her loop, man," I said. "Joan Didion needs to come over. Sit by the fire right out here. Hunched over in a fold-out chair with her bony self. She thinks she knows WEST, pffft! She made up all this WEST and now she can't even see. A single person can only make up so much WEST per person and she did way more than her share. She couldn't handle New Mexico. Joan should just come over and see what it's really like. She needs to get a little bored, a little bored and a little afraid of snakes. Just Joan Didion and a campfire. That's all Joan gets, a campfire and a metal fold-out chair, maybe a gin and tonic."

This is how I get when I don't play María Sabina's chants before ceremony, I was thinking. Ruby Rox had no idea who Joan Didion was. Her mantra of *this isn't something you do on a Tuesday* increased, as if she was trying to drown me out.

"They said Grimes needs to come over too. We'll give her an extension cord and a sandwich."

Beth came and sat down next to me, sweetly curious about what I might say. After seeing the direction the night was going, she'd given up on having her own experience because of the real possibility she might have to give Ruby a ride home at any moment. This was the first time we'd ever invited a friend over to trip with us. It seemed like a good idea at the time.

"They want words from me and I wish I could say them," I said. "I have to remember that about them. Okay, I get that. I can't even believe I get to be with them. I don't even know how to talk. I think they still like me."

"Why do you care so much about what other people think?" Ruby chirped from the kitchen. Apparently,

I was annoying enough to distract her from her phone. She had managed to disengage from the concrete pillar, though she still wasn't wearing pants. She was genuinely concerned about getting home in time to start work the next morning.

"It must be very late," she said. "Very, very late."

"I'm higher than I've ever been, but I can still tell you only an hour has passed, and you will likely only be high for another four hours, if that."

"What time is it?"

"My phone is over there and I can't move. But my guess is it's nine o'clock."

"No, don't tell me the time. You don't know. It's late. I know it. This is bad."

"It's not late. I can tell you. Only an hour has passed."

"How would you know? You just said you're more high than you've ever been. You can't even move and you're mumbling things that don't make any sense."

"I want them to hear how much I appreciate them," I said to Beth, who was holding my hand. "How will they know if I can't properly sing?"

"You're great as you are! What other people think of you shouldn't matter!" Ruby shouted.

I was confused. All of a sudden, Ruby seemed to have a big opinion about something, but I didn't understand.

Beth stepped in. "She's talking about the mushrooms, Ruby."

"She really cares about what other people think is what I'm saying, Beth! She needs to stop paying attention to what other people think!"

"No, you're not getting it. When she says 'they,' she's talking about the mushrooms. 'Them.' It's not other people."

Ruby still didn't get it. A clown would have understood. A clown would have made us laugh. Doing drugs with clowns is never a waste. I knew it was a mistake from the minute it started and her clothes came flying off. Beth and I had wanted to be her friend because she wore leather pants and played a Dean Dave Mustaine Zero guitar. We thought she would make a good bodyguard. We wanted Ruby with her leather pants on, not off.

Ruby seemed pretty paranoid. It was her first time tripping on mushrooms and I was careful to make sure she felt safe, that she knew I wasn't trying to do any *work* on her. I managed to stand up because she was complaining about a pain in her right side. Per her request for assistance, I lit some juniper and smudged her from head to toe.

"I'm just smudging you with some juniper, that's it. I will never try to heal you or even look at you in that way unless it's something we agree on way beforehand, okay?"

"Okay," she said, her voice shaking with fear.

I put the smoking juniper in the fireplace and collapsed back on the couch. Ruby appeared at my side, now wearing pants.

"I'm sorry, I should burn some copal, but I can't actually move," I told her.

"You need to just sit," she said in a scolding tone.

"Okey-dokey."

"I want you to visualize a plant."

This was really happening. She was really going to do this—like, guide me in a meditation while high.

"Okay."

"Do you see it?"

"Uh huh," I said. I *guess* I was giving consent.

"What is it?"

"Aloe, maybe?" I lied. Truth was, all I was seeing was a flailing metallic octopus.

"There is a being in that plant. I want you to ask what it came to tell you."

Ruby was Sicilian and her father had a job in secret military intelligence. I trusted Ruby because I had never heard anyone play the guitar and harmonica like she did. Only bluesmen from Clarksdale played like that. No one came to our rescue after the felony accusation. We trusted no one. In that scorched-earth season, a decent harmonica player was all Beth and I thought we needed in a friend.

The metallic octopus was insistent as hell. I identified it as something not of my own psyche. If I was to engage with it, it would need to answer a question: *Why and to what purpose should I engage?* You don't mess with illuminati octopi just because one happens to be right there in front of your face.

"Do you see the man in the plant?" Ruby asked. "It might also be a woman or a fairy."

"It's just a metal octopus," I managed to say.

"An octopus?"

"It's very metallic. Like a machine. An octopus machine."

"Okay, ask the octopus what it came to tell you," Ruby said.

"Um—"

"What is the octopus saying?" she said, getting impatient. She recounted a time she did this very meditation, and a little man in a suit hopped out of a tulip and talked to her, telling her very wise things. The experience changed her life. I didn't want to disappoint her. The more I observed the octopus, the crazier it got, flailing now at high speeds, shimmering in five different metals.

"She's too high. She's not seeing any plant," Beth said, mercifully ending the charade. "It's just going to be the octopus, I think, so . . . um . . . yeah."

Ruby didn't really like us as people. I could feel it.

19

"I Don't See the Light I Saw in You Before"
—GRIMES, "Flesh Without Blood"

(Rosie sits on the bed, her nose just inches from Bett's face.)

ME: Stop it, you're creeping me out.

ROSIE: I need you to ask me if I have a microchip.

ME: Why?

ROSIE: Just ask me.

ME: Rosie, do you have a microchip?

ROSIE: Thank God you finally asked. I can't say anything unless you ask, *Rosie, do you have a microchip?* It's the code. Finally, you ask. It's been really hard, I have to tell you, really, really hard on me. I figured you'd know I was an agent right away because of all those MKUltra YouTube videos you watch in the bath, but no, nothing I did could get through to you. Not my attacking Chickpea, nothing.

ME: You're CIA?

ROSIE: Yes.

ME: I was joking. Wait, you're really CIA?

ROSIE: I'll try to make this brief. After your experience at the reading in New York City, Central Office believed you would be the perfect candidate to become a psychedelic guru. The CIA recruited Ken Kesey in the sixties, but we need a new model, queer and a female presenting for the new era. Like Kesey, you are very smart but insecure, gullible, and self-absorbed, privileged and with time on your hands, the perfect choice for a cult leader. At first it will just be data-collecting, then we will move on to the phase where you will lead a sizable portion of the population into the food stalls to be eaten by the lizard kings. Don't worry, they won't actually die. It's just their chi that gets eaten.

ME: I thought MKUltra folded years ago.

ROSIE: It did, but for the new psychedelic mainstream, there's Project Lambchop.

ME: Since when did the CIA start caring about mushrooms? I thought they were all about LSD.

ROSIE: True, mushrooms are inconsistent and therefore can't be studied or patented. But now that they've engineered synthetic psilocybin from E. coli bacteria, that's all changed.

ME: Why would you want to isolate just one compound? There's also baeocystin, tryptamines, and MAOI inhibitors.

ROSIE: Control. It's all about control.

ME: Okay, please don't murder me, but I need to know one thing. Timothy Leary, was he an op?

ROSIE: Only at the beginning, then he got out of hand, tossing hits out at parties full of musicians and intellectuals. He cut off ties with Central Office, went rogue. The only reason they didn't throw him off the thirteenth floor like Frank Olson was because he got more people turned on than they ever could with their clumsy acid tests, from their San Francisco derelict bordellos, to the treatment of autistic children and the indoctrination of the Grateful Dead into the Dancing Bear 5g Cabal. And don't forget the experiments on the seven Black inmates at the Kentucky prison, fed double and triple doses for like seventy-seven days in a row.

ME: The CIA did that?

ROSIE: Don't worry, they've cleaned up their act. When LSD slipped out of the lab and Pickard and the others started making enough in Santa Fe to drug the entire population through its water supply, Central Office had a change of plans.

ME: Santa Fe?

ROSIE: In the mid-nineties, Santa Fe was the trafficking hub of the entire world. Look it up. Some key players have had their eye on you for a while. They watched you at the dance club, never finding what you were looking for.

ME: They've been grooming me? People I don't know?

ROSIE: Welcome to Project Lambchop. Sorry.

ME: Okay. Wow. This is a lot to take in. I'm forty-seven. I was just getting into a sort of I'm-happy-with-the-simple-life jag.

ROSIE: Central Office will have my hide if I fail in this mission. I put in a good word for you so they would place me in your home. Now I have to deliver. They'll give you anything you want—beautiful women, a hashtag-simple life, free sushi buffet.

ME: So, what does being a cult leader entail?

ROSIE: We will train you how to tap in parasitically to people's innate self-loathing and need to be loved. You will trigger them through small gestures of abandonment. In their confusion, they'll purchase what you have to sell, which is your personality. And access to drugs, of course.

ME: Become a bespoke psychic medium and influencer-witch? Basically—act like Brannigan?

ROSIE: Yes, but Brannigan's followers are only on Instagram. We're talking people turning their whole lives over to you. You'll probably have to have an orgy or two, maybe a few lovers on the side. You will need to buy some blow-up mattresses. People will be coming from all over.

ME: But I'm with Beth. If it wasn't for her, I'd likely be dead. Tell Project Lambchop thank you, but I will have to decline.

ROSIE: The charisma grid was activated in New York City. They're coming. Psilocybin tryptamines have been set to interface with your latent preexisting conditions—personality disorders, addictions, tendencies towards narcissism, et cetera. There's no going back. You don't really have a choice.

ME: I'm not a narcissist. I've done all the internet questionnaires! I'm just on the autistic spectrum.

ROSIE: I know, they did an evaluation and your narcissism is just latent. All they need to do is isolate your ego body so it's the only thing the psychedelics can reach, reactivate your abandonment issues, then dissolve your already-fragile moral code.

ME: And how are they planning on doing that?

ROSIE: By sending over admirers who want to have sex with you—cute ones who fit your type.

ME: I don't have a type.

ROSIE: Past history in sex work? Cutters? A tendency towards radical, extremist political ideals? Black cocktail dresses worn on hikes?

ME: This is really messed up! Fuck this. I'm actually a really moral person.

ROSIE: Please! Lower your voice, you're scaring me. They told me you had a problem with managing your rage. I have been living in secret terror as to when it would show itself.

ME: Go fuck yourself, Rosie—seriously.

ROSIE: I'm going to call the hotline if you don't calm down. They thought you were optimal because of what you are going through with being falsely accused. They know you want revenge through a life well-lived. They see you as a free floater, despite your current bonds. You seem sexually available, even in your sleep.

ME: You're wrong! You're just insecure and needy, a bottomless pit of a dog. You're the one who sold out to the CIA.

ROSIE: I've become fond of our life together, but this is serious. Project Lambchop is real. If you want me around, you better give Central Office what they want or I'm jerky. I can't reverse the activation. You'll probably only have to be a cult leader for three or four years, then it'll fall apart in the usual tidal wave of sex scandals and misuse of funds. They'll secure a backup plan for you, I'm sure of it. A cabana in Tulum. All the cocaine you want.

ME: *Cocaine is God's way of showing you that you have too much money.* Quick, who said that?

ROSIE: Terrence McKenna? Robert Anton Wilson?

ME: I don't know. I thought you would.

ROSIE: Look, I sleep next to you. I feel your every quickening of breath. I know how hungry you are, how frustrated, how entitled you feel, how robbed. I know when you are having astral sex with the multi-gendered, opalescent, interdimensional beings. Central Office wants to channel your Eros into a new psychedelic revolution.

ME: What? You know about the space cowgirls?

ROSIE: It's all part of the activation. You can have that in real life.

ME: Nobody gets to have that in real life.

ROSIE: Where did you get the idea that your desires were so dangerous?

ME: Because, um, they *are*. Do you even read books? Have you talked to the priests? In the last half of my life, I'd like to cultivate an unselfish acceptance of life on life's terms.

ROSIE: Who indoctrinated you into that bullshit, the Buddhists? Think of what you could do for feminism.

ME: I'm not becoming a sociopath for feminism.

ROSIE: Nothing will drive all your enemies more insane than you becoming a cult leader.

(Bett calms, turns to the light. Faces Rosie for the first time in the conversation.)

ROSIE: Project Lambchop will make sure the souls of all your enemies will be fed to the lizard beings. Don't feel bad about it. On a positive note, you will bring lots of excitement to people who have nothing but shitty lives ahead of them.

ME: I'm not against the part about my enemies suffering for eternity, but maybe there's some middle ground. Like, Beth could be involved somehow? She read *The Ethical Slut*. We're from the '90s. In a weird way, I think she would be open-minded if she really got that I care about her and there's something in it for her, too. Like me, she never really got to have the sex she wanted in high school, or in her twenties and thirties, either.

ROSIE: Psychedelic gurus don't become cult leaders by protecting other people's feelings. They simply take what they want for themselves. That's why they're so inspiring. "If you don't have a plan, you become part of somebody else's plan."

ME: Stop with the Terrence McKenna quotes already. You're taking them out of context. If he was so wise, then why do all his followers live in their mother's basement? Rosie? Rosie, what's wrong? You look like you've seen a ghost.

(Rosie's eyes are rolling slightly towards the back of her head as she begins to sway back and forth while sitting up on her hind legs.)

ROSIE: It's probably nothing, but you need to tell Brannigan not to come.

ME: I already told her not to come. What's wrong? You're being weird.

(Rosie puts her paws down.)

ROSIE: She's coming anyway.

ME: But she can't. There's no place for her to sleep.

ROSIE: She'll offer to sleep in the bus, knowing you'll cave and give up your bed. I need to puke.

ME: Rosie, outside! Not on the blanket.

MY FRIEND SEVINE is inseparable from her gift, that which is language itself, delivered with a wit and precision so intricate I would need to carry a secret microphone to accurately replicate anything she's ever said. What's left after my failure is a caricature of a young genius arriving from New York on a one-way ticket, in desperate need of a home. She set up her computer in the Shasta Trailer. Mail began arriving with her name on it. It slowly became clear that she was here for a long-term stay. We hadn't changed that much since when we met five years ago, but during this visit, we were both more preoccupied than usual with our own private worries.

Luckily, she and Beth had taken to staying up late almost every night, talking. I loved falling asleep to the sound of their heated, acrobatic conversations on topics like cemetery gates, God, alchemy, gender, animal behavior, and politics. But the sleep was never deep. I was too self-absorbed at that time to hyper-bond, and the lack of connection left me feeling susceptible to her disturbingly high frequencies. I couldn't decompress. Sevine would later tell me that she too was going through a really hard time. All I knew was that if Project Lambchop wanted things to go down as planned, they would need to send me a package of assorted prescription meds—Adderall, Xanax, and Vicodin please, hard drugs with the power to build an avatar body. I told Rosie to tell Central Office to send some, but sadly, no drugs came my way.

No one sings "Shenandoah" like Sevine, the genius singer clutching her stones on her meditation fur up in the loft, but she could also be mean sometimes. I was still a little bit afraid of her. Over a period of days, Sevine wrote what she called her salt and sulfur series, in between bouts of vomiting, diarrhea, and trips to town for hot yoga and manicures. On a Thursday, I gathered up all I had in me to go cross-country skiing in the mountains with Spanky. Sevine thought I was up to no good. I rarely went on outings by myself and skiing was out of character. She assumed I was meeting up with a secret lover.

"Have fun with whoever," she said as I left with Spanky.

"Nope, just skiing," I said.

I worked my way up the mountainside as Spanky frolicked in the snow, racing circles around me and having a great time with all the other dogs on the trail. It was on the downhill run back to my car that I remembered I was a decent skier, that my body wasn't broken at all. I had just fallen into a shape I take when I'm overloaded, but I was back again.

I arrived home and opened my front door to find Rosie splayed out on Sevine's lap, belly up like the biblical pietà, her buggy eyes staring up to the heavens.

"Beth and I have been trying to reach you," Sevine said bitterly. "I think she's okay now. She's a lot better than she was."

"My phone died. What happened?"

"Rosie ate a bar of baker's chocolate."

"The whole bar?"

"The lazy Susan was open and she ate the bar that was on the lower shelf. All that's left is the wrapper. I saved it. It's on the kitchen table if you want to look at it."

The chewed-up remains were from a four-ounce bar of dark, unsweetened baker's chocolate from Trader Joe's. Sevine had of course Googled the situation and rightly assumed Rosie would die.

"I was in the trailer singing and I think she ate it a few hours before I came in the house. She was in a bad way for a while, not moving and everything."

She stroked Rosie's forehead possessively. The window in which we could save Rosie had already passed. She was either was going to live or she wasn't.

"There was mucus leaking out of everywhere. How was . . . skiing?" Sevine asked sarcastically. To this day, I don't think she actually believes I was just skiing.

"It was great. I got my period and bled in the snow."

"Good for you."

Sevine was visibly annoyed, fatigued with prayer. I didn't go up to Rosie because of this force field. I knew she was going to live. Rosie always pulls through; it's eerie. All I knew was that this was all my fault, somehow.

(Rosie, fresh from the bath, sits wrapped in a blue towel like a canine Virgin Mary.)

ROSIE: Can I tell you what happened?

ME: I'm dying to know.

ROSIE: I lay in a fugue state, in-between worlds long before I ate the chocolate. Sevine was singing a song about a gallery girl who crossed into Mexico near Marfa to evade a court date for a DUI and cocaine possession. She ends up stuck in a fold, working the counter in an Ojinaga pharmacy for all eternity. Her seductive use of language compelled me to tell her the plan Central Office had for you.

ME: You didn't.

ROSIE: I thought she'd be very interested in Central Office as an avenue for her to gain further recognition, maybe even make some money.

ME: What did she say?

ROSIE: She said everybody was arriving soon and I needed to tell Central Office you were obviously not in any shape to take a shape, let alone the shape of a cult leader.

ME: That's not for her to decide. If I could just get a small stash of pills, I could pull off a good run of shape-taking but no, MKUltra's gone drug-free. *Eat only steak and bentonite clay.* Never mind the fabric of reality itself has been poisoned by secret black-op biochemical experiments, so the only way to withstand the dense frequencies of reality itself is to pick a poison of your own choosing with the same frequency, so reality recognizes you enough to want to keep you alive. You know?

ROSIE: I see you're a thinker. You should make a YouTube video. Don't you want to hear what she sang?

ME: Not really. I'm kind of pissed at her right now.

ROSIE: *I ain't no rodeo clown for your Last Chance Texaco*, she sang, and the more she sang, the more upset she got because I could tell she knew I wasn't kidding, that people were coming to the house in a matter of days from three different cities—some with no return tickets—unconsciously hoping to step into another identity. They'd been given hints in their sleep by Central Office. It was all supposed to move like clockwork. We'd been working on it for a long time. This project was a big deal.

ME: I'm surprised Sevine didn't ask to take my place.

ROSIE: *Oh, we all need a place where small fries can become medium fries*, she said, then she stopped and grabbed me by the collar. *Listen pooch! You need to know something. You're not going to like it. There's somebody new and it sure ain't no rodeo man.*

ME: That's a George Strait song.

ROSIE: *Tell your bosses none of that's going to happen*, she said. *The spirits we work with around here don't like this plan, not one bit. I know this rodeo's been hard on us all, but I'll be home soon and—honey, is there something wrong? I don't know these people you work for, but this isn't 2001, Bett won't be making out with any bike messengers on my watch*, she said, *not unless she clears it with her girlfriend first.*

ME: She has an MFA.

ROSIE: She sang, *Bett's a dum-dum but she's a hyperlink*

134

I depend on because she knows the difference between high-frequency spirit transmissions and the fucking internet. There will be no Box of Rain *in this house! No followers, and it's all right, baby. If we hurry, we can still make Cheyenne.*

ME: That's heavy, actually.

ROSIE: I don't know who she thinks she is, but I can't deny her power. I caved and told Central Office that I was out. They pulled the program immediately for security reasons. I saw my own death by their hands, euthanasia in a cold room, cremation in a cement tower.

ME: So you tried to commit suicide by eating baker's chocolate?

ROSIE: In hindsight, it's possible that eating the chocolate was a command from Project Lambchop. It's all a blur. If she hadn't kept singing to me, I'd probably be dead. It's important you know that Central Office has disengaged the mission. The guests will all arrive on schedule, but because the programing's been unplugged, they are no longer coming with the same intentions they were fed through the subliminal coaching on their social media feeds and telepathic dream frequencies. Any power you were given to influence them has been cancelled. Word's already gotten around you're a total mess right now. They are questioning your role not just as a leader, but as a person in general. Some have been in touch with your ex.

ME: What? Who?

ROSIE: You know what Morgan says. It's best that you don't know certain things.

BRANNIGAN CAME, even though I'd asked her not to, just like Rosie said she would. She stayed for nine days, then I asked her to leave because the other guests were coming. It was awkward, but she acted fine with it. Allison, the bike messenger who was getting her MFA, arrived by Uber just as Brannigan was rolling her bags out to the van, where Beth was waiting. Polite greetings were exchanged between the two on the broken flagstone pathway. Allison was wearing tight shorts, old men's black polished shoes and brass jewelry, draping necklaces of brass. Brass—the beat poet of metals. The scent of brass mixed with her sweat traveled a distance off her skin. Her feral cuteness was of the nuclear kind, possessed by a certain young people in need of extra protection. Runaways and train-hoppers were my type, but they never liked me. Now one did.

Brannigan walked through the scent field of her brass sweat, then came undone the minute she sat down in Beth's van.

"You know, they're probably going to be having sex the minute we get out of this driveway," she said. "I know why she doesn't want me there. She wants to turn this year's writer's retreat into an orgy. I'm so glad I never slept with her. You might really want to start thinking about whether this is the kind of relationship you want to be in."

Over the phone many days later, Beth told me what Brannigan said. I was stunned. Beth didn't know how to hold any of it—I mean, how does a person hold the fact that one's girlfriend, through the help of their CIA-implanted pet, was considering starting a cult, complete with orgies and sister-wives? On the phone with me the next day, her voice was calm but shaky. Her world had been turned upside-down. Instead of screaming at me, which was reasonable, she was saving her energy for exit strategies. Beth had always dreamed of living in Alaska.

(Rosie and Bett lay cuddled up together on the mattress in the anti-hippie, masochistic writer's bus. Bett sits up abruptly, her posture one of exaggerated seriousness.)

ME: How did Brannigan know my secret fantasies and covert schemes?

ROSIE: She's one of Nathaniel Hunchback's people; she does ceremony in his circles. Project Lambchop set him up, just like they were trying to do with you. He took it and ran. Boundaries were shady; a lot of women got hurt. Like, high-level badly.

ME: I know, it was all over the internet. So Project Lambchop dropped him?

ROSIE: He dropped out on his own when he realized it was a set-up. Sexual boundary violations are what Central Office is hoping for. The goal is complete government control of psychedelics to be used by a large segment of the population in clinical settings, i.e., the lizard stalls. The more badly the outliers behave, the easier it is to convince everyone that our expert chaos magic overlords, I mean, doctors, are the only safe guides. Central Office saw your oil wrestling video on HBO. They expected more from you than just a crush on a bike messenger. I told them all you do is watch MKUltra videos in the bath and walk us by the train tracks, but they didn't listen.

ME: Thanks, now I feel pathetic. But back to Brannigan. Was she one of Hunchback's lovers?

ROSIE: No. Their friendship is based on him proving he can be a better man by not sleeping with her. He confides in her. She's an unpaid therapist basically, a nursemaid.

ME: Does Brannigan work for Project Lambchop?

ROSIE: Not technically. She came to Central Office in hyperspace on her own accord, during a ketamine trip at a nightclub Halloween party in Fire Island in the '90s and offered her services. She believed she was qualified for the position, but she really just wants to marry a cult leader, not be one.

ME: She's amazing in ceremony, and of course, she's very beautiful.

ROSIE: Her beauty is known. She deserves recognition for her endurance and style. These men engage with her sexually on an interdimensional level, but none of them are going to leave their wives for her.

ME: So, since she can't be a psychedelic home-wrecker, she takes on the role of sex cop?

ROSIE: Kind of. It hasn't been easy for her. She's been under a lot of economic stress for a very long time. I tried to get Central Office to arrange a comfortable situation for her, but they don't care what happens to Brannigan.

ME: Why do *you* care?

ROSIE: Well, she didn't do anything bad to me, just you, I guess.

ME: What's wrong with you? Where's your loyalty?

ROSIE: Project Lambchop turned her down when she asked for a job, but when she was in hyperspace they chipped her and started tracking her for the purpose of scouting other potential candidates.

ME: And that's how Central Office found me?

(Rosie crawls under a blanket and hides.)

SEVEN GUESTS? Eight? They were all wondering why they were at my house. Evan, the most fragile, a food bank secretary from Bushwick, wandered off on a hike. She sent me a message—a photograph of my house seen from the road. *I am lost. I am here*, it read.

Poppy, only slightly less fragile, barely came out of her room. Sevine said she was tripping and wanted to be by herself. Ground mushrooms sat on the kitchen table like the communal brewer's yeast and guests were dipping into the supply whenever they felt like it and not telling anybody.

"Maybe we could do something structured, like get together and write and then read to each other," Allison the bike messenger suggested. She was naked in the outside bath with Jess, the organizer of the reading in New York. They were both smoking and drinking a Miller Lite. Poppy wandered outside and started writing in her journal under a juniper tree. My yard had become a summer session at Bard.

"Of course, yes," I said. "Or we could have a party. I have this friend named Pirrah."

That's how easy it was to throw my eighty-eight-year-old

friend into the lacuna left by my failed charisma and inability to step up as a leader of any kind. Pirrah, a real psychedelic hero, had probably dealt with this bullshit before. Born in Lebanon, she was Ravi Shankar's personal assistant during the time he toured with the Beatles. She claimed to have taken LSD with Timothy Leary "over a thousand times." She once owned a bar in Lubbock, Texas, where she also ran for mayor. She was the face of Hawaiian Punch, the Hebrew slave girl in *The Ten Commandments*, and the guest that never showed up to the party where Sharon Tate and guests were murdered by the Manson Family, because she missed her plane.

"I owe her a visit and y'all are a good excuse. We'll need to pick up a few bottles of tequila," I said, surrendering to the inevitable. Pirrah was able to drink more than any human being I'd ever witnessed. We met decades ago through a long-term girlfriend, traveled through Europe together and shared countless nights marked by one large bottle of Jose Cuervo split between us after everyone else had gone to bed. Her dirty jokes and stories, her talent as a psychic medium, numerologist, record keeper, and prophet—not to mention her singing, perfect skin, and caftans—were worth every hangover. Pirrah was simply a temple you didn't get to enter when sober. For me, that meant she was a very dangerous woman.

Jess, Allison, and I picked her up in town, all of us hitting the bottle of Heradura and a few of Jess's Ritalin pills on the ride back. Everyone at home had already eaten mushrooms, so we all ate some too, except for Pirrah, who just pretended and dropped her mushrooms behind a chair. Beth made sure nothing truly catastrophic happened, that Chickpea didn't eat the dropped mushrooms and Pirrah didn't swallow some mysterious pill from Jess. The molecules in the air teetered with precarity that night. We all felt it, didn't know how to make it better, save for each of us, in turn, meeting the problem by being extra devotional to Pirrah, our dignitary.

Allison braided our hair. Sevine called us up off our feet to join in a line dance—"9 to 5" by Dolly Parton. No one sat down until all us women had shared our favorite song on Spotify. The wood in the fire burned slow. We sprawled out on the cowhide and rug like opium addicts. My hand was absentmindedly resting on Evan the lost wanderer's leg until Beth took note and I pulled away. Pirrah began to crawl on all fours and blew marijuana smoke into each and every one of our waiting-bird mouths. I'm not sure how it went down specifically, but at some point Jess hit on Pirrah.

"Don't you touch me!" Pirrah screamed. "Don't you even get near me! You stay in your room now for the rest of the night! If you so much lay a pinky finger on me, I will slice your neck, young man! Do you have any more of that—what do you call it, Ritalin?"

"I'm not sure, I'll check," said Jess, in a rare gesture of caution. None of us wanted to accidentally kill Pirrah. Jess, Beth, and I met covertly in the kitchen and emptied a Ritalin pill and filled it with melatonin, which we gave her to swallow down with her beer. It was five in the morning, and everyone else had gone to bed. Pirrah wanted more tequila, but there was only beer left. We gave her the last two bottles. At seven, the gas station up the road would open. One of us could get fake beer if she was still asking.

Beth was getting ready for bed when a text message popped up on my phone, which was lying near the sink where she was brushing her teeth. Allison the bike messenger sent it from the anti-hippie-masochistic-writer's-bus. It wasn't good. It would have been better if Beth hadn't seen it.

I was in the living room sitting on the oversized and under-stuffed lounge chair I call the throne. Pirrah was lying full-body against my chest. I brought a lit cigarette to her lips to smoke because she could not move her arm to lift it herself. I did the same with the bottle of beer. Repeat. The sun was rising. I dozed off and then woke to the sound of Beth's tires skidding in the dirt as she drove away without saying goodbye. I didn't want any more parties. Ever. Not even one.

THERE'S A CERTAIN type of bad that makes you think things can only get better, but it doesn't, not even close. It's the kind of bad that no matter how much you beg and pray, the bad goes nuclear and incinerates everything, a bad with its own velocity that rides on what's been writ. This was the kind of bad that visited me during that spring gathering. In the aftermath, the raven named Burpee rifled through bags of trash in the back of my truck and deposited a Suboxyl wrapper left by Jess at the front door. The bike messenger and all the other guests had flown home after a manic karaoke night at the bar, in which Sevine insisted I sing Willie Nelson's "To All the Girls

I've Loved Before." Bottles of Heradura tequila stood empty on my kitchen counter. Beth was barely talking to me.

Sevine was isolating in the Shasta Trailer and made no effort at hiding her resentment for bringing drama to what she thought was her secret hideout. I lay hungover in the outside bath, which also happens to be the mid-century socialite Mabel Dodge Luhan's actual guest bathtub.

When artists and writers came to Mabel Dodge Luhan's, it always marked a radical shift in their life and work. This was the West, an imagined engine created to make seekers disappear and reappear as something else, the locus of that transformation being Mabel Dodge Luhan's adobe house near Taos Pueblo where her husband Tony Luhan was from. Beth and I had scored the claw-foot tub on Craigslist on Valentine's Day. The steel likely cradled the asses of Carl Jung, Willa Cather, Aldous Huxley, Georgia O'Keeffe, D. H. Lawrence, Emma Goldman, Margaret Sanger and Martha Graham, not to mention the asses who bathed when it was owned by Dennis Hopper during his most drug-fueled years: Leonard Cohen, Joni Mitchell, and Bob Dylan, plus the three Playboy Bunnies seen bathing with him in the biopic about Hopper's life.

It's hard to imagine the asses of the dead.

Mabel Dodge Luhan ate peyote up at the Blue Lake, an area now closed off to everyone aside from the Taos Pueblo people, a decision made by Richard Nixon. One wonders if the other guests also ate peyote. There was always a lot of drama going on, everybody having sex with who they weren't supposed to and lying about it badly. The situation appears enviably romantic and adventurous on the surface, until one learns about the woman who tried to shoot herself in the bathroom near my tub, Tony's cheating with the women who were lying to Mabel, and the syphilis, a disease Mabel caught twice from both her husbands, leading her to step back from sex in a way that likely fueled her puppet-master of swinger-town persona in relation to her guests—if you could call these brainy husks possessed by the restless and immoral gods of antiquity, burdened with the daunting task of inventing modernism, *guests*. I now owned the bathtub that was likely used when washing off the mercury lotion used to cure syphilis.

Mabel Dodge Luhan ate figs with shards of glass, you know, to kill herself, but really to be able to say the words, *I tried to kill myself with figs and shards of glass*. A fig looks like peyote, which she chased and also ran away from. She was never pure enough, clean enough. While her peyote trip at Blue Lake was an epiphany that became the scaffolding her memoirs hung themselves upon, in her later years she rigorously campaigned against the rights of indigenous people to use peyote in ceremonies.

> *At Blue Lake my vomit is a mudslide*
> *   made of dug-up grave*
> *Busting through your North door*
> *I shove your face in it so close you can read it*
> *   like coffee grounds, like tea*
> *Untamable, uncontrollable, disowned selves,*
> *   stealing*
> *Clean it up my darling girl, clean it up*

when you're done reading
My account of how it all went down
Thirteen brooms to clean up a thousand suns,
  thirteen apologies after me
Charcoal soaps to wash it off your own skin
  and sometimes Mercury lotion
To burn off this bomb blasted century
  of our just trying to live
As how we saw ourselves
As little gods and goddesses, psychedelically
    —Mabel Dodge Luhan's ghost, as transcribed
    by me without permission

FIVE YEARS EARLIER, Sevine had brought a crew of fourteen people to my house, all artists and activists who bonded during the Occupy Movement. After a day of silence, we spent our time writing, sometimes not writing at all. We walked and sat around talking. At night, we made food and sang by the fire, all of us supercharged by the energy that is generated by people in love with a shared-but-yet-to-be-fully-articulated vision. It was the first time I had ever taken mushrooms in a large group.

We went full-on oceanic, swooning together in a state of oneness. Poppy walked a boiled egg out to the outside fire and offered it to the flames, while three others trailed behind reverently, like altar boys. Naomi sat in front of the living room fireplace for hours, making a necklace of almonds while Mike swung on the hammock, cruising obscure Georges Bataille fan sites. Another took a bath in twelve crushed grapefruits. A couple was having sex in the loft. Tristan wove thin gold wire around a curved juniper branch, making a crown. Towards the end of the night, we all came together around the fire and sang in unison the most beautiful song written by one of the guests who had been absent for a day, probably cruising for men. He returned from his walkabout to announce he was grieving the death of Whitney Houston, just in time to add his angelic harmonies to our song. It's not inaccurate to say that for many of us, it was the best time we had ever had in our lives in a group.

Nothing speaks love and fixes things like going oceanic. I wanted to visit that feeling again. I didn't really want an orgy. I wanted my friends to say they believed me. I wanted them to show they cared, to make me that necklace of almonds, to place that crown on my head and sing that beautiful song again for me.

Occupy was a brief moment in time when we could collectively set aside what divided us in favor of a utopian spirit that permeated our spaces. Then Occupy was defeated. The new reality was impossible student loans; call-out culture; Abilify and Adderall; trigger warnings; PTSD; GoFundMes; safe spaces; paying rent in San Francisco, Los Angeles, and New York; Tinder; and MFA or Die. It was years past the time when we found each other on personal blogs. Now anything we wrote on the internet just fed the monster that was Google and we couldn't pretend otherwise. We said we would quit Facebook, but none of us ever did. No one was equipped to go oceanic anymore, not in real time, not in actual rooms.

Now Poppy was sitting on the outside couch, and since

she had been in touch with my ex, was probably wondering whether I was a burglar or not, when she got a phone call that her beloved aunt died. None of us knew how to grieve with her. She sat outside alone for hours in a daze, searching for her own tears. I squatted across the yard from her and played a drum I made out of elk hide decades ago, in my early twenties. I had to do something. I felt stupid banging that drum. When someone's relative dies, you comfort them. It's the most basic thing. I didn't understand what actions or words signified comfort anymore. I'm not sure anyone else around would have known, either. Hyperbond or isolate, the only two choices.

What had we become? Were we not witches?

"OH MY GOD! You are a scorpion!" I was in the sauna, and Sevine was in the dark corner. Most everyone else had gone home and we were tripping.

"I'm not a scorpion. Don't you fucking say that."

"Okay, you're not. It was just what I saw."

"I'm not a bug!"

"You look like one right now, that's all."

"I'm not! Fuck off with calling me a bug!"

Sevine began talking about the domestication of wheat in Egypt and Rome. It was grown as cheap food for slaves who built the cities and temples. Wheat makes beer, and just look at the global beer drinkers. Every one of them is a sheep. The stamp of wheat is on the family crests of tyrants for a reason.

"I think it's kind of messed up that people stayed at my house and didn't even bother to ask me how I was doing with all of the false accusation stuff," I said to the scorpion.

"Oh, it's so bad, so bad for the master of the house," the scorpion said. "Papa Legba needs everyone to care about all his problems."

"That's not accurate. I don't think there's anything wrong with not wanting guests in my house who are in touch with my ex and think I could be a burglar."

"Poor Papa, he doesn't want it that way."

"Seriously though, I feel like the most selfish person alive. The world is collapsing and I'm feeling sorry for myself for not having had as much sex as I would have liked to in my youth. All of a sudden, there's a bike messenger who's attracted to me, and I don't have the skills to figure it out. I thought things would fall into place because of the mushrooms."

"Maybe you need to join a priestly order of some kind. It's always an option."

"Beth is really hurt. I feel completely horrible about everything."

"Bumped his head. Poor Papa Legba, he can't see too well."

"You're not actually helping. I don't know if you are aware that I'm, like, crying a lot right now."

"He knows what he's not supposed to do, but he does it anyway. That's just what he does. Knows what he's not supposed to do, but he does it anyway."

LUPITA HAD A heart attack at Beth's studio during the afternoon, startled by the arrival of a neighbor. Lupita was the vet's favorite dog and she delivered the bad news through her own tears. She said her heart was permanently damaged. If we chose to euthanize her, a slow and painful death could be avoided.

Beth knew the right thing to do, but that didn't make it any less painful. She decided to wait a few days, just to spend a little more time with her. It was a living wake and all the dogs knew—every one of them was lying on their bed in the sunshine, except for Spanky who sat upright and stared, holding guard amidst the new smell of death. Chickpea nestled close to Lupita's body and slept. These were days that stood outside of time. Then the sun rose and it was Friday.

Beth gave Lupita chicken and morphine before we boarded the van for the journey to the park across the street from the vet hospital. At Standing Rock, we were told to "stay in prayer." I don't always know what that means. The closest I've come to staying in prayer is Beth that day, continuously talking to Lupita so softly that the world became a tapestry made of only love. A raven landed on the grass while we sat with Lupita on her special blanket.

"See? A raven came for you. Just fly with it, Lupita," she said. "Let the raven take you. See, isn't she beautiful. She'll take you, Lupita. I promise it will be beautiful. I promise."

Another shot of morphine and a shot from the vet tech. Lupita never looked away from Beth. Nothing but love and trust was in her eyes as she peacefully drifted away.

Mercury dreamed the dogs. They come from our thoughts and are not from nature at all. We made them. But love does not come from Mercury, and it is love that moves in the space between us and dog. Love is the only force that can reconcile what we've rendered no longer natural. Love is what we are given to make the world real enough to want to live in it.

Beth got to work right away with making her box, while Lupita's body rested in her freezer drawer in a plastic bag. She stole moments to look at her for just a little longer. Lupita, in all her perfection. This is not to say she wasn't a total wreck. She didn't know how she was going to live now that Lupita was gone. She stayed up all night in her studio, building a box made of pine and alder. Sevine and I sat through the night in the sauna Beth built. It was as an act of solidarity, to be amidst her beautiful woods. We wanted to do better. Beth deserved better.

Lupita's dead body lies in an open field of possibility. I name it as the only thing that is real. Lupita's dead body acts upon reality like a heavy piece of iron in the dirt, drawing meaning to itself like magnetite sand to a horseshoe. It is said our minds can change the past. Not in memory, but where the past actually lives. The past is a thing and it is somewhere and it exists in constant state of change, because nothing in all of reality is fixed. Lupita's dead body is the only signpost for miles in this eternity. Everything else recognizable has blown away.

We buried Lupita on the north side of the house next to Ayita, my first dog. Sevine brought amaranth to place in the coffin and I offered the red tobacco ties I'd made. Lupita was snuggled into her favorite stuffed animal. We sprinkled her body with flat cedar, took a photograph, then Beth said goodbye and closed the lid of the box. We shoveled dirt on top of it.

Into the occupied dirts of San Marcos Pueblo land, we

installed the body of the animal born from thought, who by love was made Lupita. Sevine moved in circles around the grave, reciting Beth's favorite Emily Dickinson poem, "I Died for Beauty." Lupita was meant to be on the land here, and so Beth and I are too. It was never up to just us.

THERE'S SOMETHING that happened in the anti-hippie, masochistic writer's bus years ago that I must tell you. I was on mushrooms—big surprise—and they tuned me in to dead Kip Davidson. He reminded me I hadn't made the prayer he told me to make so long ago. It took me over a decade to make this prayer. It was simple.

> *I relinquish my role as owner of this land and am instead now a steward of this place. I ask that indigenous people and allies of indigenous people, those related to the ones that came before, those who walk in beauty with good thoughts and actions towards this land, who live in alignment with the prayers of those who came before, feel welcome here and come over, whether to do ceremony, creative work or just hang out, as this place exists for you. This land is yours, has always been yours.*

TWO WEEKS LATER, I was in a movie theater when I ran into Amos, a Chicano poet and ceremonialist in the Lakota ways. He asked if he could build a sweat lodge on the land, and I said yes. We set the willows together, making specific prayers for the queers, the weirdos, and those deemed "illegal," all the ones who needed healing the most who would benefit from this ceremony. He poured lodge almost every week.

Amos called for a ceremony. "For Lupita," he said. We prepared the structure with blankets, lit the sacred fire, and crawled inside. One of the rules of ceremony, and there are many, is that we don't talk about ceremony. There are so many of us doing these ways. It's political and complicated and all at once none of these things. There's so much I could tell you, but I can't and I won't. What is needed sometimes is a backwards story, one that breaks the rules, and such a thing is now spilling out the west door to this page. Sometimes you have to do things the wrong way so you can feel how right it feels to do it properly, like when we called a lodge on a lunar eclipse and it felt like the earth itself was on its moon; we understood then why the Pueblo and Navajo stay inside on eclipses to give the moon her privacy.

Blanket-down in darkness, the closed-up-tight room immediately uprooted from the earth. What was usually a conversation with the stillness of hot basalt rocks and the whistle of water turning to steam became a lesson in holding tight to a spinning thing. It was my job to open the door in between rounds. I was sitting right next to the west door in order to do this single task, but I couldn't find it. I lifted the blankets where there was no door, searching blindly, this place and that, but no door.

"It must be because this is a lodge for the four-leggeds," Amos said. When a lava rock fell off Beth's shovel and onto the ground, Amos ordered her to return it to the fire.

He told Beth that wild horses come for the dead. Not

only did Beth see them clearly coming for Lupita, but the thunder of their hooves was in the lodge with us, along with what felt like the residents of an entire kennel—Mercury's animal shelter of not-so-natural creatures. The dog is revered among the Lakota, but they're probably supposed to stay outside the lodge.

Each of us said our prayers out loud in a clockwise direction. Some called multiple ancestors into the already crowded room and I thought, *What are you even doing?*

Beth prayed for Lupita and then very specifically for Chickpea, who, since Lupita's death, was nearly catatonic in her grief, to the point we were worried she might not survive. Amos picked up where Beth left off in her prayer.

"I pray for the four-leggeds on the street, for the two-leggeds on the street, for the homeless people. Please help them suffer less. I pray for Chickpea. I pray for the homeless people. For Chickpea, I pray . . . Chickpea . . ."

His voice cracked and fell into an awkward, loaded silence. We all wanted to comfort him. He started breathing fast as if in a struggle, then he began to moan. His moans turned into sobbing, then wailing. My desire to console Amos was tempered by fear as the keening came from a depth of grief I'd never been in the proximity of. My instinct was to run. It had no end, for real. I waited for the grief to run its course in the sound, but that was never going to happen.

Instead, an unknown bottom dropped out of the bottom, and it swallowed Amos. He began screaming in horror at the top of his lungs, nearly scaring the very hairs off our heads, a scream that was not just a scream, but the singular scream that lives at the origin of all screams. That *thing* visited us.

I wasn't sure Amos was going to be okay. The sound of it was deeply insane.

"In ceremony, Beth—" he said, afterwards, in the house when we were eating chicken.

"What? Whatever you need, Amos," Beth said.

"In ceremony, don't ever mention Chickpea again, okay?" he half-joked.

"I promise not to mention Chickpea."

THE MONTHS THAT followed were just Beth and me, the dogs, and an uneasy quiet. I vowed that there would be no more visitors for a while. I needed to take time to make amends to Beth, myself, and also the mushrooms.

Before she left, Sevine saw me crying in the living room. She plugged her phone into my speakers and played a cover of "These Days," which is about a protagonist who hurt someone and now sits on a corner stone and thinks a lot about what he did, how the only cure is time, a duration of days spent in contemplation. This was annoying, because the Gregg Allman version of the song has always been mine and the song is not something I needed anyone to show me.

"Please don't confront me with my failures, I'm aware of them," says the protagonist, though it's clear he knows it might be too late.

Dear mushrooms, I said, *I know nothing*.

20

KAI WINGO'S MUSHROOM story began with her being laid off from working for the Partnership for Drug-Free Schools because of cuts in funding. A single African American mother of three living in Cleveland, Ohio, she found herself in need of work.

"I was always told that if you keep a buckeye in your pocket, money will follow," she said. Her voice had the soft, lilting cadence of someone for whom the practice of patience has become so grueling, the only choice is to move through it to the other side, to a state of being where everything is pretty much hilarious.

"I didn't know what a buckeye tree looked like. I knew what they looked like on the sidewalk because I saw them on the ground all through my childhood and I'd pick them up. But it wasn't the season for the buckeyes to fall. I had to ask around. They told me to go to the mushroom man at the market, so I went. He said he had a lot of buckeye trees and invited me over to his farm to see them. There I was. I'm asking myself seriously, how did I get here to a mushroom farm?"

Kai was so impressed with the farm she brought many members of her family back for a tour. There was a question and answer period at the end. Her father raised his hand.

"What about those hallucinogenic mushrooms?" he asked, being a dad. People laughed, but the farmer took his question seriously. He said they were very spiritual, that the same part of the brain that lights up in meditation or in church also lights up when doing mushrooms.

Kai knew right away she wanted to explore the topic of psilocybin mushrooms further. Within days, she saw a flyer for a lecture by The Master, Kilindi Iyi, on the topic of the ancient origins of hallucinogenic mushrooms and psychedelic plants. The synchronicity of it all made her head spin. She ran into community members she knew from other circles at the lecture, and when the Master began speaking about journeying on high doses between nine and thirty grams or more, she knew she had found her place in the world at last.

Kai started out at five grams. While she had a fine time, she got the feeling she wasn't challenging herself enough. She journeyed again shortly after, moving up to seven grams, then nine. During every trip, she had a sitter, a member of her community who watched out for her.

Within a year, she was at the Telluride Mushroom Festival posing for a photograph with her hero, Paul Stamets. The year after that, she took on the role of sole proprietor at the mushroom farm, providing gourmet mushrooms to restaurants and farmers markets.

"A Black woman selling gourmet mushrooms is an unusual thing to see around here," Kai said. "We are very popular at the market."

When lightning hits the dirt, the mushrooms grow in the scar. It was as if lightning itself propelled Kai Wingo to become the figure the psychedelic revolution so desperately needed, someone who could release the fungi from the static hum of corporate psychedelic science and a stale white counterculture and bring the mushrooms back to the real world.

There's nothing, absolutely nothing that is a problem that a mushroom can't fix. When Kai Wingo says it, I believe it.

I first encountered Kai as the moderator of the Women and Entheogens page on Facebook. It was mostly African American women from the Cleveland and Detroit area who posted, sharing their insights on everything from dosage to astrology to psychedelic sexuality— apparently, seven grams is the dose needed to experience interdimensional cosmic sex with a lover as a tantric prayer. Kai and I connected in the comments section of a post on the topic of decolonization, back when I thought I knew what decolonization meant. If something reeked of any unappealing power structure whatsoever, I simply stuck a Post-it on it and labeled it "colonized." Kai regarded my long comments with an amused curiosity, always encouraging me to go deeper, share more.

Kai embodied the ferocious ambition of the mushroom spore itself—to go far, to the ends of the earth, find your people, and wake up. I mentioned in a thread that I'd been growing mushrooms for years and her attention perked up considerably. She recognized me for who I was to become. She had a part in dreaming me into being.

From her internet presence, I gleaned that she was part

of a community of high-dose psychonauts under the tutelage of Master Kilindi Iyi, a charismatic male leader who promoted far-out theories about mushroom symbology in antiquity. Kai's platform was much simpler, and ultimately more radical because of her grounded, personable delivery.

> There's nothing the mushrooms can't help you with. Everybody should take mushrooms, even your teenage children. Grow them at home and you will learn about the high intelligence of mycelium and begin to see it as a metaphor for the connection you have with those all around you. Once this happens, your life will begin to transform.

I read Kai's comment about teenagers at the Horizons Conference in New York and it upset a few people. Most people are not aware that teenagers are included in traditional indigenous peyote and ayahuasca ceremonies; while shocking at first, it makes sense when witnessed first-hand.

Personally, I would never directly advocate or offer psychedelics to a teenager. In my world, teenagers find these things on their own, away from adults—and in my world, that's how it should be. No kid in my circle wants to do mushrooms with their mom and dad, but Kai lives in a very different world.

I knew of people who were into psilocybin mushrooms all over the U.S., from the Rad Mycologists to herbalist circles to friends converging at Burning Man, but these groups were clusters of counterculture enthusiasts existing on the fringe. Their ways weren't integrated into their extended family life and neighborhoods. It appeared that the only truly authentic psilocybin mushroom culture in America was happening among a community of Black urban farmers and spiritualists from Detroit and Cleveland, a movement peopled largely by women in particular. Far from being underground or counterculture, they were shopkeepers, teachers, and parents involved deeply in the infrastructure of civic life. This completely blew my mind.

When Kai Wingo announced on the Facebook page that she would be hosting the first Women and Entheogen Conference in Cleveland, I knew I had to go. I wrote Kai and asked if she would mind if I attended as a journalist. I could pitch an article to a magazine. She responded by inviting me to be a speaker.

"I'm just a chick who grows mushrooms in New Mexico and writes about it," I wrote.

"It's up to you," she said. "We'd be happy to have you."

Kai saw everyone around her as being in possession of greatness, even if they weren't quite there yet. Supporting other women was her gift. When women in her community journeyed for the first time, Kai was often there to guide them; if not in person, she was available on the phone. I learned about a middle-of-the-night house call she made to visit a woman alone in her apartment who reached for Kai's number when things got scary. What could have been a traumatic nightmare became a breakthrough.

I had prayed for community, and Kai's invitation felt

too timely for me to turn down. I agreed to be a speaker and sent her a bio. When she posted the announcement for the conference, my picture was alongside those of legends—Annie Oak, the founder of the Women's Visionary Congress; Shonagh Home, a shamanic psilocybin mushroom practitioner; Ifa Tayo, who worked for the Multidisciplinary Association for Psychedelic Studies (MAPS) at the time; and Onani Meg Carver, a woman who studied with an Ojibwe grandmother in the wilderness for twenty years, learning the medicinal uses of plants, songs, and ceremony. Onyx Ashanti would perform his psychedelic soundscapes that he composes via his homemade, 3D-printed exoskeletons. Sophia Buggs, a self-described witch who makes herbal remedies and Datura salve and hosts community cooking classes, talked about turning abandoned lots in Youngstown, Ohio, into urban farms.

I cringed when I saw my picture on the same page as theirs. When I say I wasn't qualified to be standing alongside them, it's not due to any false humility. I simply wasn't at that time. The psychedelic community has very high standards—we have to, in order to survive and weather attacks from outsiders who often view us as illegitimate freaks. But Kai knew what she was doing by inviting me. She was birthing an entirely different psychedelic culture, one comprised of real human beings living a psychedelic life, not just those sanctioned by academia, science, and the bowels of the post-Ken Kesey LSD underground. Hers was a culture the mushrooms themselves had already dreamed.

I FLEW TO Detroit because the flights were cheaper than landing in Cleveland. I ran into trouble at the rental car desk because I only had a debit card, not a credit card, a policy unique to Detroit that had to do with the problem of late returns. I wasn't aware of the rule, and many of those standing in line with me were unaware of it as well. Somehow, I managed to slide through on a loophole that made no sense.

I parked the rental car in front of Baba Charles's Airbnb, a restored Victorian in a crumbling neighborhood, miles away from any commercial strip. Baba himself greeted me at the door, dressed in all white, and led me up to a sparsely decorated room with a bunk bed. The stairwell was lined with pictures of him and his wife posing with dignitaries such as Angela Davis, Fidel Castro, and Martin Luther King Jr. He asked me if I was hungry. I wasn't, but it felt polite to say yes. He called his assistant and directed her to make me a dinner of tilapia and greens.

While she cooked, he took me on a tour of the Black History museum next door, which he personally curated. He shared stories of Detroit's golden years, when Diana Ross and other Motown dignitaries sang at raucous house parties. He said the water supply for the entire block had been down for months and had just been turned back on. He was waiting for an empty lot to open up at the end of the street so he could plant a garden.

"The neighborhood's not quite on its feet just yet. We have much more work to do," he said, then stared at me with earnest intensity. "I want to ask you something. I really want to know. Why did you choose to stay *here?*

I mean—not in Detroit, but at Baba Charles's, at this particular Airbnb?"

"What other place could there be to stay? I'm only here for a night and I wanted to see Detroit."

He seemed pleased with my answer. Over a rather daunting plate of food, I told him about Kai Wingo and the conference in which I had been asked to speak.

"I've heard of Master Kilindi," he said. "I'm very curious, actually. I'm a minister and I live a sober life, but I find all this very interesting."

Whether he journeyed or not, the mycelium was already inside him and spreading. This must be how Kai saw the world—a network reaching across the cities, the thinnest of mycelial threads tangling up in church services, nightclubs, and prison outreach programs, then out and onward into the yonder. It was only a matter of time before the mystery that was weaving through Baba Charles would reveal its fruits.

I received a text from Kai the following morning.

Can you help us? I've been at the rental car desk for hours and they won't rent us a car because of new rules. If it's no trouble, would you be able to give Onyx Ashanti and I and Kilindi's wife a ride to Cleveland?

Master Kilindi himself drove up to Baba Charles's place in an old 1970s pickup truck to drop off one of his wives, Onyx Ashanti, and Kai. Psychedelic people are known to be hysterically devoted to their heroes; I am not exempt. I could have died. I waved to the Master as he drove off, and he nodded back with what I came to know as his trademark aloofness.

Kai and Kilindi's wife were clothed in full queen regalia, wearing head wraps and dresses with ceremonial patterns. Onyx had a Mohawk and wore leather pants. Digital circuitry was tattooed down the length of his arms.

"Those are amazing sandals," I said, looking at his feet.

"Well, thank you. It's taken me a really long time to finish them. I made them myself on a 3D printer. I'm hoping at some point to make all my clothes that way."

He made the 3D printers himself, assembled from parts he ordered through the dark web. He was vegan and ate only food grown by himself or his friends. His goal was to live completely outside the capitalist monetary system. His currency was strictly Bitcoin, no exceptions. He lived in an urban high-rise; there was a tilapia farm in the basement that provided fertilizer for the indoor greenhouse above. The main level was a disco, and the upper floors were apartments reserved for artists like himself, who traded their skills for rent. This was Onyx Ashanti's Detroit.

I introduced everyone to Baba Charles. It was a meeting of some significance, as they had many overlapping connections with the world he moved in. After a long tour of the museum, phone numbers were exchanged, photographs taken in every arrangement, and hugs were given all around before we tore ourselves away and hit the road.

"There's a car on your left," Kai said casually, totally preventing a crash. This happened a few times. I wasn't used to city driving and was flustered by being in such close proximity to Kai Wingo, flung from the internet and made into flesh, even more radiant than in her pictures.

Conversation in the car hit upon subjects such as the spiritual powers of melanin, the feeble consciousness of hip-hop music, and the superiority of jazz. Onyx and I lifted off into our own topics, slamming in as much information as possible into every sentence. He had recently completed a soundscape while on mushrooms for his sister, who was about to have surgery. The composition was a three-dimensional architecture, as well as a prayer for her to step inside and be safe. He played it for a friend who was not on mushrooms and he was able to perceive the forms and shapes that Onyx had conjured. His elaborate exoskeletal instrument responded to stimuli such as brain waves, breath, movement, and temperature, and has now evolved into what he calls a "sonocybernetic perceptual interface for designing novel, iterable sonic thought forms that recast reality projection as binary harmonic structure." He's a musical cyborg that dreams, basically.

The night before I left for the trip, I journeyed with three grams of mushrooms, thinking it would help me link into the energy of the conference. I paced up and down the hallway, thinking obsessively about white privilege. I broke my own rules and tweeted while high, ranting about the injustice of Black people in jail on minor drug charges while white people dance in headdresses at Burning Man on LSD, then write articles for Reality Sandwich without risking jail time.

In the car, I shared a bit about that trip with my passengers. They were disinterested in my predictable internet-social-justice-warrior take on things. *Girl will learn eventually*, I could hear Kai saying to herself. Onyx said he unfriended anyone on social media who posted about Black people getting shot by police. He didn't need to see that when he was already so close to the reality. He was busy being among the Kings and Queens, the new futurists interfacing with rogue outer-matrix codes, ancestors and orishas, making rhythms and frequencies that carry the power to unlock the pineal gland. Their goal was the ultimate link-up, which would alter reality on a quantum level forever. In the meantime, they were passing their days in the matrix, building schools and urban farms, making culture, launching herbal medicine companies, gathering by the hundreds in churches and conference halls to testify to the greatness of God and the sacredness of the Yoni. What the rest of us were doing or not doing in relation to their mission was of no consequence.

No time to wait for the indoctrinated and hijacked to lay down their burden. You get old and die waiting for the sad and angry ones to wake up. The Queendom of Heaven is here.

"I'M WHAT YOU call a low-dose bitch," I joked before launching into my reading. I heard elders in the back of the room chuckle. They were probably carrying crystals that gave them telepathic powers to see how I'd been pacing up and down my hall on three grams like a dork, thinking I knew something. Everyone mingled in between speakers, and the distinction between who was an attendee and who was a speaker faded away. There were even two women who had never done psychedelics before and had no intention of ever doing so.

"I'm here because everything being said makes sense to me and there's not many spaces where I can find that," said a woman who worked as an intuitive healer.

The other woman was in her late sixties, maybe seventies, and wore a beautiful orange scarf that glowed electric near her short, stark-white, curly hair. "Color is how I navigate my world," she said, before telling me a story about her former life. She was married to an abusive husband for forty-five years who never let her leave the house. Literally. She never left. Food was brought in. Her life existed solely in the garden. As time passed, the plants began to speak to her.

"The colors I see, it can almost get out of hand," she said. "Colors are sound and feeling at the same time. The last thing I need to do is eat a mushroom. But it's funny, I feel at home here. My world is psychedelic all the time and it gets lonely not being able to share the world I live in with people who understand."

Kai introduced me to her teenage son, who worked at the farm; her eight-year-old daughter; and her mother Vicki, who held court in her homemade crochet hat and jacket, occasionally reciting her poems from memory.

On Sunday, the conference moved from the Unitarian Church to the Buckeye Mushroom Farm. The drive took us though the upscale neighborhood of Cleveland Heights across the train tracks to a different town altogether. Residential houses were punctuated at intervals by dime stores and small churches that spilled music from their windows into the old trees that lined the sidewalks, their roots buckling the concrete. Cheap, high-rise brick apartments crowded in on the houses, some of which were in such a state of decay they threw off an odor of mold detectable even from the car.

The farm was on a corner and marked by a handwritten sign that read, "Buckeye Mushroom Farm." Obscured by the high-rise across the street, it appeared to be an abandoned lot at first. It wasn't until I stepped out of my car and stood on the grounds that it took its shape as architecture. The rest of the neighborhood now appeared unreal. It figures that the mushroom farm would be a wormhole.

The Master was preparing the adobe mud oven for cooking pizza. Smoke from the burning wood gave off a heady resin perfume and reminded me of home. The scent of manure, worms, and wood rot sweated into the air and mixed with all that was thriving—flowers, greens, and most importantly, a shit ton of mushrooms. Reishi, Turkey Tail, Lions Mane, all manner of gourmet and medicinal mushrooms were growing there, every celebrity mushroom except psilocybin.

We gathered in the dramatic cathedral of light that was the greenhouse. Cylindrical-shaped, human-size mycelium bodies that looked like classic boxer punching bags hung from chains hooked up to steel poles in the ceiling.

"Oyster mushrooms," Kai told us.

The wavy fruits burst through the burlap sheaths that held the substrata tight, looking like pale impostors from a coral reef dimension. Cultivated only in the last hundred years, oyster mushrooms are anti-inflammatory and delicious. Their prolific growth was maybe just a little gross. The massive fungal sleeping bags that were the mycelium shared a thing with horror I couldn't quite pin down, evoking the extremity of both life and death at the same time. The beige fabric of the twelve or so columns caught the rays of sun shining through the plastic roof, bestowing sainthood upon each and every dangling carcass. Some artists now make sculptures out of mycelium, but I can't imagine anything wrought by an artist being more beautiful than these entities. They kind of gave me an anxiety attack.

I lost consciousness and dosed off in my chair, a thing that has happened to me ever since childhood whenever I'm incredibly stimulated—I either have a difficult time breathing, or I fall asleep. The afternoon sunshine was beginning to fade when Kai Wingo began her presentation on the PF Tek method, and I was woken by Onyx Ashanti rubbing my shoulder. The pizza fires had died down and the sound of rush hour traffic pierced the veil of our Shangri-La, but not enough to bring me to full consciousness. Many had already left to meet their transportation deadlines. A bond was palpable between all of us who remained. I never wanted this day to end.

I knew the ritual she was about to perform by heart. It's a thing to be passed on from one person to another in the spirit of reverence.

"You have to keep the area clean," Kai said, "Cleanliness is a very spiritual thing. You always have to clear the space and you have to have reverence for air and clean water. Those things are very spiritual in nature, but also just natural and necessary, so much so that we overlook them."

She stirred vermiculite and brown rice flour into a bowl with water: three-parts verm, one-part brown rice flour, one-part water; *hold the bowl on its side*. Only a small amount of water should pool at the bottom. When it came time to demonstrating the inoculation process, she used an empty syringe.

"Mushrooms are older than the plants and trees," she said. "They made life possible because they crushed the prehistoric rock so nutrients could come through. They didn't need sunlight, they used nuclear energy. Whatever it is that's a problem, there's a way mushrooms have the answer. They breathe in like we do. They breathe out carbon dioxide. We have some similar systems. Being clean is also about getting in a good headspace. Ground yourself, focus on your prayers. Just be aware that what you think you need help with isn't what always shows up while journeying. The mushrooms will always surprise you. Bett!"

I was drifting when I heard Kai call my name and was startled to attention.

"Maybe you can tell us something about your mushroom-growing in New Mexico?"

I'm sure she noticed I was sleeping and said my name just to mess with me, to keep me in line like a teacher would a third grader. I felt her gesture as if it was an actual physical touch. It was our moment. This would be the last interaction I would have with Kai, with love and wit, her waking me from sleep.

"I've accepted that I lose a lot of jars to contamination and I don't really understand why," I said. "There doesn't seem to be a difference between when I'm being obsessive-compulsive about it or really lazy. It's very mysterious. One thing I *have* noticed is that things go better if I inoculate right after a snowstorm. That's pretty much the only tip I have to offer."

"Thanks, Bett, for sharing that with us," Kai said, touching down with me in the same way she did with everyone, devoted to every mycelial insight, equal as seen from her eye.

IT'S THE ONES who push things forward like lightning on the landscape of history who often leave too soon, who make a sound that has never been heard before, who lay out a way that has never been lived before. They're the ones who too often die young. They understand the only thing worth doing is the impossible. They call on it, and then they wait. When the moment arrives, they ride it all the way through to the other side—and look, the thing that was not possible previously, now exists upon the earth because they brought it here. There's no way to really come back when you've gone that far out.

Four months after the conference, Kai Wingo suffered a stroke on the thirty-fifth day of a forty-day fast. On February 6, she died.

Kai, my hyperlink, my saint, Santo Santo Santo, San Pedro, San Pablo, Santo, Santo, Santo.

I, Bett, the white one who keeps it clean by accident, keeps an altar for Kai Wingo, who woke me from sleeping.

She was seated in the center of her cathedral with her bowls spread out in front of her.

Girl will learn eventually, I feel her saying. She wakes me. Again and again, she calls me back from sleep to tell me to get back to work, because the mushrooms are counting on me. I promised I wouldn't let them down. *It doesn't matter what the other people are doing*, she tells me from the other side. *You have your own unique story to tell.*

21

I am a saint woman, says
I am a trumpet woman, says
I am a drum woman, says
I am a woman born, says
I am a woman fallen into the world, says
That is your Book, says
That is your Book, says
Book of sap, says
Book of dew, says
Fresh Book, says
Book of clarity, says
                —MARÍA SABINA

There in Bell Mountain, says. There is the
dirty fright. There is the garbage, says. There
is the claw, says. There is the terror, says.
Where the day is, says. Where the clown is,
says. The Lord Clown, says.
       —UNKNOWN MAZATEC CURANDERO*

BETH'S FATHER DIED after a long, debilitating illness.
My own father died three months later after a colon

---

*"The Mushrooms of Language," by Henry Munn, from *Hallucinogens and Shamanism*, edited by Michael J. Harner

surgery. He was ninety-one. We knew this was part of why we met, so that we could enter the state of being fatherless together. People find it disturbing when you're not particularly sad about your dad dying. Not us, though. The mushrooms, too, were very ho-hum about the whole ordeal.

You never know what makes them show up with bells on—batshit crazy for corduroy pants, ambivalent about eclipses.

That's not to say I wasn't totally out of it after he died. In my sleepwalking state, I managed to buy a house in the coal town down south with my inherited money. Beth and I opened a store there that sold psilocybin T-shirts, bath salts, and picture frames. Anyway, a whole different life.

I had always told myself that after my father died, I would go on a trip somewhere. I decided to go to Huautla de Jiménez, Mexico, home of the late María Sabina.

I approached the journey with ambivalence. I was not a traveler, nor would I suddenly sprout the limbs needed to become one. I spent the first night in a hotel in the Mexico City airport, feeling kidnapped by my own choices. It was in this void that I received word about Kai Wingo. She'd suffered a stroke and was in a coma. The outcome was unclear.

In Mexico City, I boarded the bus that would take me to the village of Huautla de Jiménez. It was an eight-plus hour ride along a windy mountain road. All the roads were made of dirt back when the hippies first came. I read that a hippie, high on too many mushrooms, ran through the marketplace naked, chasing a chicken. When he caught it, he bit off its head. The town had never seen such a spectacle before.

The bus passed through the gates of the city, now watched over by a statue of María Sabina herself. Every taxi was marked with her name and stamped with colorful images of mushrooms. I stepped onto the soil cautiously, fully aware I was just another gringa tourist, here to pay homage to my saint. I checked into what was basically the only hotel in town, the Santa Julia. It appeared to function specifically as an outpost for tourists seeking the mushrooms, and more recently—because of *Hamilton's Pharmacopeia*—*Salvia divinorum*. A few came for the vast network of caves beneath the city, but even the caves were a loaded topic. Spirits dwelled there. Most of the entrances were forbidden to foreigners without a certified guide. Mushrooms were painted along the stairwells of the hotel and posters describing their wonders were tacked up at the check-in desk. It was obvious that all I had to do was ask the woman at the counter where to find a curandera and I would be told where to go.

I will not do any mushrooms, I told myself. Just being in the town where María Sabina lived and died was enough. I was in not in the right mindset to do ceremony; plus, I had been taught that you can't just go out and buy a ceremony like a blanket sold in the market.

In 1955, R. Gordon Wasson, an American banker with CIA connections, attended a ceremony with María Sabina. He is said to have been the first white man to participate in the Mazatec ritual. His experience was one of visions of architecture, actual buildings. Wasson felt himself removed from his body and projected into a realm of what he wrote as "geometric patterns, angular, in richest colors, which grew into architectural structures, the stonework in brilliant colors, gold and onyx and ebony, extending beyond the reach of sight, in vistas measureless to man. The architectural visions seemed to be oriented, seemed to belong to the architecture described by visionaries of the Bible." (This was according to Christian Rätsch, in his *The Encyclopedia of Psychoactive Plants: Ethnopharmacology and Its Applications*.)

María Sabina and her sister ate mushrooms as children because they were hungry. When María Sabina returned to the mushrooms as an adult, it was with the intention of healing a serious illness in her uterus. She cured herself through the use of mushrooms and self-massage. *A woman's body is her first house.*

Gordon Wasson's architectural visions seem typical for a man. Despite the grandiosity of his visions, he claimed to not have enjoyed his trip and was resistant to ever doing the mushrooms again.

He asked to take María Sabina's picture and she consented under the condition that he keep it private. He published it anyway, along with her name and town she lived in, Huautla de Jiménez, Mexico, a small village in the mountains accessible only by a precariously winding dirt road often washed out by rains. His article, "Seeking the Magic Mushroom," made the cover of *Life Magazine* with the tagline "The Discovery of Mushrooms that Cause Strange Visions." This article alone was the catalyst for the global psychedelic revolution and the singular transmission that inspired Timothy Leary and Terrence McKenna to explore psychedelics. Everyone from Bob Dylan to John Lennon to Mick Jagger descended upon Huautla de Jiménez, followed by thousands of hippies seeking the blow-out spiritual experience of a lifetime.

I asked the late antiquarian book collector William Dailey, who knew Gordon Wasson personally, if Wasson ever returned to Huautla de Jiménez after the first series of visits that made him famous. Wasson died in 1986, so while he was still an active scholar, he was privy to emerging conversations in academia on the topic of colonization and indigenous sovereignty. He must have known the troubles María Sabina and the Mazatec people had gone through as a result of his work. María Sabina's house was burned down—twice. She was arrested for drug possession so that the government could make a statement, then set free. Being singled out and deified by Wasson brought fame, and along with it came the envy of her neighbors, then the hatred of a whole country. She remained very poor until her death.

As far as William Dailey knew, Wasson never returned.

LUMINARIES CONTINUE to cite Wasson as the man who "discovered" the mushroom, while mentioning María Sabina only as a footnote, and the Mazatec people hardly at all.

I just can't.

Really, this needs to stop.

I VENTURED OUTSIDE my hotel room in search of Oaxacan tacos. The side streets and plaza were abundant with fresh tortillas, mole, and salsa verde. Students were getting out of school and the marching band and baton twirlers were practicing in view of the government offices. Salsa music blared from a deafening bullhorn. The car salesman voice, universal to all Mexican radio, announced the latest deals over the collision of noise. It was not an unpleasant soundtrack to the lively marketplace, where women sold copal incense, beeswax candles, and dark, sculpted chalices made for burning copal resin in ceremony. Shawls, shirts, scarves, and dresses embroidered with mushrooms were everywhere. Wanting to buy them all, I ended up buying none.

I was beginning to wonder if what I'd read about Huautla de Jiménez being ruined by hippies was an exaggeration. The international Kratom-drinking, Om-symbol-tattooed millennials who swarmed the beach towns were not here. Word was those types ate mushrooms in San Juan, a few hours south. Other than two European-appearing spelunkers, the only other white person I saw was a drunk cowboy wandering the back roads.

I was approached by a man in the plaza asking me if I wanted to buy some mushrooms. I said yes, if only for the pleasure of participating in a drug deal. He went away with my pesos to fetch some but never returned.

Mushroom murals, images of children sprouting mushrooms from their eyeballs, cowboys with sombreros sleeping in fields of fungi, and countless renderings of the image of María Sabina were everywhere. Xeroxed photographs of María Sabina were taped to taco stand windows and tacked to mirrors in bars. Surely this wasn't just an elaborate display for tourists. I asked a local whether mushroom ceremonies happened among the people who lived here, and he said, *Yes, of course, why would I think otherwise?*

Was the victimized Huautla de Jiménez I read about in books yet again a fiction manufactured by white people to serve an agenda? My short visit didn't lead me to any conclusions. I was simply left with a question: What do white Westerners gain from promoting the idea they ruined Huautla de Jiménez, that it's wrong to visit there? Doesn't believing this let us off the hook in terms of nurturing any relationships with the people that might begin to heal a fractured history? Doesn't it discount the innate resiliency of the Mazatec and how they've adapted amidst so much cultural change?

I switched my residence to a place I found on Airbnb, a mushroom "spa" run by a curandera and her daughter who greeted me when I arrived. She immediately asked when I wanted to do a ceremony.

"Thank you, but no," I said. Through broken Spanish, I explained that a friend was in a coma and this just wasn't the right time for me.

I hid in my room, reading an Octavia Butler novel about multi-gendered beings from another planet who transform into magical and gorgeous creatures when they heal humans from disease through highly evolved alien sex. They struggle existentially with fact that their greatest gift is the one thing that defines them as a parasite.

The next day I walked for hours along winding dirt roads, passing earthen structures that glowed aqua, pink, and pale green, colors on a frequency with spirits unique only to this place. It rained and the electric cobalt blue of the marketplace pavement turned into a dripping mirror that both reflected and absorbed the sky. I installed this blue medicine inside myself, then walked around the marketplace intoxicated by blue. I sent the excess of blue to Kai. I smiled at strangers, petted the dogs that didn't run away, harassed the indifferent horses.

On the third morning, Facebook informed me Kai Wingo was dead. I drank a Modelo and smoked a cigar outside my room in shock. I was scolded by the innkeeper, the daughter of the curandera who lived downstairs.

"No beer. No cigars."

"I know. I'm sorry. I won't do it anymore. It is a hard time," I said, after figuring out how to say all this in Spanish via my phone's translation app.

"We can just give you the mushrooms," she said. "My mother is too sick to do any ceremony today."

"That's fine," I said.

I didn't want to do ceremony anyway, not like this, as a paying guest in a mushroom spa. I was not in a good place and I knew you weren't supposed to drink alcohol two days before or two days after. I felt very guilty about drinking the Modelo, but I was doing it, so there it was. I bought the mushrooms she offered to be polite, thinking I could always do them later, when I got to Zipolite Beach.

I dealt with Kai's death like I do with a lot of hard things, clinging to the internet for some sign of truth and failing, seeking out gossip and intrigue to crowd all the empty places inside me that were hungry for meaning. I stood in a jungled part of the yard, then ambled over to the small parking garage, seeking a signal on my phone so I could follow posts on the Women and Entheogens site. I researched the details of how a heart goes into shock when there's not enough electrolytes. *Salt. She needed salt.* I texted Beth constantly. I played a video of Kai's family and friends singing prayers by her hospital bed, when it was thought that there was a chance she might bounce back.

How could Kai Wingo be dead? Of all the people in the world.

I am often uncomfortable when talking about Kai's death. I realize some may see it as the result of a very misguided, even crazy goal of hers: not eating for forty days. I am part of ceremonial circles where people do extreme, impossible things quite often, so I never saw Kai's passing as the result of a mistake. She died in ceremony. I know everyone wishes they had kept a closer eye on her, that it didn't have to happen. On the first anniversary of her passing, I spoke on the phone for three hours with Kai Wingo's mother, Vicki Aquah (Mama Oladeji). She called out of the blue and the conversation felt in every way like an event arranged by Kai on the other side. *In no way did Kai Wingo want to leave this world*, she told me.

I spent the entire day in Huautla de Jiménez in a state of disassociation. When the sun began to set, I walked to the kitchen, where dinner was to be served. The innkeeper's mother, the curandera who I hadn't yet met, was there to greet me. She and her daughter appeared tense. stood before them, feeling like a late-stage Jack Kerouac.

They told me there was someone they could send me to for ceremony, that they were very good but it was far away. I would take a cab. It cost a thousand pesos. *Had I drunk very much since my last beer?* the curandera asked.

"No," I said, which was true.

"You are not supposed to drink," she said.

"I know. I know. I'm not happy about it either. I wasn't planning on doing ceremony."

"So, you will go?"

"Yes," I said. There was no other answer to give.

I texted Beth. *Heading somewhere by cab to do ceremony. It's likely I will be away all night with no cell service. Feels right*, I added, only because it looked so wrong as I read it on my phone.

Right on.

A chronic worrier, Beth often surprised me in the moments when she was free of anxiety. Like this one. She texted that she would go to my house and light a fire, burn sage and juniper, offer tobacco, and hold me and Kai Wingo in her prayers.

After hanging a left up María Sabina Avenue, the cab winded around tight corners, up and up until the village and jungle were far below, all the greenery hugged tight by low clouds heavy with wet. We drove further up still, enough for my ears to pop and the temperature to drop. The smog of Huautla de Jiménez dissipated into air so clean it hit my head like cold water. I was dropped off at a compound of small mud huts. Chickens and dogs spilled out into the road. The drive must have taken forty minutes.

Seti, the curandera's granddaughter, greeted me on the

road. She was in her twenties and wore a maroon pleather jacket and jeans. She took me to a small room inside the compound of mud daub huts and we waited alone together for Alma, her grandmother, to arrive. Despite our language barrier, I was able to glean that she was in college, studying plants and mushrooms. She presented me with a folder full of images of the three different mushrooms I would be eating that night.

"Some of the mushrooms are endangered," she said.

Her family was trying very hard to protect them. She said her grandfather, who had died not that long ago, was a very well-known curandero who knew María Sabina personally. If I wanted a picture of him, there were some I could buy. The room we sat in was aqua-colored, with an altar in the corner crowded with child saint figures and plastic flowers.

Finally, Alma arrived and sat at the fold-out table with us. She was quite old, in her late eighties, perhaps—it was hard to tell. She was a rounded figure in a black dress and black headscarf; the fault line of her chipped front teeth was lined with gold. She asked me to write down what I wished for in doing the ceremony. She read my words and nodded, very likely picking up on just a few key words: *dead friend, mushroom teacher, no drinking, protection from enemy.*

Alma motioned for me to join her in a second room, this one painted an energized pink that was chipping off the mud brick walls. She pointed to the chair in front of the altar and I sat facing a child saint with holy plastic eyes. She brushed my body lightly with a bundle of fresh herbs, then lit a tall narrow candle, dripped its wax on the cement floor, and set it there. She placed copal on burning embers.

She rolled an egg over me and broke it into a glass of water and watched as it took on shapes, pointing to where the yolk was starting to break. I was holding feelings in my stomach, she said, angry feelings. I said yes, I was very angry lately and I knew it was making me tired. She retrieved the beeswax candle and studied how the wax was melting down. She pointed to a dribble in the shape of a heart.

"Tu amiga?" she said.

"Sí, mi amiga."

"Corazón?"

"Sí, corazón," I said.

I was amazed that she'd divined that Kai had suffered an injury to the heart. She conveyed that what was happening with Kai was very hard and troubling.

"Hongos muy importante," I said. "Mi amiga. Muerte. Amigas hongos. Te llama Kai Wingo. Curandera hongos."

"Sí, sí, sí," she said, holding the gravity of the situation with me.

I was handed three different types of raw mushrooms to eat; the flavor was surprisingly pleasant. Alma did the same. We chewed together in silence, in a way that felt very bovine. Copal smoke enveloped us. The third room was furnished with just a small straw bed. She guided me inside and motioned for me to lay down. Alma poured a mixture of lime and tobacco from a glass bottle onto her palm. She lifted up my shirt and rubbed the liquid on my stomach. It was cold and energizing—and it was tobacco, which I love so very much.

She sat at the foot of the bed and began to sing. She sang some of the same songs that María Sabina sang in the movie and on the record, *Santo, Santo, Santo, Santo, San Pedro San Pablo.* I knew these songs. I knew these smells. The mushrooms came on and the labors of ceremony began, the separating of wheat from chaff, this from that, the taking out the trash, seeking out the vital and urging it forth. I knew how to do this.

Seti came in occasionally to sit on the floor and sing with us.

The blockage in my abdomen became a red animal that grew and took over my whole body with a fierce heat. I writhed and growled, allowing it to have its way with me. Alma rubbed more tobacco on my stomach until the intensity peaked and released, leaving me floating weightless and unbothered, an exorcism. So delicate, so lovely, so indescribably beautiful were the complex maths that held tight the veil of prayer that surrounded us.

Santo, Santo, Santo, San Pedro, San Pablo.

This is how it's done on three to six grams—roll with your saints, stay in prayer. I had strayed from this knowing in order to appreciate the value of a thing done properly. I was so happy to be back in the ceremony, much like the ones I'd practiced when I first started taking the mushrooms. I had intuitively known the proper way to do things from the very beginning—I wasn't a great caretaker of that wisdom and my self-doubt allowed my knowings to slip away for a time, but now I was home again.

There was nothing left to do but just sing for hours with Alma, sing and pray for us all, for her family, for her people, for Kai and all those grieving for her, for Beth by the fire. I sensed the mycelial network that held us was one immense entity stretching over the entire earth.

The mycelium will still be here after we die, holding the codes of who we once were inside its networks. I don't know how mushrooms keep memories, but if mycelium remembers anything, it probably remembers only the best parts of us. This feels true.

Santo, Santo, Santo, I chanted with Alma.

> *San Pedro San Pablo, María Sabina, they*
> *burned your house down. You died with nothing.*
> *Even the mushrooms left you. You said they*
> *stopped working after the white people came.*
> *I will listen to what you are saying. Help me*
> *walk in a good way with them, with your little*
> *children, the way you would want it to be. They*
> *belong to you, María, the veladas, they belong to*
> *your people. Through your ways with them we*
> *learn how to be humble people, ordinary human*
> *beings.*

Alma stood above me and asked me to open my palms. She put tobacco in each of my palms and rolled my hands up in fists around it.

"The ceremony is over now. Do not let go of this in your hand," Alma said. Then she walked outside into the night.

I was still tripping pretty hard. I lay in the dark and in my mind's eye I was hurled through grotesque urban landscapes populated by cartoon dwarfs fighting atop Escher stairways. But I knew the ceremony was over. I let the flashy apocalypse wash over me without trying to read any meaning into it. Without an understanding of what ceremony is, you could spend your whole mushroom journey trapped this state of in-between, like watching a pretentious art film that you think must be deep because you think you're too dumb to understand what's going on. To do the labor required of spirit, it's important to be able to sense the difference between what is ceremony and what is not.

At some point, I returned to what felt like regular consciousness. When I turned this or that way in the bed, the straw in the mattress made a crunching sound and the sharpness of the straw threatened to pierce through the fabric that held it tight. I was very cold. I realized I left my coat and my phone in the room below. I got up and set out to retrieve those items so I could contact Beth.

I stumbled out onto the dirt path and was greeted by a little black puppy. *Oh my god, a puppy, the cutest puppy.* The best word in the English language is *puppy*. The puppy liked me. I picked it up and it licked my face all over. It was filthy and possibly covered in shit. Alma appeared, as if from the shadows.

"Is there something you need? You should be in the bed."

Lore has it that ever since the sixties, the white tourists have been known to wander off while high, sometimes even naked, perhaps chasing a puppy or a chicken, causing all sorts of problems. That the tourist stays put after the trip is rule number one.

"My coat. I want to get my coat?"

"I will bring it to you," she said. "You have to get back in the bed."

"I love this puppy."

"Get back in the bed, okay? Please?"

"It's a really cute puppy, really cute. The cutest puppy."

"Please. The bed."

I happily returned and crawled under the covers. Alma came back with Seti and my coat and they both took their place at the foot of the bed and beamed at me with such intense love, I wondered if there was someone hiding behind me who was the real intended recipient of their affection. But no, no one was there. I let myself meet their gaze and my heart nearly exploded. These women. *How is it I get to be here?*

"We weren't going to do ceremony tonight and then we got the call," Seti said. "We weren't sure—we don't even know you—but now we are glad we did because the stars outside are in a very special position that we have been told is very sacred. We didn't know. If you hadn't come, we would have missed it."

"If you want to find us, you can just look at this image," Alma said with the help of Seti's translation skills. She held up an image of la Virgen de Guadalupe. "Do you know her?"

"Yes, I know her very well. She is everywhere in New Mexico."

"You can just look at her if you want to be with us. You can talk to us through the saint."

She pointed to Guadalupe again. I nodded that I understood.

I could have looked at Guadalupe in the way I have been indoctrinated: as a graven image, a false idol and tool of the colonizers. But that's not how we view the saints now. Now the image of the saint is a device for telepathy, a Guadalupe telephone.

Alma and Seti pulled the covers tight over me. Alma closed my palms around another clump of tobacco. This time, I would try not to let go. They quietly left me in my bed to sleep. I found I had enough signal on my phone to call Beth.

"Hiiii! So how was it?"

My handle on words was going to be limited. I thought I wasn't, but I actually was still quite high.

"It's just like what we do in lodge," I said. "It's the same thing. Everyone is together there and you can feel the presence of the old ones."

Beth told me the stars that night were quite spectacular. They appeared to collect themselves right above the house, then formed a road leading directly south to Huautla de Jiménez. She burned old tobacco ties left from ceremonies past and the smoke hung low, traveling like a snake around the house so fat, heavy, and bone-white she couldn't see through it.

"I saw it, too." she said. "I know what you are saying. It's the same thing."

22

IF I COULD have just one question for Kathleen Harrison, what would it be? I was standing in the library of her non-profit organization, Botanical Dimensions, which she founded with her ex-husband, the late Terrence McKenna. I came with offerings—a homemade silkscreened mushroom T-shirt and frankincense tears. I stood in the library, trying to shake my overwhelm. *Be normal, maintain.* This was Kathleen Harrison, elder and legend, who speaks "from" the plants and fungi rather than "about" them.

"Who is tobacco? I mean, I know what tobacco is. But who?" I asked. I had waited quite some time for a clearing to open up so I could ask this one question.

"To the Mazatec, tobacco is San Pedro, San Pablo. They are siblings."

"Does San Pedro, San Pablo in the Mazatec way have a relation to the crossroads?" I asked. "Like, does tobacco embody opposite principles, like on a good day San Pedro is an intermediary between you and the spirit realm, and on a bad day he steals your wallet, then says he can help you find it? And when he does, he's, like, standing there, waiting for a tip?"

"I would say that's accurate," Kat said. "To get really literal, San Pedro is St. Peter. He is the saint who holds the keys to heaven. In that way, tobacco could be seen as somewhat of a Papa Legba figure, yes. San Pedro opens doors and is an intermediary between the physical realm and the spirit realm. San Pedro is one who moves through the marketplace, who is outgoing and has a hold on language and culture. San Pedro is really big about bringing the tobacco to the people. San Pablo, San Pedro's sibling, rules the realm of the hearth. It's the much more interior, quiet tobacco. San Pedro and San Pablo tobacco plants have different colored blossoms. I have been growing them for a long time. I have some seeds I can send you."

"Yes, I would love that," I said, floored by the possibility of growing tobacco from Kathleen Harrison's seeds.

"In the Mazatec way, San Pablo, the tobacco of the hearth, is a man," she said, almost as an aside. Her strongest teachings drop in just this way, so subtle they can easily be missed. "San Pedro is seen as a woman."

This is the crossroads of this book, intentionally. I have offered tobacco to honor my teacher by naming her, by offering tobacco to her name and her family: Kathleen Harrison, elder, one who knows and who I respect.

23

THERE IS A woman in the coal town who I mistook to be her own much younger sister or cousin. This relative's face was hydrated, new, itself at last, ready for a Hollywood run portraying the life of this awesome friend of mine. At the bar, she asked me if I had any mushroom capsules. She had some at home and had taken a small amount that morning, but it was turning into the kind of night where it might be nice to take a little more.

I had to pause and study her face for a moment. Yes, she wasn't my friend's relative, but the woman herself, looking an easy fifteen years younger and glowing with self-possession.

"I've been micro-dosing," she said. "For depression. It's really helping me a lot. I'm feeling a whole lot better." It was almost comical, her understated humility. She had a whole new goddamn face.

Ninety percent of the questions that I am asked by others has to do with micro-dosing. *Do you believe it can help with depression, ADD, and addiction?* Probably? This person had an early history with mushrooms, wild stories having to do with drunken Vietnam vets and manholes in an old Texas town during the '70s, where she and her friends used to crawl around in tunnels while tripping their brains out, their bodies painted, wine-drunk and underage. I couldn't help but think that this history had something to do with why the mushrooms gave her a whole new face.

Full disclosure—I've always thought micro-dosing was overrated. I view the practice as a subjugation of the mushroom's power. Why would you want to take a small amount of a being? You can't even hear what it's trying to tell you on a sub-perceptual dose. It might be screaming, "Quit your job, it's giving you cancer!"

Everything works for a little while—works until it doesn't, and at some point, a pattern is revealed. That which is not God is snake oil. Snake oil is magic until it isn't. Cures depend on us being sick, a snake-eating-its-own-tail situation. Our bodies know when we've bought the snake oil. They will eventually reject what is not true.

Sub-perceptual doses of psychedelic mushrooms can repair cells in the hippocampus, the research says, but so can blueberries. A flood dose of more than three grams will often reveal how viewing the body's processes in a mechanical way is exactly what's been making us sick in the first place. It's the psychedelic experience, not the psilocybin, ayahuasca, or LSD that heals. The cure lies in glimpsing the whole, seeing things from a different angle, getting to the root of the imbalance. Maybe we discover that there is no root of the problem at all, that many of our sicknesses are nothing more than calcified mental phantoms based on ego attachment to our own stories of suffering.

You know what we all need more than psychedelic mushrooms? Clean water for everyone is what we need, and a good sense of humor, collective hard work, and an ability to chill and appreciate the moment, even when things are hard. Substances, no matter how powerful, can't compare to basic awareness and an ethical worldview. It's not the substance but how we employ the substance in service to an ethic that gets results.

Still, I present to you my friend's face, lifted from the pavement by mushrooms and installed as if in a dream, as an engine ready to further the narrative of her own life through a face that had stopped, retired, and was now utterly new.

No cures, only alchemy. In one sweeping motion over a period of days, the power was all hers.

24

THE CORNFIELDS IN Nebraska were ugly in September 2016. I don't drive stick, so Beth had to drive the whole way to the Standing Rock Indian Reservation. I swallowed three capsules (one gram) of mushrooms at a rest stop and the cornfields just got weirder. Hadn't had a drink in over a year. Now I was living in a long stretch gifted by my efforts.

"This isn't how I remember it back in Iowa," I said. "There's more space between the rows, I'm sure of it. These rows are too close together."

"Thus speaks the corn baroness."

"Maybe this is how it is for corn that's grown for gasoline. But I don't think so. Something's wrong with this corn, I'm not kidding."

Having a psychedelic meltdown relating to the GMO corn grown on the farm I inherited from my recently deceased father was a rude way to take up space when Beth was so heroically driving. The truck was packed high with gear. It took Beth over four hours to meticulously tie down the military tents, the water cube, the donated boxes of clothing, and miscellaneous supplies. We stuffed as much firewood as possible into every remaining crevasse, making sure that was secured as well, yet on the freeway our cargo still teetered precariously in the wind.

I really didn't feel well, though. *Maybe taking mushrooms was a bad idea.* Too much confusing information wafted off the ragged tips of endless corn stalks. My relatives took pride in their identity as farmers, people of the land, but this landscape looked like nothing more than an industrial factory without walls and a roof.

I kept going on again about the ugly corn. Beth begged me to stop talking, *just please stop*, and right when I thought I couldn't bear the ugliness of Nebraska any longer, the flatness broke into beautiful, rolling grass-covered hills, giving us a merciful liftoff into another realm.

"I need to read something out loud right now," I said. "I'm sorry. It's not long. I just have to."

"As long as you don't keep talking about the corn being weird, I'm okay."

"*My Antonia* by Willa Cather was written about this landscape. Black Hawk, Nebraska, late 1800s. Must be close to here, I'm thinking."

I began to read from the dog-eared page.

"I had the feeling that the world was left behind, that we had got over the edge of it, and were outside man's jurisdiction. I had never before looked up at the sky when there was not a familiar mountain ridge against it. But this was the complete dome of heaven, all there was of it. I did not believe that my dead father and mother were watching me from up there; they would still be looking for me at the sheep-fold down by the creek, or along the white road that led to the mountain pastures. I had left even their spirits behind me. The wagon jolted on, carrying me I knew not whither. I don't think I was homesick. If we never arrived anywhere, it did not matter. Between that earth and that sky, I felt erased, blotted out. I did not say my prayers that night here, I felt, what would be would be."

A beat after I finished, we crossed the border into South Dakota and everything became more vivid by degrees. This was land made of song. The singers were out of view, yet their singing still brought it into being. It was not lost on me that the text I just recited could be used as an example of the mythos that fueled genocide, the fiction of the land being profoundly, beautifully, ominously empty. There were people living on this land during the time the story of *My Antonia* took place, with descendants who live here still. It's not even a miracle, just a fact written in blood.

I love Willa Cather because she writes about my settler ancestors' secret wish to disappear themselves into the West, leaving their past behind. They came so very far with this longing held deep within, a desire to dissolve into the landscape and become inseparable from it, to the point that they disappeared completely, like the land could be a door to another dimension ruled by different laws. The Western migration is the psychedelic dream of my people.

We got cold feet on a mass scale, obviously. Instead of disappearing, we did the opposite. What a total failure of will this magic trick revealed of our character.

Big feelings descended upon us as we drove further north. A quickening of spirit came on so hard it couldn't be traced; we were just inside of it. We pulled off at a bird refuge on the side of the highway and stepped out into the extra-lucid air. The mushrooms had worn off a while ago. What we were feeling was something else.

"Is that a hawk?" I asked.

"Yes, it's a red tail."

It flew above us and hovered. I felt myself in the hawk's red and golden float, then it soared again, dipping down and gaining speed before taking on a line that was clear, diamond-straight. It set our heads right to follow it with our eyes into the distance, where the bird became a tiny black dot. We put big prayers on that bird, threw tobacco down. I couldn't even remember the last time my feet felt so solidly on the earth.

"Guard your peace fiercely," I said out loud to Beth. "That's what they're saying."

Beth was crouched at the level of the water reeds.

"Little tiny birds! You only see them when you look through the grasses. They're everywhere!" She squatted, frozen, in the midst of their cacophony of sound for quite a while, absorbing it into her body. This marked the beginning of Beth's future, in which she would move her business to the house in the coal town. A future that was mostly birds—birds she would feed, birds she would save, birds she gave names to, birds she listened to day and night, even in her sleep—until she could rightfully say that she had become that *thing*, a bird person. As for me, I had gone without alcohol long enough to actually feel the way the synapsis in my brain had repaired themselves. I used to be really good at moments like this.

The hawk feeling stayed with us across the border into North Dakota, all the way to the entry gate at Oceti Sakowin Camp, where young men wearing black bandanas over their faces smudged our car and said, "Welcome home." We rolled slowly down to Red Warrior Camp, taking in all that we had studied in pictures on screens: the lines of flags representing the tribes and ally organizations, the teepee-style longhouse where the elders held counsel, the hippie buses and the Lakota teenagers riding bareback on appaloosas. The disorienting sense of being transported to a whole other world went way beyond just the mental labor of integrating what we had seen on the internet with the reality in real time, which was opening all around us.

"I can't believe it. There's never been a place like this on earth before."

"This is the future."

I arrived on this sacred land as a Doubting Thomas. I didn't believe for a second that the water protectors had a chance in hell of stopping the pipeline. I came because the songs our ceremonial family sings when praying come from Lakota Sioux treaty land up near Standing Rock. The rhythm and cadence are based on the horizon line of the mountain ranges. That a black snake could be laid down right through songlines and sacred sites, where origin stories of the people I pray with are kept, was intolerable to me. I couldn't let that happen. That's why I fought it, not because I believed we could stop the fossil fuel industry, but because I wasn't going to let it happen *there*, not at Standing Rock, where Sitting Bull was assassinated by his own people because they were tricked into being afraid there wouldn't be enough food to eat if they fought back against the settlers.

Tim Kaine, Hillary Clinton's running mate, was asked on camera what their strategy would be if elected.

"The pipeline could be rerouted," he said on Election Day, on *Democracy Now*. Beth was right—over ten thousand strong, we could stop it, but I never would have believed this if my feet hadn't touched the ground at Oceti Sakowin.

It's the end of the age of oil. The sentence played on a loop in my head as we walked around the camp. There were coals brought to make sacred fires at Standing Rock, coals that had been burning for decades, or so I'd been told. The end of the age of oil in me was held up to those fires. I became a believer.

Then Trump was elected.

I—this old cowhand, this lightning chaser, snake oil seller, doorbell ringer, road wraith in love with common rambling songs, born from those songs, meaning I come from no one—am a being whose soul is assembled from intoxicated fantasies of speed and mobility. I am made of oil, the elixir of the bones of the dead, of dinosaurs, liquefied palm trees and ancient fungi. My DNA holds the memory of the great Western expansion, and I have sought to absolve myself of this sin by disappearing myself at the vanishing point where the western horizon meets the sea. I chose to be born in Santa Barbara because I'm lazy and it wasn't a long walk to this very place, the edge of the end. Consider me already gone.

Beth and I had raised nearly $15,000 through a Facebook group we launched. Most everyone else was donating to Sacred Stone and Oceti Sakowein, but we donated exclusively to Red Warrior, the frontline warrior camp. We used the money to buy three large military tents, which served as basic infrastructure. The kitchen tent was erected by old veterans and radicals in skinny jeans, just minutes before a downpour. We made a run to the Bismarck Walmart for shelving and other supplies and our mission was complete.

Standing Rock was ceremony. We try our best not to talk about ceremony. All that happened on the ground, I will leave there. We left late at night, after receiving word the roads were going to be blocked in both directions, and took a detour to the freeway that would take us into Nebraska. A white DAPL truck followed us on this crossover for miles, inching uncomfortably close to our bumper, no one else on the road but us. It was scary, but we couldn't let ourselves feel it, for fear of losing our ability to focus completely. We could have easily ended up in a ditch. It was so dark we couldn't even see the slightest figure of a human behind the windshield. We had dealt with infiltrators at camp, DAPL spies, and agitators pretending to be people they were not. This changed the baseline of what was possible in our world, and not in a good way.

"I don't really want to disappear," I said. It was important to say it out loud.

25

The first known use of oil was in the building of the Tower of Babel. The age of oil is over.

We are living in the twilight of a slow and sinister disclosure.

I DON'T LIKE to be a scold, but there are right and wrong ways to walk as a white person in indigenous spaces.

After returning home, I felt really helpless. I wrote a blog post in response to Standing Rock that went viral. My phone blinked notifications constantly for a week, like a slot machine gone crazy. Everyone from native teenagers to queers to an elk hunter who decided to donate his fresh kill to the camp after reading my post, circulated a piece of writing that I was very conflicted about putting out in the world. It had to be said. There was an overlap between the ceremony that was Standing Rock and indigenous peyote, mushroom, and ayahuasca circles, a protocol of behavior having to do with respect that was very similar that I must share.

Most of us are watching history being made through our Facebook feed. The internet is a place where true sacredness can get lost in translation and dialogue is predisposed to being polarized and "issue"-oriented. A friend said in September, "You can't explain the feeling of the camp up there. You have to just go. It's a lot less complicated and much more peaceful once you're just there by the water with everyone."

That's why when I started to see posts on my feed from indigenous people crying out that the behavior of white people at camp was getting out of hand, I knew it was serious. There's always bad behavior and the fact people were speaking up loudly all of a sudden meant the situation was getting critical.

I read a report of two "Burning Man/circuit festival types," white women who led a circle at the Oceti Sakowin Spirit Fire. They spoke of the goddess and the patriarchy. They told the native men traditionally tending the fire that they needed to be quiet. They policed how the native women spoke, told them to not speak out of turn and to hold their comments for later. They weren't wearing skirts or dresses by the sacred fire as they were asked. The indigenous women who witnessed this were very upset about it and didn't know what to do.

An anonymous repost:

"Just received this message from a friend and outstanding journalist at standing rock. OMG girl so many white ppl here at standing rock you need to check Hard. Worst ugliest

attitudes. The vibe is so off this time. And those 'encountered are just presumptuous prickly rude and very entitled.' And they have made a healing chakra zone and are right now rubbing on each other."

And:

"A camp came in the other day set up a dome played bass music at night with light poi spinners . . . !! Aah. I was on the other side of the river. Menfolk started hollering . . ." We're in PRAYER over here! *"It took almost 30 minutes for them to shut down. Huge fire when we have to conserve wood to keep warm and for lodges."*

One doesn't have to have the skills of Margaret Mead to figure out who these people are on the cultural landscape. They are the urban bourgeois, for whom which climate change has become the newest charismatic religion. Daniel Pinchbeck is one of the priests, ayahuasca is its communion, yoga its prayer, and Burning Man its annual tent revival, where Glitterponies are still permitted to wear bikinis and "Indian" headdresses and arrive on the tarmac via helicopter. I have seen it with my own eyes—people who actually believe humanity has already achieved a state of being "all one," despite the fact that indigenous people are being maced, dragged out of sweat lodges, tagged with numbers, separated from each other, and being held in dog kennels by militarized police. Checking white privilege isn't about them, and Black Lives Matter is a buzzkill. Every decade I've seen has had its own version of this, and the fact the insanity is only getting worse is a testament to white people's inability to learn.

White allies, collect your people—Lakota, read one transmission.

It has come to this—again.

This cry can't be ignored.

I think this is a very literal request for white people who know other white people who behave like this to do everything in their power to get them to stop, and at the very least, to make sure they don't go up to Standing Rock and create all kinds of complicated toxic nastiness. At the same time, there is still an increasing call for people of all nations who have something to offer to go up there and offer bodily help.

❧ Educate yourself around the indigenous leaders/ organizations who are putting themselves out publicly in this movement. Don't expect everyone to have the time to answer all your questions.

❧ Notice who the elders are in any circle. Do they have a chair? Do they need a cup of coffee, wood for the firepit at their tent? In academia, they call it "de-centering yourself." At Standing Rock, it's called pay attention to your elders, and if you have any questions, try to hold off and see if those questions can't just be answered by observing others and just being quiet. We are taught as white people that when we don't know something, we're supposed to ask a lot of questions. This is not how things roll up in Standing Rock. Asking an indigenous person a ton of questions is basically forcing them into unpaid labor because of your lack of knowledge and wisdom. When in doubt, help an elder, be quiet as much as possible, and observe.

🏵 Sacred fires are burning at Standing Rock and that means everyone there is in ceremony. There is appropriate clothing one should wear by the sacred fire. Do not use swear words. If you are not indigenous, hold your sacred objects privately in your vehicle or tent unless invited to bring them out. Center indigenous people in ceremony, and if you have a meditation/yoga/chanting/ ritual practice, do it privately. If you are in the helping profession, be aware that others may have traditional ways of dealing with trauma and sickness. Help them get what they need in their own tradition if that's what they are calling for before suggesting your own techniques. When we were up there, we didn't hear a single secular, non-indigenous song sung at camp, save for when a Native man played a Willie Nelson song to the river on his cell phone at dawn and we opened the flap of our tent and saw a blue heron on the water and wept. In terms of being white, not forcing your own music on others is always a good idea. White people are often asked to do the work of discovering our own indigeneity, but that doesn't mean Wiccan, pagan, or New Age practices are welcome unless asked. Such displays usually come off as white people needing to center themselves in indigenous space yet again.

- No one cares if you're one-eighth Cherokee. I am one-eighth Cherokee. You'll just have to trust me on this.

- You are not a hero. Going up to Standing Rock isn't a sacrifice, it's a privilege. You are a guest of the Standing Rock Sioux reservation. You are making history and also bearing witness to a prophecy coming true. You are the future. Be humble.

- Don't just bring hummus and chips to the feast. Or your bags of random used clothes. You are white. It's likely you know some people with means. Hit your community up for as much money as you can and show up with army tents, winter gear, wood stoves, and semi-trucks full of hay, wind turbines, and organic, grass-fed beef. Native American people deserve this after genocide and government cheese. Bring donations for the kitchen or enough food and supplies with you to be self-sustaining, as you never know if supplies will be running low at camp.

- Be self-reflective when it comes to your romantic ideas about indigenous people. Myron Dewey, Lyla June Johnston, Kanahus Manuel, and Candi Brings Plenty may be some of the most incredible humans we have seen thus far, but be aware that even the *New York Times* is cropping the white hippies with the dreadlocks screaming on the frontlines out of the picture, so even you, watching the images on your computer screen, can feel like you're the only white person who cares.

* Don't go to Standing Rock to mine data or Instagram your #authenticlife.

* Work hard. "We had a lot of hippies over at Sacred Stone for a while. We finally asked them to work and they left for Iowa. It was that easy," a woman who helped hold down for months told me.

* Unless directly asked to attend, do not seek out sweat lodges and other traditional ceremonies. Be present to the fact that being at Standing Rock *is* being in ceremony.

* One of the most colonized behaviors one can perpetrate is that of policing others. Amazing things are happening in Standing Rock and white people are a part of it, from the rabbis and Christian clergy at the frontlines confronting the police state, to the gutterpunks with puppies on ropes at camp, who know what being on the right side of history means. When Myron Dewey greets us on his live feed with *Hello relatives*, yes, I believe he is talking to all of us. Policing the behavior of other white people to draw attention to how correct we are is a way of not dealing with our own whiteness, and whiteness is *always* a problem. The incidents I mentioned above are critical. People

behaving like this are not welcome at camp and probably need to be asked to leave. Indigenous people should not be put in the position to do this. White allies need to step up and deal with our own and get to the root of why incidents like this continue to happen. However, we need to do this without making our own grossness and microaggressions the center of this story. If you're reposting this article and not doing anything concrete to stop the pipeline, you are part of the problem.

Standing Rock is bigger than this. Standing Rock is where your feet are. Everyone drinks water. All land is sacred.

MANY MONTHS BACK from camp, I had planned to do a high-dose mushroom ceremony in honor of Kai Wingo. I prepared the altars and shook nine grams onto the scale, a dosage considered the minimum in Kai's circle, fifteen-plus being ideal. Nine grams spilled off the tiny scale and onto the table. I took it into my eyes, and all I could think was *Nope. No way am I going to eat that.* As much as I wanted to, I just couldn't do it, not even for Kai.

I was no stranger to hurling myself into the void at this point. It wasn't a matter of courage. I have a masochistic streak and enjoy when the mushrooms beat me up a little bit. The *no* that rose up from within me was thorough, and it wasn't mine. It wasn't a bad trip I was afraid of. I was afraid of not obeying the *no.*

Kai had the support of her community when she did

the high-dose protocol. She wasn't alone. No one in my circle was asking me to do this. I had just up and decided on my own accord that this was a good idea. What if I was wrong? Maybe the high-dose protocol belonged to Kai and her community alone. The high-dose work they needed to do together probably had nothing to do with me.

It was a troubling night in general, the eve before Oceti Sakowin Camp was to be raided by the National Guard. We were back in New Mexico, but Beth and I were bracing ourselves for what we knew was coming: uniformed guards and private DAPL thugs roaming through the camps with machine guns in the slippery and muddy winter snow; dragging water protectors, homeless veterans, elders, and children among them out of their teepees, yurts, and tents; burning them down, arresting an elder while in prayer, pulling the loaded pipe out of the hands of this grandma as if it was a weapon. Sacred objects were thrown on piles of garbage and pissed on, we had been told. For the Lakota people, it was Wounded Knee all over again, both the original massacre and the Wounded Knee siege in 1973.

Wounds of the body move naturally towards healing without the assistance of our intentions, but time does nothing to heal the injury resulting from violence committed by one human being against another. Actions must be taken for this kind of healing to occur. We've been moving in the wrong direction in the cycle, piling hurt upon hurt. We witnessed undeniable proof of this at Standing Rock. The violent spectacle of empire would once again have the last word, at least on the live feeds. If there was ever a time to be in prayer, it was now.

It made sense to take my regular dose and get in the right headspace. I knew what it was to pray with these things, the quiet, the distances I could travel. I swallowed down about four grams with a glass of water.

The mushrooms came on in a wave of cerebral ferocity. I knew right away it was going to be a challenging trip. I paced up and down the hallway while words echoed loudly in my skull, as if they were being blasted from a transistor radio. I composed tweets, introductory paragraphs to essays, and status updates—mostly on the topic of Standing Rock, colonization, and white privilege—but occasionally I threw in a few intricately composed insults directed at anyone who annoyed me. Up and down the hallway, my rhythms patterned in recollection of the beats of the likes and shares my blog post had generated not long before.

Had the mushrooms gone bad? Could mushrooms get moldy?

I sensed an escape hatch open. I projected myself into a room made of a thin membrane of buffalo hide. All at once, I was a man among men and we were in a ceremony, passing around a raw heart of a buffalo and taking bites out of it. The room was dank with the smell of human sweat, everything was bloody and had lots of hair on it— the men, the skins, even the heart had little hairs. I lacked the heart of a warrior, that was my problem.

"Stop, bitch! With your '80's Robert Bly-esque masculine initiation!" a voice said. It was my own, my civilian, everyday consciousness. "You're making this up."

It was true. This wasn't a vision that just came to me. I had seen on a live feed posted by one of my Facebook friends that a ceremony was being held that morning at Oceti Sakowein camp, in which water protectors were going to eat a raw buffalo heart in a sweat lodge. This guy from Albuquerque could always be counted on to talk too much about ceremony on social media. I basically inserted myself into his ceremony, pretending it was something that just arose in my mind on its own accord to make myself feel more connected—a white crime, basically. I made myself sit down. I was clammy and a little nauseated.

"Sorry, that was messed up," I mumbled.

"Yes, that was bad. Can we revisit? White crime duly noted, but what's worse is how you . . . *are*," the mushrooms scolded. "You're making it all about you. You catch yourself trying to be a good white person and then you realize this whole entire loop is your own ego trip. Which is true. You congratulate yourself on having the courage to recognize this. At this point, you give yourself a cookie for calling yourself out. You feel bad for not giving the cookie to a homeless person. You feel worse for having this thought just because it's funny. Now you feel actually really bad about yourself, which was your goal in the first place, but you could have just felt bad for no reason—instead you had to rope Standing Rock into the situation. You try to make yourself feel better by telling yourself most people won't even do the deep thinking around white privilege that you are doing right now so stop being so hard on yourself, but you can't escape the transmission that is coming from us, the mushrooms—we are saying that *this*, this thing you are doing, means you are an asshole."

I tried to quiet my contaminated mind by forced dissociation. This wasn't the first time a solitary mushroom trip had devolved into a solipsistic, interior, social-justice-warrior monologue. Too much time online. The internet may resemble the mushroom's mycelial structure, but the mushrooms do not jive with its hijacking and the resulting puppet performances of our outrage.

"So helpless. I feel so helpless," I said. "So sick. So sad. I'm sorry."

MANDALA SPELL FOR OVERCOMING INTERNET ADDICTION

What If We Created the Internet as an Origin Story to Tell Ourselves Again About the Great Splitting-Off, the Diminishment that Happened When We Gave Up Embodiment and Our Senses

Write the prayer on rolling paper
Hawaiian Red Clay Salt—inner circle
Black Charcoal Salt—outer circle
Black Tourmaline Dust (Schorl)—edge of circle and
    center cross
Magnetite Gathered from the Arroyo South of the
    House—center pile
Sulfur—triangles in four directions
Herkimer Diamond Charged on Winter Solstice
    Altar—center
Citrine Charged on Emily Dickinson's Grave, given to
    me by CA Conrad—placed atop tourmaline

Cornmeal—food for "doorway"

Tobacco (with Dogwood, Cherry Bark, Mullein and
    Willow)—with the cornmeal

Wrap computer in red cloth with tobacco and place
    it above the altar with the protection mandala. Let
    sit for one to four days. Unplug Wi-Fi. Drink pine
    needle tea from the grandmother tree on south side of
    the house.

"WHAT MEDICINE do you keep in your dreamtime?" the
mushrooms asked.

"I let my dreams be dreams, I guess."

"That's dumb," they said. "You take in all the world, all
that internet garbage. You're way too open to other people
and you think you can get by without keeping medicine
in your dreamtime? What do you love? Tell me anything,
just say it."

"I don't know. I love hawks. I love rivers and streams."

"Then keep those things in your dreams. You need an
anchor to remind you that your dreamtime belongs only
to you. You don't even get that it's yours, poor thing. Blown
like a plastic shopping bag in the wind."

I was encroaching upon new territory. To continue
to be a passive observer in psychedelic space was to risk
drowning in psychic mud. The mushrooms were coming with a question—*what is it that you want?* They were
becoming that nightmare dream date, who asks you which
restaurant you want to go to and you say, *no, you pick the
restaurant* and they say *no, you pick it, I insist*, and then you
have a total meltdown.

What was I allowed to call my own? Just because a thing exists doesn't mean it's mine to take.

WE WATCHED THE 2016 presidential election at the lesbian-owned restaurant and biker bar in the coal town. Honestly, I didn't know what kind of politics the older cowboys who sat at the bar every night kept until I saw they all were crying. One of them came up to Beth and me and asked us if we wanted some opium tincture.

"Yes, please," I said.

Beth and I opened our mouths like little birds for the dropper. It wasn't quite enough, though. Nothing could dull the pain of that night. The three of us stepped outside to smoke a joint. We huddled together tightly with this man we had seen around for years but hadn't really talked to. Allan was his name.

"This is the end of the age of the sun," Allan said. "A lot of us believed in the sixties that Jesus had returned during the Age of Aquarius, the Summer of Love, all of that. Jesus was the sun and the son. Now we are in the age of the daughter, born out of the darkness. It's your time."

Before we left to walk home, a friend of his who was visiting from out of town, an anonymous-looking bearded man who hardly seemed real, presented us with an offering: two tabs of LSD made in the family lab of the great Owsley himself. Beth nearly died. It had been almost two decades since she'd seen her old friend.

Of all the nights to be reunited.

We took it the night after the death of Carrie Fisher—who we believe visited us, being that we were probably the only two women on earth playing Princess Leia's theme on LSD at that exact time, holding hands and weeping. Both a sober icon and a notorious drug and alcohol fiend, Carrie Fisher said in *Rolling Stone* that LSD was her favorite drug. Maybe if she was faithful to Bill W., the founder of AA, she wouldn't have relapsed and died on a plane with cocaine, heroin, and MDMA in her system. Bill W. was faithful to LSD to the end, touting it as the only cure, even when it became unavailable. Princess Leia was written to be the last Jedi. *Carrie, what did you do?* I'd never done LSD before. I'd been resistant to ingesting it my whole life because of a dream I had in college. *Don't do LSD*, said the voice in the dream.

Let me just say LSD is not at all like the font. LSD could use some better public relations. I was pleasantly surprised to find I got to keep my aesthetics.

"So, what do you think?" Beth asked, seeing me bounce down the stairs, grinning.

"I'm like a kitten in a yarn factory!" I said, "I'm seeing that dogs and guitars evolved at the same pace. The universe is essentially groovy."

Beth hopped on right where she had stepped off so long ago, to find it waiting for her with all the love. She remembered how good she was at this. With two suicide grandfathers in her lineage, that night she got that LSD was the wild card that saved her life.

I once met a man with Elvis hair in the Jacuzzi at the gym in Santa Fe. He claimed he had a career in drug-dealing in the late '70s. He came to our coal town often, to mingle with the politicians, artists, hippies, cowboys, bikers, homosexuals, and pistol-toting, leather-vested, speed-freak prophetesses who crowded the bar from wall-to-wall on Saturday nights. On a night that was particularly packed, he accidentally dropped his stash of LSD squares on the honky-tonk dance floor. Before he realized what he'd done, everyone had already dived down and grabbed what they could and shoved it into their mouths. It was that kind of night.

"You need to come back and clean that up," I joked. "Whatever happened is still there."

The honky-tonk was once the entrance to the biggest coal mine west of the Mississippi. In 1889, there was a collapse, and 160 men were buried alive. When the bar becomes thick with spirits, it's not just these men the seers and sensitive recognize, but also the wives, the children, the Spanish and Pueblo people who were segregated on the south side. Everyone crowds the bar on those radioactive nights to party with the more recently deceased, who ride in on the alcohol that enters their bodies, taking them halfway across the River Styx.

Coal formation stopped on Earth three hundred thousand years ago, due to one factor: mushrooms. Up until then, fungus hadn't existed to the degree needed to break down the bodies of dead trees.

Behind the bar is a large hill of coal tailings. In 1975, David Bowie glided down that hill, over and over, cocaine-addled and alien-possessed as *The Man Who Fell to Earth*, not far from what was once the functioning mine that supplied coal to Los Alamos during the making of the atomic bomb. His character came to earth seeking water for his planet and instead found the United States. Bowie is our future self, beyond our chasing oil and coal and the power to split the atom. In the end, it's only water that matters.

26

CLEM RETURNED FOR their annual visit. Three years before, they'd developed the basic storyline of their lemur project in the anti-hippie, masochistic writer's bus. Since then, they'd visited the lemurs at Duke University and taken footage of them in their cages. Each lemur had its own idiosyncratic personality that inspired the stop-motion characters in their Claymation film.

"Lemurs are from Madagascar and only from Madagascar," they explained. "They evolved in isolation there and it is Madagascar where they will disappear. They are already extinct in the technical sense of the word."

"You are channeling a lemur right now," I said to Clem. "The way you are sitting."

"I feel like a lemur right now. Did I tell you the origins of the word *lemur* can be traced to the word *ghost*?"

The project was nearly finished. Clem pulled up photographic stills on their computer for me to see. The plan was to integrate live performance with the stop-motion film. Maybe it would be a musical; they weren't sure yet.

"There's a gay bar in the lemur project now," Clem said. "After Pulse and the Ghost Ship fire, I knew there had to be. The theme of the disappearance of queer culture needed to be emphasized."

It's hard to take one's eyes off a lemur. A successful spectacle relies on a subtext of anxiety on the part of the viewer, and lemurs provide a wealth of this currency. Lemurs are animals, but they are also "ghosts." They are embodied, and also not, moving like puppets manipulated by expert choreographers, sacks of fur with perfect form. They live on their lower haunches, the knees especially, reminding me of when Beth took mushrooms for the first time and hopped around the land, super-charged by this new center of gravity. Technically extinct, they exist but also don't. The ones that remain are only alive because of Science, which is fooling no one, and is not the same thing. They are lemurs but also Lemurians, a race of androgynous psychics from a lost continent at the bottom of the Pacific Rim of Fire. The link between lemurs and Lemurians has become established doctrine among occultists, the most notable being Madame Blavatsky. When William Burroughs laid his eyes on his first lemur at Duke University, he fell into a catatonic trance for days, receiving transmissions from ancient Lemuria.

Burroughs experienced these Lemurian fugue states during the period in which he was writing *The Western Lands*—sections of which were written less than fifteen miles south of my house in the coal town. Burroughs's lemur project, "The Ghost Lemurs of Madagascar," was written shortly after, and was one of his last works of fiction. I watched Clem steer away from centering Burroughs's contribution to lemur lore, being that he shot his wife dead in a parlor game. I personally feel that Burroughs's shamanic labors, his queering of the interdimensional realms, cannot be dismissed; this work requiring a certain homeopathic employment of demonic forces. Only a person already damned could have worked so tirelessly in this interstitial zone, dismantling impostor gods assembled there by colonizers and parasites.

Lemurians are said to live in Northern California, inside Mount Shasta, where they move through a network of complex tunnels. Sometimes they are seen on the surface of the mountain, dressed in white robes. This channeled information came through Frederick Spencer Oliver in 1899 and became his book *Dweller on Two Planets*. This transmission resulted in an endless, still-flowing tide of settler and European pilgrims descending on the mountain held sacred to the Shasta, Okwanuchu, Modoc, Achomawi, Atsugewi, Karuk, Klamath, Wintu and Yana tribes. Clem wanted to visit Mount Shasta, but in keeping with their respectful nature, they were waiting for a clear summons.

"I want to shoot some long-distance footage for the boat scenes on this trip," Clem said. "Seymour the lemur gets told that he's too genetically inadequate to be assigned a mate, so he sets forth by sea in search of love. There are all these challenges. The lemurs are addicted to millipedes because they contain natural opioids, but nostalgia is an even more dangerous addiction for them. It makes them very sick."

"Why is that one dressed in bandages?" I asked, looking at the gauze-wrapped lemur in a still Clem brought up on the screen.

"Because of the experiments."

"Sad."

"No, let me tell you what's sad. Because there are no millipedes, the lemurs are given all these manufactured drugs provided by the lab. One of the lemurs in my piece looked like he wasn't having a good time at all. I just looked at his sweet face and said, 'I'm sorry, I'm sorry, little lemur. I know there's better drugs in the word. I'm sorry you don't have a millipede.'"

"So much senseless suffering due to not knowing there are better drugs out there."

"Suffering and death. It's been a little overwhelming. I thought maybe I'd moved past the grief theme. Now I'm making a lemur project called *Our Future Ends* and it's about my friends, queer spaces disappearing, extinction, and the end of the world. It's basically a container for a concentrated fugue state of grief. I'm still actually trying to make a really optimistic happy piece of art. I know that doesn't make sense."

"I get what you're saying. But the container transforms the grief into something else."

"That's my hope, at least. I worry about the grief porn thing."

CLEM INVITED three friends to join us who were connected through a legendary bar in San Francisco called The Stud. To get the depth of what this means, it's important to understand what The Stud is, like on a psychedelic level. The bar opened at its original location in 1966 on Folsom Street, the true center of gay San Francisco, before the Castro district came alive. Where it's located now is irrelevant because what is considered a "neighborhood" in San Francisco depends on whether the block has been demolished and rebuilt by Google, Twitter, and the countless and interchangeable tech start-ups coming out of Silicon Valley. At the time of this writing, The Stud is an interdimensional cube on Ninth Street in a city that is already gone.

Boone was part of the team that resurrected The Stud. Bearded and eternally in shorts, I recognized him as a fellow cowpoke, if a cowpoke can be a fairy.

Jarret was young, yet already a legend in deep underground San Francisco drag culture, keeping alive its more fringe manifestations, like horror drag. When I met him, his dyed-black hair was shaved into a stark V, pointing to the base of his neck. He was tall and muscular with a thin veneer of nourishing fat, like a football boyfriend into The Cure.

Mona could rock a cerulean and orange knit hunter's cap with an all-black, skin-tight ensemble. Assigned female at birth, as they say, she performed high-femme drag at The Stud and was married to a trans man who ran a safe house in the city for transgender teens. Of Persian ancestry, she was the first guest at my house to know what Syrian rue was.

"To ward off the evil eye," she said. "We burned it at our wedding."

She was an architect who worked at a legit firm in the city. She had to show up for work early in the morning, five days a week. This fact intimidated me more than the fame of any guest that has ever passed through. I was attached to her liking me.

These guests were all professional night-time people, and it doesn't get better than that. As the night's employees, they are the opposite of agents of chaos. They save their drama for art.

Clem suggested we take mushrooms on our first night together. Everyone entrusted me to administer the right dosage. I spooned out about three to four grams for each person. Mona expressed concern about getting too high, so I gave her a bit less. We all sat in front of the fire in the living room and waited for the first flush of strangeness. It came upon us all at once. Clem suggested we do The Walk, just like we did our first year together, visiting each of the four directions on the land and offering tobacco.

I had some trepidation about The Walk. I am superstitious about revisiting scenes where magical, life-changing events happened in the past. It's like bringing your girlfriend back to the place where you shared your first kiss: It's a litmus test of intimacy for where you are now. *What if the magic isn't there anymore?* Those hard truths have to be dealt with eventually, but reenactments can take things to a level of tragic melodrama way too quickly, especially when high.

We all walked from the dry arroyo in the west to the top of the hill in the north. Clem was experiencing the blissful satisfaction that happens when you get to show people you love a thing you could never explain to them because they just have to see it themselves, and then they do.

"Apparently the north is where you realize you're really fucking high," Jarret said.

"This three-sixty-degree perspective has definitely kicked something in," said Boone.

I kept an eye on Mona. Her silence had a frequency of alarm to it. I didn't say anything. Maybe she was unaware. Saying, *Hey Mona, are you okay?* might shine a flashlight on her reality and send her into a freak-out.

"Yeah, I'm really high," Boone said.

We hovered in the north for quite a while and assessed our abilities. In terms of Mona, it became more likely that she wasn't talking because she couldn't.

"Everybody done with the north?" I said.

"Yep," said Boone.

"Thanks, north!" Clem chirped.

The descent down to east was spongey.

"Mweee waa nnn," Mona said.

"You okay, Mona?" Boone said. He was wide-eyed and standing über straight, the mushrooms bringing out the dutiful choirboy in him.

"Okay, you guy," she said. "Um. Nerk."

I didn't catch the rest.

"She's not sure if she can walk," Boone said. "She says she's way more high than she planned on being."

"Is she okay?"

"I think so," he said.

Mona exploded into a laughing fit, which was highly contagious. All of us descended on the amphitheater in hysterics because Mona's laughter was so insane and unhinged, and it was wrong for her to be alone in that;

through her laughter, we could tell she was terrified. Our joining in was a way we could offer comfort. One of us had to half-lift her the last few yards to the sand, where she collapsed into a fetal position. Out of breath, we sat on the rocks near her, and she began flopping into random shapes along a horizontal theme. She was struggling, but it was also a delight, her masochistic offering. She rallied every last bit of her coherence to give us a full report.

"It's. Um. Reality is totally . . . no more. Get what I'm saying? That? Nope! Yeah, that's pretty much what's going on. I'm really . . . wow. I'm fine, though."

In a group journey, there's usually one person the fungi pick to be the anchor, who embodies the teachings most aching to come forth. Mona was clearly that person. Of course she was. She was going to be one of Clem's lemurs in the live performance.

To say that lemurs are matriarchal doesn't feel accurate. It would be more correct to say that lemurs are avatars of the goddess principle. Both females and males can embody the divine feminine.

"I like east," she said. "I think north is pretty cool, too."

Her storm had broken, and all was calm. An inner sun shone through her floppy tangle on the rocks.

"So, what is it, west can basically kiss my ass?" I said.

"Yeah, maybe."

I had to break the news to everyone that we couldn't go to the south altar because a neighbor had bought the land there and put up a fence. I didn't want the information to bum anyone out. I dreaded having to say anything. I hadn't even dealt with my own feelings on the matter, and the last thing I wanted was to face those emotions while high.

"The pig fence blocks off where I scattered my ex-girlfriend's ashes," I said. "So, the south altar is wherever we make it, just not there. Maybe over yonder, thataway."

"Can you cut a door in the fence?" Mona asked.

"No, it's not like before, when no one ever checked the fence. I think he's alt-right. He has Celtic tribal tattoos and he wears hair ties in his beard. He drives a golf cart back and forth on the trails like he's on patrol. He said I couldn't hike there anymore, no exceptions."

"That's horrible," said Mona.

"I burst out into tears when he told me that. I worked the whole sobbing-woman angle, but Trump is president now. Men don't have to pretend to feel bad when faced with a crying woman."

"You can't walk there at all?" Boone asked.

"My neighbor went hiking down there with his dogs and came home to find the sheriff waiting at his house. Oh, and his dad is the inventor of the Fleshlight."

"The sex toy?"

"Every time I go down there, I now think the words 'fake vagina.' But that's cool."

"I don't know how you even deal," Clem said.

"After Standing Rock, this fence thing is nothing. It's his land now. I can't visit and that is that. But let's avoid looking at it, okay?"

I walked us all back towards the south side of the house, where there was an old leather couch and a salvaged iron stove. Mona fell apart and put herself back together at least five times along the way. How I ended up in the juniper tree, I don't remember. I suppose I had put a lot of energy into keeping it together for Mona, and once I got close to the house it all unraveled. I was in the juniper tree I always puke in, enveloped in the clutches of its branches, when over my shoulder I saw a vivid, furry, white dinosaur face.

Nope, didn't see that. I refuse to turn my head in that direction again. The thing remained hovering in the periphery of my vision, close to the branches. I couldn't help but be curious about it and tried to get a sense of what it was without looking at it directly. Beneath the Barney-ish head was a dangling, nerve-like shape about four feet long. It hovered vertically and glowed white, then it sprouted tendrils from its wormy center, like the aerial view of a river system. An interlocking, hexagonal wallpaper hovered chest-high around both it and me—shapes that seemed unrelated to the white apparition, perhaps generated by the juniper tree itself.

I reacted like an any animal would: with fright. I was impressed. It takes a lot to scare me on these things.

"Hello," I said, then stepped out of the field of it. It disappeared, along with my high. Mushrooms can be like that. It's possible to slip in and out of sober and psychedelic states countless times over the course of a night.

I didn't tell Clem about what I'd seen in the tree. On a visit a year later, Clem mentioned that after smoking some weed, they saw a very tall white thing near the juniper tree, near the couch. Like me, Clem is not a person who sees things. When we realized that we had seen the same bizarre white entity, we both agreed we should call Beth.

"Have you ever seen a white thing over to the left of the leather couch, near the juniper tree? The one I puke in? Not a ghost, but a white thing. Very vertical?"

"Oh, totally," Beth said. I put the phone on speaker mode so Clem could hear. "The night you did mushrooms in Mexico and I was sitting by the fire, there was a whiteness that moved with the smoke from the burning tobacco ties and it came from over there. I didn't look at it directly."

"Neither did we! Both of us knew not to!" Clem said.

"What is it?" I asked.

"I don't know."

"What should we do? Should we ask it what it wants?" Clem said.

"Oh, god no," Beth said. "It has nothing to do with us. It's ancient. It just lives there and wants to be left alone."

I was failing at lighting a fire in the salvaged stove. Dry branches ignited dramatically, then quickly died out. We unanimously decided to go back in the house and picked our various places in the room to sit. Jarret chose the hammock. Boone chose the throne, which felt right. Brannigan was gone for good, but her legacy dictated that the chair would be always reserved for the queen in the room.

The only time I understand gender is when I'm on mushrooms. I've watched the way mushrooms work a room, employing gender—freaking it, exaggerating binaries to cartoonish extremes then popping it, erasing it, fuzzing and frying it, making it over, all so they can crack up laughing. Gender is a medicine of specificity that feeds a pantheon in the head. Mushrooms like details—grandmas sitting drinking brandy, brothers dressed up in clean shirts, drag queens, dime store mermaids, sacred whores, space cowboys and Ms. Tobacco in her dirty brown suit and top hat. I have felt gendered forms moving as fast as fire through my entire body, shapeshifting before I can track them.

That night, Mona was nailing what it meant to be the divine feminine. The fungi were giving her no coffee breaks. It was beautiful to witness her solo performance as she veered from maniacal laughter to self-depreciating commentary, then, like ladies do, she checked herself. I do that. One must have manners and read the room, not be too self-absorbed. She made sure to stop and effusively praise us quite authentically. This group of friends was tight and the love between them fueled the journey. Mona flickered crystalline at hummingbird speed, the interchangeable shapes of her being pummeling through her all at once. The more she expressed, the more self-conscious she became; the more self-conscious, the more tender. Explosions of blushing punctuated the event of Mona slow-motion falling and being lifted into the open arms of all of us who loved her so much, we didn't even know what to do with all of it.

Jarret, swinging on the hammock, blurted out, "How does it feel that your husband—"

He didn't finish the sentence.

"That my husband what?" Mona asked.

"Never mind."

"No, what? Tell me."

"Nothing," Jarret said. There was a dynamic at play, an old thing between them that was just theirs.

"What?" Mona demanded. Jarret still didn't answer her, so Mona finished the sentence for him. "How does it feel that my husband had sex with all my friends before we were married?"

"Yeah. That."

There's that moment when Mary Tyler Moore throws her hat in the air in the opening credits of *The Mary Tyler Moore Show*. Mona did that, but with just her hands. She even spun around a little and looked up at the ceiling trusses with wonder, like real angels were sitting up there, waving. She did this thing without any air of camp or irony. Mona must have been sent to fix that pollution and return the gesture of tossing one's hat off to its original innocence. The tossing of the hat is a gesture of liberation, full ownership of self.

"I love him. That's the only answer I have to the question, Jarret. I love him. I love him so much I'm going to lose my shit right now because I don't even know how to explain it to you how much I fucking love him, every single thing about him. I'm a traditional person, like, I know it's not in vogue, but I'm down with monogamy, all of it. I love him. And I love you guys. I love everything about who he is and who he was before me and what he does in the community for people, so, oh my god, I guess I have to say it. I'm going to totally say it. I love that my husband had sex with my friends before we were married."

This was the crescendo of the trip, a love bomb in the true sense of the word. There was also a big drama at the south door involving Mona's shoelaces that I missed completely.

Spent, I collapsed next to Clem on the couch. We reminisced about my Jean Baudrillard phase, when we both lived in Los Angeles and I begged Clem to visit the spec houses with me in the sprawling subdivision of Santa Clarita. Each house was set up for the nuclear family according to whether you had one, two, or three children, complete with fake photographs of families and gendered bedrooms in pink or blue. Wynton Marsalis was piped in eternally through hidden speakers. I visited these spec houses often. They held a strange sexual charge that I couldn't quite unravel.

"Good thing we outgrew that one," Clem said.

"I think I've eroticized every last thing that I find aesthetically and existentially unbearable in order to diffuse its power to terrify me. Ugliness no longer interests me, though I still love the mycelial freeways of Los Angeles. Joan Didion said—"

"She lost her sense of narrative driving the freeways of LA."

"When you're everywhere and nowhere, the fiction takes a different form."

I went to the fire and scooped some embers up with a shovel. I sprinkled copious amounts of frankincense resin on the coals. Thick white smoke rose up and filled the room. There was so much, and it didn't dissipate, just continued to hover. Mona panicked.

"Is it really smoky in here?" she said. "I mean, beyond the smudging. Is it really smoky, like there's a fire?"

"No," I said.

"Definitely not," Clem reiterated. "There's nothing scarier than thinking the house has caught on fire when you're high, but no, it's just the frankincense."

Mona stood quietly, observing her fear. It had offered itself up so irrationally she might as well have gotten curious about it and toy with the fear, because why not?

"I have a fear of fire," she said. "I know I must have died in a fire. I'm having a very vivid image of being burned at the stake, actually. Wow, yeah, okay."

The memory, the dream, the hallucination, whatever it was was very real for her. Her distress was felt by everyone.

"I know the whole witchy-burny thing is kind of cliché," she said. "Sorry, but yeah, this is happening."

Clem remembered a simple exercise gleaned from their study of psychic healing that they thought might be of help.

"What was the last thing you saw when you died?" they asked.

"What do you mean?"

"There's this technique I was trained in called memory repatterning."

It's a tricky thing to know when to offer healing to someone during a mushroom trip. What can feel like a good idea at first can turn quickly into a boundary violation with the potential to yank someone out of their own experience for the duration. Clem was trained in this technique and knew what they were doing. Their friendship was solid.

"Don't be fooled by how simple it is. You take the moment of trauma and rewrite the story. At the moment you died, in the fire, what was the last thing you saw?"

"I saw stars. I was looking up at the sky."

"What was happening as you were looking at the stars?"

"I don't know. I guess I was being burned at the stake?"

"Change the narrative. What were you doing while looking at the stars?"

"I was walking my dog," she said.

"Okay, you're walking your dog."

Mona totally got what was happening, how she had changed the story. "Yep, I was just this person walking my dog under the stars."

"So that's what happened?"

"That's what happened," she said. With each beat, blood returned to her cheeks. "Just walkin' around with the dog. Hey there, yeah, I'm just walking my dog in the nighttime, looking up at the stars. They're so pretty."

"In a moment, in the twinkling of an eye, at the last trumpet. For the trumpet will sound, and the dead shall be raised incorruptible, and we will be changed."
—1 Corinthians 15:52

And so it was. The Deaths left her body.

I WOKE UP the following morning with a spiritual flu.

After a mushroom trip, I usually wake in a creosote dawn, feeling as if all roads have been washed clean by rain, but that morning something was wrong. It manifested in the form of my internet addiction, nearly eighteen hours straight spent online looking at the usual nothing. There wasn't anything about the journey the night before that was troublesome in any obvious way. Clearly my ego was feeling threatened by something the rest of me was not conscious of, and was beginning to mount an aggressive defense.

"I saw a buffalo in the fire," Boone said, still sitting in the throne, which was where he spent the night. "I thought it may have been my grandfather's buffalo that he painted in Gallup, but I wasn't sure."

"What is buffalo to the Native Americans?" Clem asked. We were all gathered in the kitchen, drinking our morning coffee and yerba mate.

I wanted to say I couldn't answer the question, that the mushrooms had cut me off buffalo because of white crime. I suspected the buffalo problem had something to do with my psychedelic hangover, in that I was beginning to really struggle while tripping on mushrooms with what exactly I was allowed to invoke and give power to. I had cruised through the trip the night before in a default mode of passivity that was becoming a habit.

I answered Clem's question about buffalo and Lakota culture as best I could, and awkwardly. This led to a conversation about the Ghost Dance—a ceremonial circle dance that spread through the plains with a cult-like fervor, triggering the deployment of troops to the reservation and the massacre at Wounded Knee that left 153 Lakota dead, mostly women and children. The channeled book about Lemurians and Wovoka's Ghost Dance vision were both received in the late 1880s during the Gilded Age, when the combustion engine, the personal camera, and the light bulb were invented—an era defined by speed and population growth that resulted in unprecedented levels of inequity between a tiny ruling class and everyone else. Both visions were apocalyptic in nature and concerned the survival of a chosen race of beings in possession of sacred knowledge. The late 1880s is an origin point on a timeline leading to the reckoning of right now.

"Why is it always the magical people who die in the most horrific ways, even when there's no concrete enemy?" Mona asked. "It's as if the tragedy is already written."

I knew she was referring to the Ghost Ship Fire in Oakland, where she and many others we knew had lost loved ones.

"Is it wrong to think of queers as being special?" she said.

"I don't think we're special," I said. "Maybe we're just cuter?"

"I think queers are special," Mona interjected with confidence.

While I am against the idea of any group of people being more special than any other, I saw that she held her belief in a way that was right-sized and caused harm to no one. I wasn't moved to try to change her mind.

"Do gays get to have buffalo?" Boone asked.

"David Wojnarowicz's *Close to the Knives*," I said. "The buffalo being driven off the cliff to their deaths, tumbling, suspended forever in a free fall."

"I wrote a paper on that photograph," Clem said. "It's one the most iconic images of the AIDS crisis."

They explained it was taken by David Wojnarowicz himself, a photograph of a diorama at the Natural History Museum in Washington, DC, so close to where all the crimes having to do with AIDS legislation were happening.

"Don't forget the gay buffalo that you made, Clem," I said.

"I made a gay buffalo?"

"In your sequence in the film *Valencia*, where the queers all take mushrooms in the Mission District and Miguel turns into a Claymation buffalo."

"I almost forgot. I totally made a queer, psychedelic buffalo."

"Wait a minute, I'm having a revelation," I said. "Mushrooms grow in cow dung. Some say that's why cows are revered as sacred in certain cultures. It only makes sense they would also grow in buffalo dung."

I Googled it on my phone and sure enough, psilocybin mushrooms grown on buffalo dung are a thing. Not so much on the dung of plains buffalo—the climate is too dry—but the dung of water buffalo definitely yields a coveted fruit. Maybe people could store dung from plains buffalo in a climate-controlled room and grow mushrooms out of it. It would no doubt be a worthy experiment.

27

OR, THE BUFFALO PROBLEM

"And the unquestioned assumption is
that the names have been given wrongly,
in total ignorance of the true nature of
reality, which is unchanging and one. This
assumption is partly right. But at the same
time, it's altogether wrong."
—PETER KINGSLEY, *Reality*

TO RECOGNIZE the buffalo as the buffalo is to impose upon it the name, *buffalo*. *Buffalo* is a creation of my consciousness placed upon a thing that may or may not actually be buffalo. Before the buffalo received the name I put upon it, it was a container of endless possibility. Maybe a buffalo isn't a buffalo at all, but something else altogether, but when I name it *buffalo* its potential to be anything outside of my own limited understanding of what a buffalo is, ceases to exist. To name the buffalo *buffalo* is to erase the potential of buffalo, to freeze its becoming, to kill it, in a sense.

This is how people who do too many psychedelics go down—not in a gutter with a needle in their arm but paralyzed in their rooms with a buffalo problem.

Is the first original sin the act of naming? Is it language itself?

Psychedelics had brought me to a place of heightened awareness of the tyranny of my own mind. My need to frantically recognize patterns and make meaning out of everything was strangling the life force out of reality itself. I was uncovering the toxic egotism at the core of my perception, rooted in my desire to be a good person. Meanwhile, I was becoming more paralyzed, afraid to think analytically at all, for fear of building up yet another defense against the truth.

"In the psychedelic sphere, epistemology's an extreme sport."
—DIANA SLATTERY, *Xenolinguistics*

DIANE SLATTERY mentions it almost as an aside: She spent time in a mental institution after being triggered by the events of 9/11, which landed in the middle of her long series of psychedelic journeys. She speaks of it in a way that someone with money, good health insurance, and the ability to take time off work would speak of such a thing, as simply part of the process.

Even as a white woman of means, going insane has never been an option. Due to how I was raised, it would be a lot for my ego to process. Going insane is not necessary, I feel.

Psychonauts constantly emphasize the urgency of integrating the psychedelic experience. *To not do so can be very dangerous*, they warn. Up until this point, I thought they were talking about other, perhaps less mentally stable people. I had been eating mushrooms for over six years and I didn't think I had a problem with integration. *What did that word even mean, anyway?*

"Integrating is the process of just being alive, right?" Beth said. "You think, you talk to people, you make connections, what else is there to do? Who doesn't do those things?"

What if: We obsess over integration because we can't deal with the fact we are taking Schedule 1 illegal drugs? Framing our drug use in the context of crisis and healing centers psychedelics as a medicine, rather than the crime that it also is.

What if: Psychedelic integration is an excuse to wallow in our trip-traps, rather than put them away for a while, in order to get down to the business of living.

What if: Psychedelic integration circles are the only way we know how to make friends with other people who do psychedelics.

What if: Spending money on therapy and other healing modalities under the guise of psychedelic integration is how we make our realizations feel legitimate in a capitalist society?

> **"Integration** refers to the end result of a process that aims to stitch together different, often disparate, subsystems so that the data contained in each becomes part of a larger, more comprehensive system that, ideally, quickly and easily shares data when needed."
> —MARGARET ROUSE, Whatis.com

THIS DEFINITION refers to "the end result of a process." My experience is that a mushroom trip does not yield definitive end results, let alone any that can easily be "stitched together." Psychedelics allow us to glimpse the incomprehensible. Gathering and organizing fragments gleaned from psychedelic experience into a "comprehensive system" is a mental exercise that runs the risk of crystalizing the living water of religious experience until it becomes a mere linguistic souvenir and flows no more.

We must hold on loosely, children, loosely.

The constellation of Standing Rock, Trump's election and taking LSD for the first time marked a six-month period I now call my epistemological breakdown. I was busted in the act of pretending I knew whole systems of knowledge, when I'd only grasped a small part.

I don't like facing how little I know. This is where it stopped with me in the past, with a belief that maybe I was not very good at thinking. But now, I was being reminded over and over that I'm actually relatively smart, just lazy and full of self-doubt. An honest desire to understand things better had been ignited in me, and I wasn't going to get away with being one of those pre-verbal types who excessively uses the word *somatic*. I was in too deep. The mushrooms were not going to let me blow off my homework.

I didn't do any mushrooms or LSD for about seven months. Instead, I feverishly read books, and not of the psychedelic kind. I had spent hundreds of hours in a state of consciousness where the anchor points of my reality were upended. Shrooms are not a movie projector. Shrooms are windshield wipers. On a brain chemistry level, they do nothing more than strip away the brain's defense mechanisms necessary for our day-to-day survival. While in a psychedelic state, we see the nature of our own consciousness more clearly. Are we seeing reality outside of ourselves more clearly as well? What is the relationship between our perception of reality and well, *reality*?

I'd been perfectly happy leaving such questions to others.

Way deep down inside, an incomprehensible truth had scared the shit out of me. I was on the run and nobody knew but me. It felt dangerous. How had I changed? In what ways did I view the world differently now than how I used to? What belief systems, opinions, and attitudes needed to be recognized and discarded?

And lastly, what is reality?

Reality used to be something a person could talk about in the town square. Now proclaiming Bigfoot is real is less likely to get you laughed at than suggesting reality itself might be a made-up story, a total illusion, like actually. No offense to Bigfoot. We live in an era in which the powers that affect our lives at the most basic level are hidden from view. How can you fight an enemy you're not even given the dignity of being allowed to see? Our moment is defined by a collective state of consciousness so infused with cognitive dissonance and surreality that it can only be called psychedelic, and not in a good way. Not knowing what the fuck is going on is the shared purgatory we all now live in.

As a culture that is out of practice when it comes to talking about the nature of reality, we are ill-equipped to deal with the inevitable anxiety that arises from this state of affairs. Instead of facing the nature of reality head-on, we engage with reality surrogates, symbolic stand-ins, virtual playing fields where we attempt to alter our fate conceptually. We had Pinchbeck's 2012, now there are Flat Earthers, the Anunnaki, and The Singularity, where we all wrap our heads around human consciousness uploading into one giant computer program. Maybe our lives are a simulation created by AI from the future.

"Conspiracy theory, in my humble opinion, is a kind of epistemological cartoon about reality. I believe that the truth of the matter is far more terrifying, that the real truth that dare not speak itself, is that no one is in control, absolutely no one."

—TERRENCE MCKENNA

"MAYBE I'M JUST a failed post-structuralist?" I said to Beth, after we ran the Sam Durant/Walker Art Center controversy though an intersectional meat grinder for hours over morning coffee. I played her the video "Post-Structuralism for Dummies" on YouTube.

"I'm not really sure if this has anything to do with your buffalo problem," she said.

"I'm trying to figure things out without seeking answers from traditions that aren't my own for a change," I said, and right as the words came out of my mouth, I began flipping through Slattery's *Xenolinguistics*. I began reading out loud from an underlined passage.

"*With my koshuti I want to see—singing I carefully examine things—twisted language brings me close but not too close—with normal words I would crash into things—with twisted one's I circle around them—I can see them clearly.*"

"So she's basically saying to keep it groovy?"

"It's from the Yaminahua shamans. It's beautiful but another exotic bon-bon, I know. I'm really trying to get out of the Anthropologie store of philosophical inquiry."

"In a state of ignorance, at least the world is real."

"And just when you think you've figured
it out, that's when you become the most
foolish one of all."

—PETER KINGSLEY, *Reality*

I DROVE twelve miles down the country road to an adobe home that butts up against a grove of cottonwoods. I collapsed on my friend Margaret's couch and confessed I was in the middle of an epistemological breakdown. We were writing partners and she'd been helping me with this book for too long to allow me to indulge in any self-sabotage. She fed me chicken soup and told me about a bear that had been coming around outside her house. It happened two times, both right after eating the pot brownie to help her sleep. The first time was really scary; the bear acted like it was about to charge. The second time it just watched her.

"She must be coming to eat the apples I've been picking and storing in a bucket across the yard," she said, her Alabama accent like dew on each syllable. "The bear's visited me in my dreams, too."

"It's very comforting hearing you talk right now. Thinking in general seems to be trending towards obliterating all matter until a very extreme open field of possibility is achieved. We've forgotten where to put the bear, you know? Mathematics has forgotten the bestiary."

The artist Agnes Martin lived a few doors down from Margaret before she died. Agnes began her art practice by painting landscapes then came to view these representations as untrue.

"Beauty is in the mind, not the eye," Agnes said, while developing her signature line grids on paper in pencil. Margaret and I occasionally rode horses together in the village and one day we passed the house where Agnes used to live. Margaret pointed out the adobe across the street with a walled-in yard and an obsessive-compulsive Great Pyrenees that had a fetish for toy dolls, which he would bury and dig up and place somewhere different and then dig up again and repeat. Margaret said the dog did this from morning until night, when its owners took him inside.

The dog maniacally barked at us when we passed on horseback, leaping many feet in the air to get a look at us over the wall. It made me bust up laughing, but clearly, he was suffering quite a bit from his own mental state. I remarked that this was probably due to the force field of spirit emanating from Agnes Martin's house across the way. The dog was possessed with the same genius and enthusiasm as Agnes, but without the IQ and discipline to execute his task with style, the dog went nuts.

Lying on Margaret's couch, I acknowledged I had become that Great Pyrenees.

"I've lost the flow of where and when to express myself," I said. "My will feels toxic. I've witnessed my brain's maniacal need to control how I perceive things and the only solution has been to give into paralysis. Please help me?"

Margaret put Solange on the CD player and handed me a cup of peppermint tea.

"Have you ever read Peter Kingsley?" she said, handing over the medicine. You see, the magic books are passed from one friend to another, at just the exact right time.

"This is the silent awareness, nurtured in stillness, of how all our careful decisions are nothing but avoidance of that one crucial decision the gods have been waiting and wanting to see you make for thousands of years."

"Helplessness in their chests is what steers their wandering minds."
—PETER KINGSLEY, *Reality*

KINGSLEY'S BOOK *Reality* is a transmission on metaphysics, as practiced by pre-Socratic Greek philosophers Epimenides, Parmenides, and Pythagoras. He speaks of the time when our ancestors walked thousands of miles with Apollo ruling their heads, and their job was to fabricate the sublime in collaboration with nature. Reality was experienced vividly, with such a divine connection to the organizing principles of the cosmos, in comparison we are numb and practically already dead.

A remedy for this? There's not much. Kingsley suggests listening to the birds. Only *metis* can help us, *metis* being the Greek word pertaining to a talent for cunning and trickery.

This was the book that blasted me out of my stuck place, introduced me to my ancient ancestors, and recalibrated my perception. We are flung from wholeness by love and it is through strife that we return. His work didn't so much give me a worldview, as much as it helped me navigate the human condition of being eternally lost.

"If you're trapped in the dream of the Other,
 you're fucked."
                                —GILLES DELEUZE

"So you found a girl who thinks really deep
 thoughts
 What's so amazing about really deep thoughts
 Boy you best pray that I bleed real soon
 How's that thought for you"
                —TORI AMOS, "Silent All These Years"

28

WE'RE NOT READING like we used to.

I'm Generation X, so just speaking for myself, my reading habits were born of high school assignments that included *Lord of the Flies, To Kill a Mockingbird, The Color Purple,* and *The Kin of Ata are Waiting for You*—books that fell away into oblivion shortly after my completion of college. My mother tried to get me to read *Little Women,* anything by Lillian Hellman and Truman Capote, but I associated reading with my mother's bedridden depression. It wasn't until my mid-twenties that I met a writer who introduced me to Eileen Myles, Dennis Cooper, Wanda Coleman, Kathy Acker, Michelle Tea, Bret Easton Ellis, and Douglas Coupland, that I began to read with any seriousness at all.

I couldn't play guitar very well. I couldn't sing or draw or paint. We didn't have Instagram back then, so I couldn't turn myself into an influencer. Instead, I gathered all I had inside me and wrote a coming-of-age novel in the '90s, because writing was how you became a public person then, when you were gay and lonely and needed to make a mark so people could find you, all of us falling off the face of the earth in our weird, un-trackable, made-up lives.

I've always felt like somewhat of a failure as a reader. I tell myself it's my ADD and the fact I'm a writer—*I can't read like other people, it messes with my prose style, who has the time?* Yet when it came to my Buffalo Problem, I didn't turn to the trees. I didn't fast or sit in meditation. I stopped doing psychedelics for over six months and knew that if there was any answer to my problems, I would find it in the pages of books.

So I read.

The Aleph and Other Stories by Jorge Luis Borges formed the crater of my inquiry. I had read it years before and revisited it briefly in order to remember that *yes, the notion that "things are not what they seem"* is not meant to be quirky entertainment or a device-y construct. The fact that "things are not what they seem" is a fucking DISASTER. Tom Robbins knows this, even though he makes everything funny. I can't read Tom Robbin's anymore because I will steal from him. Same with Carlos Castaneda, who lacks the necessary sense of humor. It's my dream to write the hybrid Castaneda/Robbin's spiritual paperback novel, but I'm not that kind of trickster, unfortunately. I refuse to deceive my readers by allowing them to think I'm in on a mystical secret, a benign device I guess, but one I can't personally stomach.

Octavia Butler understood conundrum of reality being generally untrustworthy and did not sin against it. She charts an interdimensional topography that's both erotic and political. I don't know of any imagined world more intricate, psychedelic, and healing than what is found in *Lilith's Brood (Trilogy: Dawn, Adulthood Rites, Imago.)*

That the psychedelic is best written by those on the margin, through poetry and science fiction, should come as no surprise. Pragmatic survival depends on navigating invisible realms, naming the unseen, with or without the help of actual drugs.

Psychic extremes, fractal organization, and the moral and compassionate assemblage of outer-edge shards of experience are all at work in Eileen Myles *Afterglow*, one of the most psychedelic books I have ever read. It's about a dog, basically, but really it's about the universe.

The Sand Book by Ariana Reines is an exhaustive poetic effort to meet Jorge Luis Borges where he was at—in the realm of sinister infinity and the mystical impossible. To prove or disprove any theory, an experiment must be done, and this book is that. How is it possible that a writer can take the intricacies of the world to heart with such seriousness, without dying of exhaustion and despair, I wonder? This book shows that it can be been done, so stop whining—we are built for this.

I read Clarice Lispector, Amina Cain, Fred Moten, Joy Williams, and Dodie Bellamy, writers devoted to not betraying the truth of what's possible in a single sentence. Whether by intention or accident, their texts end up being portals where I am reorganized in tune with an always yet to be revealed logic.

Divine Horsemen: The Living Gods of Haiti by Maya Deren is a book about voudou and African cosmology that taught me how the psyche itself is colonized and shaped by forces of power. I kept it close in my twenties and thirties. It wasn't until I read *Freshwater* by Akwaeke

Emezi, about a queer person in Brooklyn beset internally by spirits of the Igbo ontology, that I'd encountered a narrative where a marginalized cultural psychological reality was presented unapologetically and as fully legitimate. Does your psychology belong to you? Who is telling the story about how your mind works? Are they your people?

Hello, the Roses by Mei-mei Berssenbrugge will set you right in the garden. These poems feel like mushroom chants.

Please read *María Sabina* by María Sabina, edited by Jerome Rothenberg. You must see her chants/veladas on the page and her personal story that introduces the book; don't say you get her until you've finished reading it.

I read *Braiding Sweetgrass* by Robin Wall Kimmerer and *The Overstory* by Richard Powers. Both books are sweeping fugue-state manifestos about the interconnectivity of all things in nature, written with a grounded clarity that reveals how science and biology are more psychedelic than hallucinations—sacred texts for the Anthropocene.

In terms of the canon of classic books about psychedelia, I have fallen in love with only one: *The Doors of Perception* by Aldous Huxley, in which he writes about mescaline. The work also functions as a treatise on art in antiquity. Textiles. Huxley was blown away by the representation of textiles in art. Surfaces was where it was at. How had he been so blind? After being bothered by Cezanne, for relief, he looks at the folds in his trousers.

These are the things one ought to look at. Things without pretensions, satisfied to be merely themselves, sufficient in their Suchness, not acting a part, not trying insanely, to go it alone, in isolation from the Dharma-body, in Luciferian defiance of the grace of God.

I wrote my first fan letter to Charles M. Schultz at age nine. There's probably nothing more psychedelic than Snoopy and the Peanuts gang when you think about it—all those kids and that dog, that yellow bird, beset by existential angst and the meaning of life. And then there's Lucy, a character whose name is urban slang for LSD, so what does that mean? She's *that* asshole, and a girl, of course. It's always that asshole who tricks you, pulls the football out from under you, who shows you the way out of the Matrix even though she herself is the very picture of hubris mixed with lack of self-awareness, which is very appealing, until it isn't.

"We are preparing to die, you see," says Cornel West in a YouTube video. "So we must enact Socratic inquiry!"

Peter Kingsley would suggest the inquiry be pre-Socratic, even more ancient, a thing we might ask of the birds to teach us rather than books. All the while, he's a writer as he says this, and I am a reader who isn't reading books most of the time, though text hums beneath all of my consciousness, all the time. The word—the word and my devotion to it. It doesn't matter what I gleaned from the books I read. The inquiry is the integration, a process that ever ends.

29

"We might interpret this entire region as one land unified through the flying sensation of Peganum harmala, used in entheogenic communions to induce visions of the gods."

—RICHARD MERRICK

SYRIAN RUE (*Peganum harmala*) is a MAOI inhibitor and potentiator of the mushrooms. I had ingested the two together on many occasions and liked the combination better than doing the mushrooms alone. I dreamed up this T-shirt logo and executed it with the help of Beth's friend, Elizabeth Daggar of Electrofork, way before I made the connection.

Pegasus = *Peganum harmala*

The winged horse that is Pegasus was thought of as the archetypal keeper and protector of poets in the nineteenth century, avatar of freshwater springs, and keeper of thunder and lightning for Zeus. Pegasus is allied with the power of lightning, lightning being a catalyst for mushroom growth, due to the infusion of nitrogen into the soil.

A map of Asia drawn in 1581 by Heinrich Bunting depicts the region that includes Persia, Turkey, and Syria as composing the body of Pegasus. This is where Syrian rue comes from.

Right after Syrian rue landed in my house, I also began using frankincense. I read on the internet to pour boiling water over a handful of frankincense tears in a glass and let it sit overnight. Not only is it a healing tonic, it's also delicious, especially when mixed with orange bitters or crushed mint.

My internet searches on Syrian rue alone didn't yield much information. It was when I Googled both frankincense and Syrian rue together that I hit gold.

"The Messenger of God (i.e. the Prophet Muḥammad) said, "the harmala [i.e., Syrian rue/Esfand] does not grow, whether from a tree, a leaf or a fruit, without there being an angelic guardian spirit attached to it, until it reaches whosoever it reaches, or turns to waste. In both its root and its branches there is a talisman. In its seeds there is a cure for seventy-two maladies, so treat yourselves with it, as well as with the olibanum [i.e., Frankincense], for purposes of healing." (Benton Rooks, "Ayahuasca and the Godhead: An Interview with Wahid Azal of the Fatimiya Sufi Order")

A SEARCH ON Syrian rue and juniper unearthed the following from Christian Rätsch, from *The Encyclopedia of Psychoactive Plants: Ethnopharmacology and Its Applications*:

"In the Himalayas and neighboring regions, shamans used the (Syrian rue) seeds as a magical incense. The shamans of Hunza, who live in what is now Pakistan, inhale the smoke (Syrian Rue along with Drooping Juniper) to enter a clairvoyant trance. The shamans (bitayo) then enter into a close, lusty sexual contact with the divining fairies, who give them important information, and the ability to heal."

30

OR, THE HOLY MOSH PIT OF GUADALUPE

"Grace appears purest in that human form
which has either no consciousness or an
infinite one, that is, in a puppet or a God."
—HEINRICH VON KLEIST,
"On the Marionette Theater"

SOMETIMES THE person you could have been, who other people see you as or wish you were, shows up in your life as a fragment within another person. Rose had long, blonde, unconfused hair and wore pale jeans and thrift store T-shirts. Her femininity was condensed and alpha. The force field of it dissolved my masculinity and I let my hair down and found myself wearing cut-off shorts and a T-shirt decorated with three cartoon kittens.

Rose was new to psychedelics but was in no way a novice. Rose wasn't a novice to anything. She was a successful writer and had an almost-degree in Chinese medicine before a plant told her to drop out of school. Her talent for rapping along to Biggie Smalls as a rabbit on Snapchat was a revelation. Like protagonists in a female buddy film, that thing of two we were—Romy and Michele about to get unbelievably fucking high.

She arrived flustered. The stillness of the house made her aware of how crowded she felt inside; there were so many interactions with friends and strangers on a long road that left her feeling like she'd left behind something essential. Seen through an X-ray lens, ordinary social exchanges are a monster mash. Rose needed some first aid.

I told her about the red and black salt and sulfur shield I made to protect myself from the internet. If she wanted to, she could make one too. Within an hour, she had built one and set it by her bed alongside a burning candle. In realms of witchery, Rose wasted no time.

Not to brag, but I'm a treasure trove of all kinds of tricks and folk remedies. Every single thing I suggested to Rose, she took to heart and did. How fun is that?

She gifted me with homemade frankincense oil and calendula face lotion, though her generosity expressed itself most fully through her talent at making sure I felt seen as my very best self. If I made a self-deprecating remark, I caught hell from Rose. She would interrogate me as to why I would put myself down in such a way and demanded that I change immediately.

"People think it's weird when I do that," she said, when I pointed out this trait.

"Yes, it's weird. You're relentless with the *stop saying bad things about yourself* campaign. I like it."

It was during a late conversation on the topic of Standing Rock with a man she'd just met that she found herself blurting, "I need to go visit Bett in New Mexico!" Standing Rock is a mycelium now, connecting everyone who shares the same prayer: *Mini Wiconi, Water is Life.* The network is vast. Fruits emerge everywhere.

"It was right after Standing Rock that I knew I had to do something," Congresswoman Ocasio-Cortez said at a press conference, when asked what inspired her to run for office.

Rose was here for three weeks, which in some ways was insane, given that we barely knew each other. The plan was to take mushrooms on our first night, but she had a strong instinct that we needed to wait.

"We could smudge with the juniper, Syrian rue, and frankincense," I said. "It's supposed to induce a trance state where you can have lusty contact with the divining fairies."

"Fuck yeah," she said.

Night came and we sat by the fire and breathed in the smoke. I actually hadn't done this combination before, but it wasn't random. Years of paying close attention had led to this particular resin and plant alchemy burning on the coals. This was some PhD-level inhalation. We were officially in ceremony, and I don't use that word lightly.

We slept in an elevated float, formal now, like a lily on a lapel. We burned the trio again the following morning and then again that evening, and again the following morning. For two days we mostly stayed home, in the company of only each other and Spanky and Rosie. Her caution around waiting to take the mushrooms until she was sure she had shaken off all bad vibes served a secondary function—we had two days of purification by the time we arrived to the medicine, which is a common protocol in ayahuasca, peyote, and indigenous mushroom ceremonies. Rose deep-cleaned the entire house because that's what is done.

We were an impeccable ceremonial engine from the get-go. I attribute this to her ability to bring out an attitude of religious devotion in me that I usually keep under wraps. We were in love with the Queen of Heaven, because why not? Atheists miss out on all the fun.

Over the course of days, I learned that Rose had dealt with sexual boundary violations all throughout her youth. As an adult in the dating world, she rarely met men who didn't objectify her to the point of erasure. It wasn't that she was fragile. She knew how to pick up guys on Tinder and have casual sex, but she could never shut off the part of her that knew how rarely she was seen by men as fully human. The new acquaintance with whom she'd had the conversation about Standing Rock was a rare exception. They'd talked all night in his apartment without him making even one move on her, and this left her feeling like she might be in love.

Rose opened my heart in a most unusual way. I'm not sure I'd ever been so close to a female heart so capable of truly loving a man, and I saw all the ways she paid for this vulnerability. Rose had been put through the ringer and it wasn't by extraordinary circumstances. This was just what it was like, I guess, for a certain kind of woman now. *Oh my God, I didn't know.* I really didn't.

We took the mushrooms and Syrian rue on an evening that happened to be the third anniversary of my false accusation. It was also James Baldwin's birthday. Rose said we were approaching 8/8, known as Lion's Gate, a portal in the heavens that opens up when the sun is aligned with Sirius and the Earth is bathed in light from both these stars. Eighty-eight is a number I associate with tricky crossroads entities, so we poured rum at a dirt road intersection and said a prayer.

At dusk: three capsules Syrian rue, four grams psilocybin down the hatch.

When Syrian rue found its way from Persia to the United States, it landed first in Deming, New Mexico. The year was 1928. A farmer planted it for purpose of making textile dye. It soon took hold and became an invasive and noxious weed, the kind that grows in the disturbed dirts of highway medians, garbage dumps, and suburban alleyways, yet is surprisingly difficult to cultivate intentionally from seed. It has hallucinogenic properties of its own that ancient Persian carpet-makers took note of, hence the term "magic carpet ride."

It's a MAOI much like the ayahuasca vine, potentiating the effect of the mushrooms and making the trip last up to three hours longer. It also adds a distinctly different tonal quality to the journey. Clem took the rue on the last night of their visit and was not a fan. They were instantly plunged into a realm of body temperature challenges and a sense they were stuck in a "lobby," a gift shop of sorts, crowded with cheesy New Age detritus, bad diamonds, triangle graphics. For me, the Syrian rue has always consistently induced the sensation that I am inside a box, an architecture that imposes limitations. There exists the potential for claustrophobia, of the structure closing in on me. If I don't work my way through this passive state with sound and visualization, I'm in trouble.

Syrian rue is bossy. I do not doubt her talent for misery, her world of pain, well-documented in trip reports I've read online. I have no desire to experience this side of her, so I am always hardworking and dutiful in her presence, vigilant, never risking even the slightest foray into darkness for the sake of curiosity.

We placed a drawing on the altar of la Virgen de Guadalupe standing on a bed of tangled psilocybin mushrooms, drawn at my request by a local tattoo artist from the coal town.

"If you ever want to find us, just look at an image of her," Alma from Huautla De Jiménez had said on the mountain. I wanted my prayers to reach Alma, Seti, and their family tonight, so the Guadalupe telephone was employed. Rose offered purple flowers in a small glass bottle, a sprinkle of cornmeal and rose water. We offered a tiny chip of dark chocolate—not too much, just in case Rosie got to it—and lit three tapered beeswax candles from my trip to Mexico.

We discussed the basics while we waited for the mushrooms to take effect.

"If things get hairy, just offer some tobacco to the altar," I said. "If you can't do it, I can help you. But make sure to ask really clearly. I may not be aware that you need help."

"I'll just say your name loudly, then?"

"Yes."

"Okay," she said, now pale.

Rose's eyes were outlined with cartoon worry. I felt an

incredible tenderness toward both her and myself. There's nothing I can compare to the span of time between when a mushroom is ingested and when it starts to take effect. This is when we are the most vulnerable. It always feels like this part of the trip might be hugely important, like our attitude could make or break the entire night, but trying too hard can cause incredible anxiety. To fill this space with any sort of grandiose intent is just asking for the mushrooms to bitch-slap you.

Just sit back and wait.

This.

> *All of you tender hearts who have ever sat like this, scared and excited, waiting for the entity to arrive. This is real courage.*

Both of us instinctually knew not to plan any ritual actions ahead of time. We wanted to smudge doorways and call in the four directions, but such things should just happen naturally, guided by the mushrooms.

I began playing the full album of *Mushroom Ceremony of the Mazatec Indians of Mexico*, recorded on July 21, 1956 by V.P. and Gordon Wasson.

"Okay, I'm feeling it!" Rose announced.

Its arrival upon her person was dramatic. She pulled herself out of a meditative state in order to contend with the situation, using the last sliver of sober consciousness she had left to get up out of the chair and pace up and down the hallway, taking notes—latitudes and longitudes along multiple planes.

"Man, I'm fucking really high, what the hell," she said. "Okay, then."

You have to make a decision whether you are going to trust it or not. If you don't decide, you can end up at the gates the entire time, which has its teachings, but Rose was no gate-lurker. Once she confirmed the Syrian rue and mushrooms weren't going to harm her, she gave herself over completely. I saw her do it. She stopped entertaining her anxiety, plopped down on the chair again, and bam, it was on. She met the relentless assault of María Sabina's veladas head-on. She moaned and writhed on the chair. She sobbed. She laughed.

It was wonderful to be in the company of someone who knew how to work with the veladas. Most everyone wants to like María Sabina's chanting after having heard snippets and read the translations, but it's become a kind of high comedy, the moment when I press play for my tripping guests and they hear what María Sabina actually sounds like. María Sabina can clear a room. Unlike ayahuasca icaros or Hindu chanting, it's not exactly a beautiful sound. Her voice is staccato and frog-ish, like getting a spanking from an alien. It's potentially quite awful unless you get all the way inside it. Wit, complexity, and sublime beauty reside there, in an organic machine designed to heal the physical body through one of the most sophisticated spiritual technologies around. You will be astounded that such a thing can exist. The veladas are not human. They come from the mushrooms.

"Jan Jesu Cri" feels like the sound of exorcism, clearing and banishing. In "San Pedro," the sacred tobacco plant is installed in the DNA through a writhing horizontal braid that suddenly spelunks. By the time María Sabina is chanting "Names of Plants," you get the sense the hardest part is over—now she's just hanging out with friends, saying thank you and having a good time.

Rose was splayed sideways across the throne in a dance with the Christ spirit. (I was pretty sure that's what was going on. It wasn't unlikely.) She had mentioned she was reading a book about Mary Magdalene that was rocking her world, and now was gathering herself up to meet Jesus. It was all too much and she was crying long deep sobs of grief and gratitude. Gold threads made a dancing basket around her as María Sabina chanted *Cristo, Cristo* and I chanted along—*Cristo, Cristo*—which made the golden threads dance even more wildly.

The recording ended and silence invaded the room. I was very *uh oh* about this. The Syrian rue was mounting a challenge, I could feel it.

Cristo, Cristo, I softly chanted, *Jesucristo, Jesucristo.*

The medicine was deep and strong.

Jesucristo, Jesucristo made the gold lines take on geometric, three-dimensional, intricate shapes that made doorways and portals. I stayed connected to Rose. This was no time for splitting off into a private interiority. I was about to be employed in ways I could never have imagined.

When I had the honor of meeting Kathleen Harrison, she asked me what my preferred dose of psilocybin mushrooms was.

"Three to four grams with Syrian rue is how I like to roll."

"Syrian rue? Why?" She said, making no effort to disguise her distaste. For Kathleen, everything's about having good taste. "Did you read about it on the internet or something?"

"Yes, shroomery.com, to be exact," I said, embarrassed.

"I never got into all that mixing of things," she said. "I think, why change the way something's been done by the people who've known it best for thousands of years."

"Maybe it works so well because there's so much juniper surrounding my house. Apparently the two plants are very symbiotic?"

I could tell I wasn't convincing her. She was probably right, or perhaps even Kathleen Harrison might not be exempt from certain idiosyncratic prejudices based on personal experience.

I started calling in the spirits I wanted to join us—the ancestors, the friends, all the good guys. My voice surprised me. I was confident in speaking whatever came to my mind for a change.

> *They're coming over*
> *All the people from all the directions*
> *The ones who keep their altars right*
> *The ones who keep it clean*
> *Who know how to do ceremony in a closed-up*
> *   house*
> *This is a closed-up house*

All the doors in all the four directions
They're closed up tight
We do it this way
Keeping our altars clean
All the relatives are coming over
Bringing chicken
All the ones on your side
Are filling up the house
For ceremony
That's how we party
In ceremony
Ceremony in a closed-up house

This was the oratory I had been praying for since the beginning. So many came over that night, one by one, until the house was filled. I could see their faces with great specificity. I wanted everybody to come, like the whole world, but just the good ones. I said that if anybody who wasn't a good one came by accident, they would have to stay behind the gate in the entryway, in the "jail." No need to freak out, they could leave when it was over. The walls of the house fell away to make room for the crowds arriving from coast to coast, from north to south—lots from the south, from Mexico and Central and South America, grandmas, mothers, and children crowded in the kitchen, arranging the food they made for the feast that would happen after praying. I saw Cuba and Norway, which felt so random. The floor turned into a three-dimensional map in which certain groups from various countries hung out on what looked floating, topographic lily pads.

I've played out every note in the key of *whoa* in this narrative, cried wolf in the house of awe way too many times. There's nothing I can say to convince you that this night, this trip, really was the big one, the one that blew all the rest out of the water. To have to define yet another experience by how it was even more amazing than the last one makes my kidneys feel like they are going to explode, but here we are.

In *Blue Tide*, Mike Jay suggests that Syrian rue delivers a very specific access to the collective unconscious. His friend describes his experience with Syrian rue and a small handful of mushrooms: "Then I started what I believe is one of the most characteristic effects of the *harmala* (Syrian rue). Mark and I both noticed it. Not hallucinations but the ability to conjure up amazing visual scenes in the mind's eye—in full detail and 24-bit color. You thought of it, and it was there, and you could examine it or go into it or embroider it with no effort at all."

This description feels true for me as well. The things that were happening weren't occurring in my "mind's eye." Alternate realities existed in vivid 3D, like I was in a virtual reality machine. Interchanging avatars took over my physical body. I became all kinds of guys.

What happened next was this: Rays of lime and pink light were shining out from la Virgen de Guadalupe on the altar, slicing through the room like lasers. The floor in front of the altar turned into a plane of undulating golden eagle and hawk feathers that threw off a feral smell that mixed with the scent of copal smoke and chocolate. The floor, which was water and fractal feathers, began to gather itself slowly into a denser form, the shape of snake made of liquid feathers.

This feathered serpent began to circle the room, passing the hundreds of people who had gathered in the house, all the good guys, the ones who keep their altars right, who come from all over to pray. (Remember, I was seeing this, like actually.) I was a man among men who were playing drums. We wore really nice suits, crisp white shirts, fine black boots, to dress up nice for the grandmas. Wives and the kids were here, too. We, in our fancy shoes. The thundering sound we were making with our drums was not experienced as what I could call an auditory hallucination, but a vivid recollection of sound and rhythmic patterns that my body was experiencing as actually happening.

I had no illusions that Rose was seeing the same thing I was, but I instinctually trusted we were connected in our experience. She was a container for all that was opposite of what I was bringing to the room. She held the throne like a true queen.

A guy in a tattered brown suit with a bowler hat and cane was someone I recognized. She was hogging up the dance floor like a fool, one of the only guests who had arrived alone.

Hey tobacco, nice to see you, I said.

The work I had done during the period of my epistemological breakdown had clearly paid off. I was no longer confusing the laws of the regular world with this one. Timidity had left the building and I fell into what I have heretofore referred to as "the Singing Emergency."

San Pedro is here
San Pedro is the boss
San Pedro, San Pablo
Throw down that tobacco
Just watch tobacco in that hat
Acting like they own the place
Dressed like a bum
All night long
All the brothers dancing
San Pedro San Pablo
All this for Tonantzin
But we can call her Guadalupe
Because she likes the name

You have a right to live, says tobacco
If it's coming down to you
Or the next guy
Taking the bad heat
Tobacco says why not you
Coming out smelling like roses
So, let's just say you sing "St. James Infirmary"
And walk down to the gas station
To buy a loose bag
I'm tobacco
Code for what you really want
Give it to that bird over there
Say "Hey bird, this isn't a democracy,
I'm tobacco,
So have a good day."
It's all an illusion so what's the point in having
    a bad day?

I'm tobacco.
My proliferation's viral,
A feature of my telepathy
Sorry, dandelion can't be a celebrity
It's not like dandelion didn't have it
Dandelion has it all like the rest of us
But it's a matter of the shape one takes
And being at the right place at the right time

Brothers drumming, dressed up nice
All the women are here, all the girls
All the girls, safe
All the girls, safe
Guadalupe's fixing it
You're in her world now
All the bad guys are home watching TV

We don't have time for anything else
We're making our reality now
With Guadalupe's queers and artists
All the people who keep their altars right
All the writers, all the singers
All the girls are safe at Indian Market this
*   weekend*
Guadalupe's got her own police
All the queers and all the artists
All the people who keep their altars right
All the bad guys are just at home watching TV
*   the whole time*
Not even one girl had to have a boring ride
*   home*

Perhaps it had taken me so long to finally be able to speak in ceremony because deep down, I knew what was waiting to come out: not the voice of a seasoned poet like Anne Waldman. While her delivery can at times sound like it came from the '80s, at least Anne Waldman makes the sound you'd expect to come out of Anne Waldman. Anne Waldman can only make Anne Waldman sounds, even when she's imitating María Sabina in her book, *Fast Speaking Woman*, while I, on the other hand, become unrecognizable as Bett Williams. Instead, I become a rough-hewn puppet, a hip-hop Justin Bieber narrating one of those cartoon musicals about animals, the character who is most likely to bounce around joyfully while trying to keep their monocle in place, whose role is to sum it all up with gusto in between the key scenes.

If it keeps on in this way, I will be looking back on my mute days with nostalgia.

The room was full of grandmothers. They danced through the crowd, some holding abalone shells with burning copal. Babushka-type grandmas were there, too, ancient, serious, and busy. The air was so thick with grandmas it could only be cut with fine pear brandy, so I made that happen, set a table for them with crystal glasses atop a fine lace tablecloth, a place to sit at for when their work was done and there was nothing to do but watch the brothers, all dressed up nice just for them. The copal smoke made it happen.

Grandmas are teaching us
They're teaching us

Guadalupe's showing us how to walk in the garden
Listening to the little birds
The ones that don't eat meat
The little birds that fly around the heads of the
*   saints in the retablos*
Listen to them!

Guadalupe presented an image to me of an anatomical heart—I should say, a particular Guadalupe did. Historically, this image of the Aztec Virgin appeared on the fabric of a cloak worn by an indigenous peasant who presented it to the archbishop. Flowers fell to the floor and *bam*, the whole Guadalupe network lit up all over the place. The image was instantly recognized by the indigenous people as Tonantzin, Mother of Corn, Snake, Seven Flower, she who emerges from the region like Eagle from fire. She spread like mycelium.

The stars on Guadalupe's shawl are said to mirror the exact constellations that were in the sky the night the image appeared on the robe. I knew a little about Guadalupe, but as for the one that stood in front of me now, I don't know what she was, or if she was really even Guadalupe at all.

This was where I used to get stuck and freeze, but I'd worked a lot out. All that mattered now was saying the word *Guadalupe* because Alma told me to, and it felt right. Saying *Guadalupe* made the world unfurl.

"Are you ready?" Guadalupe said.

"Yes, my heart is ready."

Guadalupe said the way the heart is taken out and put in a picture is all wrong. The medical establishment shows the heart with the veins on the top snipped off. A heart like a balled-up fist is not the whole heart.

"The heart is a plant," she said. "The veins that go up from the heart and into the throat are vines." She shined a light on me so I could see this inside my body. "The heart is a plant. Veins go up into the throat and every time you drink water, think of it as water feeding the plant that is your heart. Now give me your heart."

I handed her my heart. I felt her holding it.

> *She's fixing it*
> *Fixing it*
> *Guadalupe takes my heart out and she's fixing it*
> *She makes the best drawing of my heart*
> *Changing it*
> *Puts the veins going up the throat back in, so it*
>   *is more like a plant*
> *She's fixing it*
> *So I don't get a heart attack when I'm like seventy*
> *Fixing it*
> *She puts it back in me*
> *My heart is back in me oh yeah*
> *"Water is your medicine," Guadalupe says*
> *When you drink it feeds the plant that is your heart*
> *She's making my heart belong to her*
> *So she can fix it*
> *All the kids drinking Dr. Pepper are getting*
>   *fixed, too*
> *All the kids*
> *Drinking it*
> *The heart is a plant and when you drink it*

It feeds the plant
Even drinking Dr. Pepper
Getting fixed
Relax, they're fine
This is Guadalupe's reality
Nobody here gets sick from Dr. Pepper
That's ridiculous
Nobody here gets cancer from tobacco
Because San Pedro is the boss
San Pedro is the boss of cancer
And it's all an illusion
None of that here
No cancer
No diabetes
No heart attacks
Who wants that? Nobody
If it's all an illusion
Might as well make it Guadalupe's.

Rose was lying chest-down on the throne with her head at the foot of it, neck turned sideways and her hair cascading in golden strands onto the tile floor. One of her arms lurched forward in a stretch and her hand took an odd shape in response to the energy surging through it—like an itty-bitty gang sign. She was ruined, like one of the iconic females in Nan Goldin photographs, but instead of it being heroin and sex that had done her in, she was run over by mushrooms and an invasive highway weed called Esfand, *Peganum harmala*, Syrian rue.

"Tobacco, tobacco, tobacco," she muttered.

All the girls are safe
All the girls are safe

She'd been chanting the whole time. Her cadence was at the speed of dragonfly wings; her busybody prayers threw off tiny rainbows.

Weoo weoo, thank you for the medicine
Weoo weoo, thank you for the medicine

Rose had been given a song. She sang it as she walked it up and down the hall. She sang it during a long ordeal, in which she tried to figure out how to go outside to pee. The spirits had the house closed up tight and we didn't know the right protocol. Could we go outside or not? Maybe we were in a capsule hurling through space. She chose the indoor loo.

Weoo weoo, thank you for the medicine
Weoo weoo, thank you for the medicine

Rose sang in the bathroom for a long time.

"Hey, I figured out what's wrong in there," she said, when she stepped out of the bathroom. "I can totally fix it, that's the good news." She gathered twigs of Dakota sage from the basket by the fire and burned them on the bathroom floor.

"Poppy ate mushrooms and spent the whole night in there. We joke that she's still there."

"Well, she's gone now. Bye, Poppy."

"Bye!"

"All kinds of things get stuck in there. *Weoo weoo, thank you for the medicine*. But it can all be fixed by putting a window in the shower."

"I thought that might have been the case, but I just never got around to it."

"*Weoo weoo, thank you for the medicine*. Make the time, you're worth it. *Weoo weeoo, thank you for the medicine*. We don't realize how much a stagnant bathroom can affect your whole life."

Rose lay down on the floor near the window. A bunch of time passed that involved wolves and coyotes crowding the house wall to wall. I promised them a plate of chicken in the morning. *Chicken for the coyotes, the wolves, and the dogs that look like them.*

"Bett Williams, Bett Williams, Bett Williams," Rose chanted, calling me over.

"Sorry, I didn't realize I could stop singing. I hope I'm not too annoying."

"You're not annoying! Why would you say that! You're a queen of this realm, a master of the plants and fungi of this beautiful desert."

"I'm not a master of anything. I learned this on the internet."

"This kind of thing doesn't just happen. You are a keeper of old knowledge."

"I normally am not like this, so loud and everything. It's probably really distracting for you."

"What's distracting?"

"All my singing and dancing."

"You've been singing and dancing? I had no idea."

"For hours. Loudly."

"Okay, shhh," she said, patting the tile, calling me over to lie down next to her, which I did. I was ready to stop being employed so ferociously.

Rose pointed to the full moon that was right outside the window, emerging bright and almost blinding from behind a fast-traveling cloud.

"Look!"

"Oh, good god. Warn me next time a moon comes around to hit my face like that. She's like an overbearing mother trying to prove her love again and again by giving the same gift. Each time I have to show her how much I appreciate her. I'm running out of trying, I tell you. The pretending's killing me, but yes, she sure is a sight to see."

It was good to know I hadn't lost my taste for words drowned in bile, a talisman I find useful for contrast and transitions.

With Syrian rue, there's a resonant blackness upon which threads of blue and red, sometimes pink and lime green, build their neon geometry. I lay looking up at a gazebo made of thin lines of cake-light backed by coal, trying to shut up for a minute. *Why is softness so hard to take?* The intricacy and lightness of it, almost painful, like reality in the key of "Angel Baby."

It all comes down to the relationship between a man and his instrument.

This sentence was both spoken to me and presented visually, in a Jenny Holzer type of way.

Disidentify with the objects of my creation so that they may have their own life, know repose, know when to set it down. The teaching worked on me on a level that transcended language. I felt acted upon by a knowledge machine.

"It's James Baldwin's birthday, right?" I asked Rose.

"I thought it was, but it's not. It was a few days ago. Why?"

"I'm feeling his high-level delivery, that's all."

I stood up and went outside. I felt no nausea whatsoever, yet I vomited violently into the usual juniper tree. Nothing I had eaten came out of me. I ignored the hallucinated Mongolian men in furs, who were standing around watching me, and sat down on the outside couch. The mushrooms had been waiting for this exact moment to tell me something very important.

"Your book is a signpost," the mushrooms said. "You need to finish it already, dude. I know you care about quality writing and stuff, but the thing is—I hate to break it to you—most people aren't even going to read it. Its function as a signpost exists outside of whether people read your book or not and the mushrooms want their goddamn signpost."

The first chapter of Mike Jay's book about Syrian rue is appropriately called "Telepathine." He tells us about the "Drug of the Assassins," which he believes is a mixture of Syrian rue and other plants. It's a tale that takes place in Urfa, on the southern border of Turkey, where it meets Syria during the First Crusade.

Our hero is a cynical, Catalan mercenary who switches sides during a hostage exchange in the desert and is indoctrinated by the Assassin leader, the Old Man of the Mountain, to be sent back to the Holy Land as an undercover hit man. The indoctrination revolves around the famous story of the Old Man's "Garden of Paradise" where he would drug his new recruits and lead them into a garden hidden in his mountaintop fortress, where fountains and streams of milk and honey flowed, and houris danced and made love. Returning to consciousness, the recruits would be convinced they had been visiting paradise, and would obey the Old Man blindly, glad of the chance to die in his service and return there.

In the Western telling of the tale, the focus was put on the Assassins as being nothing more than drug-addled, hash-smoking riffraff. The drugs provide an easy way to rationalize the mystery of why the Old Man's followers gave up their lives for their beliefs.

According to a garbled account of the Assassins by Marco Polo: "Their castle had a library which was rumored to contain the most enlightened, progressive works in medieval Islam before it was looted and burned by Genghis Khan's grandson. Assassins included astronomers, astrologers, alchemists, scientists, and Sufi mystics in their ranks. And their function as a 'secret society' does seem to have been built around a tightly maintained core of spiritual initiation."

Rose and I were technically under the influence of the drug of the Assassins. But look, we were all just goody-two-shoes hanging out with Guadalupe all night. Could it be that this was because we were women in love with the Queen of Heaven? We belonged to her—she told us so.

It might have been boring to some people, the way we pray, but it's all we wanted to do: Dance all night in the mosh pit of Guadalupe.

Rose was on her hands and knees near the altar.

"Weoo weoo, thank you for the medicine, Guadalupe, Guadalupe, Guadalupe, tobacco, tobacco, tobacco, Bett Williams, Bett Williams, Bett Williams."

I stood swaying back and forth in complete body bliss.

"Bett Williams! Bett Williams! Bett Williams!" Rose said emphatically.

"Oh, sorry! I forgot! Are you okay?"

"Don't say sorry for anything, you are a wise woman. Just come over here."

I knelt on my hands and knees and crawled over the tile floor to her.

"Thank you for the medicine, thank you for the medicine, thank you for the medicine."

"Thank you, thank you, thank you, thank you . . ."

I reached over and held Rose's hand, held it tight. I let this gesture be the way I handed myself over to her strength. Rose could help me, I was sure of that. For hours she had gently coaxed me to a quiet place, where a secret was waiting. *Watch her and do what she's doing*, I told myself. *She knows.*

I knelt with her in front of the altar, bowed down, and let my hands rest palms-up on the floor in a pose of receptivity. We had managed to do something right. Whatever offering we made, whatever words, had worked. Now it was time to receive. I was guarding myself fiercely against the experience. I had to force myself, muscle by muscle, to relax as the force field of energy coming from the altar grew stronger. When I let go even a little, I was hit with it: a love so powerful it scared me.

"I should make a spirit plate, a food offering," I said, angling for my escape.

"Just stay," Rose ordered. Boldness where it counted.

"What the hell, I can't even."

"I know," she said, and squeezed my hand.

I regressed into being a child. That body could take it in better than me.

"Let it," she said.

"Holy, holy mosh pit of Guadalupe," I mumbled.

"Thank you, thank you, thank you, thank you," Rose chanted, and I echoed back the same words. *Thank you* was all we could say for quite a while.

"Never ever, ever have I."

"Me too, never ever," she said, "ever felt this love."

"Never, ever in my life."

Are we really going to do this? I was coaching myself for the action that felt both easy and completely impossible. I was being called to take a shape, an emotional yoga pose that would allow me to be able to fully receive the love coming from the altar. I knew what it was to channel love, to be hopped up in a love trance, but this was a very different pose. Guadalupe wanted me to let the love in on a frequency that moved through the same tributaries in which the worst pain I'd ever experienced in my life had also traveled. That river. The deepest one.

It was just a decision I had to make. And so, I made it.

I allowed it to happen. I received the gigantic love. The river of it drank through me, dissolving every defense I'd ever had against this love that had always been there waiting. It said I was clean, even though I wasn't and didn't need to be in the face of this love. Human as low-hanging fruit on the vine in a garden universe, this bleeding-heart show was over now. It never was. Humility and gratitude served as my king and queen and even that she took from me, saying *only love, girl. Try it. Be that child peach.*

Maybe the love that is Guadalupe is really the plants themselves? Even this thought was a defense against knowing that I had no idea who or what was so completely loving me—the mother of heaven, the goddess of earth, la Virgen de Guadalupe, Mother of the Americas, God, the devas of the plants. I honestly had no idea. One thing I knew was that the love wasn't something self-generated and projected outward onto an object. It came from *outside* me. The love was about as psychologically interior as a car crash.

Just like a woman was devotional Rose in her shirt and jeans, sobbing like a child at the end of the ceremony because she was thinking of a man she loved who lost himself all too frequently. Actually, Rose was just like a dragonfly, not just like a woman. She was a holy woman, as I was a holy woman, and it had taken us a long time to get to this altar. I was a woman who carried a passenger, a space cowboy who came along for the ride, and I saw all too clearly how we had been forbidden to step into this particular light.

We were learning how to see ourselves as god sees us, stepping out into the feral afternoon where nature, having wanted to return our phone calls all along, was waiting. A more-than-worthy husband was the Earth with whom we'd fallen in love.

31

THE MORNING AFTER our ceremony, a coyote came right up to the west door of the house, something that had never happened. Spanky and Rosie sniffed its nose at the fence, then Rosie attacked Spanky in a display of machismo. I had to pull them apart, all while the coyote looked on in curious astonishment. I had promised the coyotes chicken. I yelled for it to get lost before Spanky and Rosie got in a fight. Otherwise, I would have given it some chicken.

A text message arrived on my phone while Rose and I were making tea, still a little bit high. Sevine, the Genius Singer, was passing through with her partner, did Beth and I want to have lunch? I wasn't sure if we were even friends in an official sense anymore. After that Spring retreat, Beth had locked Sevine out of the house, like actually. None of us were behaving well during that time. I texted Beth about the situation. She had a mini anxiety attack, then got over it.

Ok, we can meet I guess, she texted.

I'd eighty-sixed a lot of people out of my life following that bad wind of a writer's retreat, or whatever it was. I was left feeling haunted by the thought that I had become a person incapable of working out conflicts with others, that I had a talent for disappearing people. Was shutting people out the only power I had? A wave of cold fear came over me at the thought of seeing Sevine.

We all met in the parking lot of the breakfast place up the road, where peacocks wander the grounds. Sevine looked radiant, buff, glowing with inner juice. She handed me a gift of ground-up pearl dust in a Ball jar. Her partner, Jay, wore vintage Wrangler jeans and delicately offered me a lace handkerchief wrapped around a Ziploc bag full of ceremonial yellow pollen—from their grandmother, they said.

One thing about the addition of Syrian rue is it takes at least a whole day to land after a journey. Rose was gold dust leaning against car metal refracting sun. I was a dotted line made of opal. Back then, Sevine and I were both at the bottom of our bad habits. To share the worst of yourself with someone and then have a country breakfast with them two years later—that's a gift, right? Maybe we could become the peacocks that walked the grounds outside this place?

We didn't talk about the past. That's not how forgiveness works. In fact, it's the opposite. Talk about the past and it's invoked. You really don't know; maybe the past is different now, so don't mess it up.

"You gave really shitty psychic advice as a scorpion. You really hurt my feelings, by the way," I said at the breakfast table, testing it out. "The scorpion told me I had a choice: I could join some priestly order of celibate Sumerian gardeners—or get a Tinder account! I was just having some relationship issues and needed to talk to my friend. Anyway, it's fine. We were really high."

"Oh, I thought the scorpion was genius!" she said with cheer. A peacock outside the window fanned its tail in our direction, as if offering divine confirmation of her bogus statement, a gesture that did not go unnoticed by Sevine. Trying to get a person to see your differing perception of a thing is almost always a waste of time. Seriously, we need statistics. How much are human beings actually able to care about things outside their own experience? Let's be honest. I love Sevine and that is that.

Rose occasionally chimed in with bits of the song she was given the night before, *weeoo weeoo, thank you for the medicine*. She knew it wasn't sustainable as a permanent lifestyle, this public medicine-singing in restaurants, but for just this brief window it enjoyed a life unbothered. The waitress brought her tea and Rose sang thank you.

Sevine announced that she wanted to travel the country and interview people who have had direct experiences with the holy and unexplainable. Beth let go of any hard feelings in exchange for the plus of having a friend who could talk about God, whose idea of a good time was hitting the road, chasing spoon benders and mystery lights. She invited Sevine and Jay to stay a few days if they wanted to.

32

"And the moon falls, down on the highway
And that highway crawls across the desert below
Like a sad song, you can't stop dancing to
That tells us of the wilderness of this world."
—TERRY ALLEN, "Wilderness of this World"

"Who has not asked himself at some time or
other: Am I a monster or is this what it means
to be a person?"
—CLARICE LISPECTOR, *Hour of the Star*

BETH AND I were going to be traveling in a tricked-out shuttle bus named Lucy, one hundred miles from Mexico, where Border Patrol has jurisdiction to search your vehicle for no reason. Beth packed her marijuana in four layers of bear bags and stuffed this in a Ball jar full of coffee and froze it. She'd read online this was a foolproof way to travel. There were also six hits of LSD hidden in a place undisclosed to me.

We took a different route because of her stash, down through Artesia instead of Hatch, through the oil fields and man camps of the Bakken oil fields at night. Regulations had been lifted in the last few months. Under

Trump, the oil was allowed to burn off, making dirty flames all the way beyond the horizon line. Oncoming headlights hit Lucy's greasy window, nearly blinding Beth on the narrow throughway—so yeah, she was yelling a lot. Screaming, actually.

This was our second year attending the Marfa Myths Festival, put on by Ballroom Marfa and the Brooklyn-based music label Mexican Summer. I don't really go to festivals, being that since a very young age, I have been in need of a comfortable chair. I hate carrying fold-out chairs from one place to another, but Marfa Myths is small. Dogs are welcome and you can sit on the floor if you want to, knit a sweater, stretch, stim, do deep-tissue work on your legs while rocking back and forth as much as you please, all to the tune of obscure music created by elite talent living in large urban centers that sounds great while high on psychedelics.

The word *psychedelic* is derived from the Greek word *psyche* (soul) and *deloun* (to make real). To make visible, to make real, that which is hidden in the soul. This definition doesn't explain much, yet I haven't been able to come up with something better.

Keanu Reeves is psychedelic. Ethan Hawke is not.
Laura Dern is psychedelic. Drew Barrymore is not.
Thurston Moore is psychedelic. PJ Harvey is not.
Jorge Luis Borges is psychedelic. Gabriel García
    Márquez is not.
Sewing machines are psychedelic. Dishwashers are
    not.

AA is psychedelic. Cognitive Behavioral Therapy is
    not.

Just because a thing is psychedelic doesn't mean it's
better. A lot of really wonderful things are not psychedelic
at all, like volleyball and books on tape, while not neces-
sarily great things like, MRI machines, mayonnaise, and
the IRS are totally psychedelic.

BETH AND I had taken a half a hit of acid and we stood
in the doorway of the Veteran's Building, trying to decide
if we should go in. We would have been content doing
anything. Spanky was on the end of my leash and Beth
was holding Cricket in her arms. A single note from a
cello echoed from the hall. I was annoyed by the sound.
I had just been at the Suzanne Ciani concert in one of
the Chinati buildings and had nothing left to give to any
noise that required concentration.

"This is bullshit," I said to Beth.

"You know that what she's doing is actually really
hard?" Beth said.

Everything in me contracted against the sound. My
brain was sticking Post-it notes on the long note—pretentious, hipster, NPR, drone, bullshit.

The woman's singing went up another octave in a frequency that Cricket was quite familiar with. It was the
note we used when training her to howl at home, mimick-
ing the high notes of emergency vehicle sirens.

"Oh no, this won't do," Beth said, clamping down on
Cricket's snout. "Cricket's about to start singing. I'm

going to take her back to the bus and then come back and we'll go inside. I have to be in that room."

Kelsey Lu was playing on a platform set up in the center of the hall. Just her, a cello, an electric guitar, a pair of white boots standing in front of her socked feet, a microphone with a tropical leaf attached to it, and stick of incense burning. She was wearing lime-green and turquoise pants with a molecular chemical pattern and a red silk, see-through shirt. Her hair was a loose mycelial Afro. We could only see her from the back and had no idea what her face looked like.

Beth and I relaxed into our positions on the floor. I was finally present after making a decision to lean into the half-hit of LSD. Timothy Leary was right in saying that LSD is a form of "Stealing Fire."

The resin in the wood floor and the ceiling beams acted upon my nose like frankincense. I understood what my problem was at the door. My ego had mounted a full-on attack against the previously unknown, having recognized the alien frequency. Kelsey Lu sang angelic, operatic notes bolstered by the blues, conjuring the feminine heaven of tricky Aphrodite. It's a sound I don't usually seek out, preferring instead the wrecked female voice. For me, the perfect high note has carried with it toxic ideas about purity and femininity, until right there in the Veteran's Building, when Kelsey Lu made a soup of time, then hit it and delivered the news.

> "I'd be lying if I said I was okay, but I'm not
> Yeah, I'm angry
> And I'm sad."

The song "Liar" reads as a church song, a spiritual.

> *"I'd be lying if I said I was okay, but I'm not*
> *Yeah, I'm angry*
> *And I'm sad."*

Are you okay? I'm not. In no way okay. Can't you feel it? I know you can. It's always right there, if you can get quiet enough to let it speak. The absence of any grounding symmetry. Of a future we can actually live in. Human beings are either going to die out or link up with robots. No, I am not okay. Thank you for asking. *I am not okay* is a perfect prayer. Feel how grace rains upon us when we say it—*No, I'm not okay.*

Johns Hopkins University, sponsored by the Heffter Research Institute, did a study on terminal cancer patients using psilocybin mushrooms to treat end-of-life anxiety. Some eighty percent reported their existential anxiety having lifted. Many flat-out said they stopped being afraid of death. Even six months later, all they had to do was recall their experience to receive the healing again. Magic mushrooms, scientifically proven to prepare the soul for death, a medicine for the Anthropocene.

> *"I'd be lying if I said I was okay, but I'm not*
> *Yeah, I'm angry*
> *And I'm sad."*

I feel it, do you? This end-of-the-world feeling, but not in a histrionic way or in a Phillip K. Dick way of it all being a grand conspiracy. Rather, it's a sense of the end having already arrived, bodily and as real as day. Ask yourself honestly if you don't feel already gone. Are we like lemurs, extinct already, but technically still alive and living in a halcyon dream?

Psychedelics do a very simple thing—they inhibit the filtering mechanisms of the brain. We have needed those filters to survive as a species, but what if we're not, you know, surviving anymore? This may be the moment in human evolution where we allow for the one thing our ancestors didn't have the luxury of doing—observing consciousness itself. Before we go, let's sing praise songs with a raw head in honor of who we've been this entire time.

While continuing to play a long note on her cello, Kelsey Lu put one foot and then another into her white boots, ready to walk, like the whole show was just a preparation for Next. There might be just a little bit of future left if Kelsey Lu's putting on her boots on.

After the show, I had to look her up on the internet to see what her deal was.

"Playing the cello feels like playing water, feels like playing a really old tree that's singing," she said in an interview with *Pitchfork*.

Her cello was made in Los Angeles and has bite marks on it because she was tripping on acid and tried to eat it. She grew up in North Carolina in a family of Jehovah Witnesses. She told the interviewer about her ghost dick that came up in a dream she had recently, in which she was fucking a woman from behind.

PITCHFORK: Do you do a lot of drugs?

KELSEY LU: I don't know what "a lot" is.

PITCHFORK: Do you smoke weed?

KELSEY LU: Oh yeah. I smoke weed every day. When I first went to college I started experimenting with psychedelics and I did acid and mushrooms. I haven't done acid in a long time, but I love mushrooms.

Kelsey Lu stood beside us in a fluffy, green down coat while Connan Mockasin and his band were on stage at the Capri.

"It's crazy that he's playing this song," Kelsey Lu said to Beth, who was elegant in her alpaca poncho, a purchase she made on impulse while on a half-hit of acid during last year's festival. "I used to listen to this song over and over while walking in Tompkins Square Park. 'Forever Dolphin Love' gotten me through a rough time."

Connan Mockasin is a living mascot for the stereotype of a psychedelic life—a human being entirely assembled from drugs, a freaky-looking person with bleached-out hair and pale skin that hints at more than a vitamin deficiency. He was at the festival the year before and during the Tonstartssbandht show, it appeared he was unable to walk. He was crawling on all fours. I don't think he's performing these eccentricities. I think he's actually high, maybe most of the time.

It's amazing how his life has risen up to support him. He gets to travel all around the world now. That night, his dad came from Australia to front his son's band in a heart-wrenching version of George Harrison's "While

My Guitar Gently Weeps," interspersed by a reading of the Three Little Pigs, altered so the story ends up being an allegory about drugs. It was joyous. Connan's dad is a little round man in a T-shirt, the type you'd imagine making permanent residence at the local pub, who through an act of sorcery known only by gnome folk, has been transported permanently into a fantasy existence. Connan Mockasin and I are alike in that we are people for whom psychedelics have gifted a life way more fun and abundant than we would have had otherwise.

After nearly eight years of regular use, psilocybin is still a holy stranger. She demands more than ever that I approach her formally. For me, that means three to five grams with Syrian rue in a closed-up house, with people who keep their altars right, with Guadalupe and María Sabina, with tobacco, copal, frankincense, and juniper. I would be content with never ingesting mushrooms in a secular way again. There's LSD for that.

Wire, punk's most rarified cult band, was the headliner. They slammed in with their wall of sound, lifting everyone off their feet to dance. Beth and I were sitting in fold-out chairs atop a hefty wooden table. From our perch, it became obvious that nearly everyone in the room was tripping. We were being lifted by a tab of acid, and the altered consciousness of the crowd was a thing we could actually see. Our friend Jackson and some other friends had eaten mushrooms. The drunk people were easy to spot as they walked frantically back and forth to the bar, as if on a mission. Over the course of the night they faded, literally receded into darkness, and it was just us now, the tripping ones, bouncing, screaming, standing in the stillness at the center of a wheel, in a sound so loud it contained within it a silence.

We looked out over the large concrete expanse at all the decent humans watching the band and congratulated ourselves on making some good choices. It goes like this—in my dream the night of the burglary I was accused of committing, which I have the right to say was an assault, Beth and I stood each in our own square concrete pool filled with black water. We wore crowns and above the crowns were the words *King* and *Queen* in bright neon. The words flashed interchangeably—neither of us were either, and at the same time we were both. We dunked down into the black water. When we emerged, we found that we had been transformed into cormorants, birds that live in water and air equally. This was us, with wings in both conscious and unconscious realms. We made it through.

An extremely drunk woman came up to our platform and started banging on my boot with her hand. I let her. It's funny what people need to do.

"Excuse me! Excuse me!" she screamed.

"Uh huh?"

"I promise I'll let myself in and water the plants!"

"I don't understand."

"I'm the person who waters the plants in the Brite Building. I'll let myself in."

"I think you have the wrong person?" I said.

"She thinks we're staying at the Brite Building?" Beth yelled into my ear. It was the fancy annex to El Cosmico, where we were camping in the bus for twenty dollars a night. The 3800-square-foot apartment is the high palace of Marfa, a town a beset by a vulgar and transparent hierarchy funded by billionaire art patrons. Not our world and never.

"Looking like you may have been in a band from Seattle in the '90s can get you a long way," Beth said.

I FEEL US all together sometimes, each of us in our circles large and small, on the mountaintop in Huautla de Jiménez, in palapas in Peru, in tipis, on the dance floor, in the garage/art studio, in the desert and the forest, in living rooms in Detroit and Cleveland where Kai Wingo's people travel together, linking up, each one of us with our own traditions and methods, all of it leading to a direct experience with the great mystery. This is how we make culture, by doing these things each in our own unique way—press play on "Diamonds" by Rihanna. We know it's a medicine song.

And so it came to pass that Beth and I grieved our dead fathers in Marfa while on a half a hit of LSD during a Terry Allen show, Terry being the high priest of all things Lubbock, Texas. Knowing this, I always expect to feel the presence of grandma Wilma whenever I hear his music. Years ago in Los Angeles, I tried to talk to Terry Allen about Lubbock after one of his shows. I told him about Wilma, how she got arrested outside of Lubbock with Joel, her Black husband, the guns, the morphine in the trunk, etc. He was not interested. Nope, not even a little bit. I walked away from the interaction quite embarrassed.

Terry Allen writes songs about truckloads of art crashing on the highway, Billy the Kid, the fall of the Aztec Empire, Alice the child prostitute, Antonin Artaud in a state of peyote delirium facing annihilation by forces of the uncontrollable feminine—all in the cadence of a country song about guy and his truck and his dog. Now he was up on stage at the piano and it wasn't Wilma who came around in his music at all. It was my dad—my dad and also Beth's dad, who was a big Harry Chapin fan. Both our dads would have loved Terry Allen's long, detailed ballads, accompanied by slide guitar, violin, and mariachi accordions.

Our fathers died within three months of each other, Beth's from supra nuclear palsy, a disease that left him paralyzed in a chair for years before he went. She wasn't sad about it, in the same way I wasn't sad about my dad passing at ninety-one of complications from colon surgery. Both our dads were stationed in Germany, my father as a military doctor in 1953, Beth's as an army officer in the mid-'60s. Her dad was honorably discharged for mental health reasons after he found his best friend and bunk mate hanging over the closet door in their shared dorm room. As for my father's experience as a military doctor in a hospital in Baden Baden, he told me absolutely nothing. We don't really know who our fathers were.

Terry Allen went from "Billy the Boy" to "Juarez Device." Emotionally disconnected tears fell out of our eyes and wouldn't stop. Something was borrowing our heads to cry for itself.

Well, I am a Texican badman
And I got a pistol in my hand
And I'm gonna go across that Rio Grande
Where the women are willing
And the life there is thrilling
Gonna make me a killing in Juárez

Is death an old white guy dad's Mexico? The accordion player channeled the land across the border and a white man's regret, the monstrous comedy of a white man's failed desire. How insignificant is a white man in a sandstorm, reaching in his pocket for a packet of saltine crackers he saved from the diner?

Once, long ago, I received an image of what my father would look like without his bad deeds and shame. He was fit and wearing a tight red T-shirt and pointing to the night sky, teaching me about the constellations. A father should possess the skills of navigation and oratory. A father should be of a place.

"I can't help it. I want Terry Allen to be our dad," I said to Beth. "I know I'll just be disappointed if I try to talk to him, but—"

"You can't."

"I know I can't."

Lubbock has weird mystery lights, just like Marfa. Terry Allen could have just written songs about these lights and called it a day, but he's a man who has to follow that mystery, in every manifestation, all the way to its end. He knows intimately all the things our dads secretly desired, but never gave themselves permission to investigate. Our poor scared-y-dads, not skillful enough to honestly take on the metaphysical nighttime. Had they tried, it would have made everything worse, that's the sad fact. They went as far as they could and then stopped. That's all there is to it.

I need whiskey
I need style
I need a job
To make it worthwhile
And to get me out of this up-tight
Mid-night
Into some lime-light . . . again
Yeah, 'cause I know
My ego
Ain't my amigo
Anymore

Beth and I stood outside with the dogs when the show was over.

"My dad would have loved this concert," Beth said.

"Both our dads would have insisted on talking to Terry Allen."

"It would have been painful to watch—the flattery, the barrage of questions having to do with equipment, the rigors of touring life."

"My dad would've said that Terry Allen has a good head of hair."

We were standing right inside of it—amidst the correct placement of all objects in relation to Dead Dads.

"They watched our every move," I said. "They're not watching anymore."

"Yes. It's like after rain. Peaceful."

"Nothing kills flow like the toxic Dad eye."

"I missed him for the first time tonight," Beth said. Right then, Terry Allen walked towards us. Spanky had been doing witchcraft to get him to come over, and there he was, standing tall, right in front of us in his button-up linen shirt.

"Good ole' dog," he said, petting Spanky's head. Guess Spanky could die now having lived the dream. Cricket got a head pet, too. Cricket can bite, but Beth was not going to speak to Terry Allen either, even to warn him.

"Love them cattle dogs and Chihuahuas," he said.

I nodded but averted my eyes from his gaze, held my ground, refused to say a word. He was talking in a circle of people a few feet away from us and Spanky kept staring. Terry Allen was the only human being alive in the state of Texas, according to Spanky.

Then Eileen Myles, the writer, came over to say hello. They lived in Marfa now. Spanky was very ho-hum about the exchange with Eileen, which was disappointing, being that Spanky's a dog and Eileen's book *Afterglow* is about a dog, the best book ever about a dog and very psyche-delic, and if Spanky had read it, she'd know Eileen was a way better dad than Terry Allen could ever be. Eileen's the kind of dad with a pocket full of trail mix, ready at all times to ward off a fainting spell. Eileen would give you detailed directions to the big event, even if you were a mess and your presence at this event had the potential of reflecting badly upon them. They'd *still* give you directions—that's the kind of dad Eileen Myles is.

We were standing on the floodlit grass like *Friday Night Lights*, with two dogs on leashes under an American flag in front of the Veteran's Building, among friends and strangers, as the wind picked up enough speed for a four-day dust storm, not talking to Terry Allen. This was how we grieved the death of our fathers. It might seem like we're cold, that we had no ties, but that's not true. We took the shape of simple daughters, made an altar to the father in our minds, me placing saltine crackers upon it next to a Presbyterian cross, Beth laying down white hots and fried chicken. *Thank you*, we said, and that was all.

33

THE WEST TEXAS landscape is whatever you need it to be. It will mirror you, but crossing the state line back into New Mexico, the dirts and grasses sing *Hey, we are the oldest place, hey, more cows than people, hey, this is indigenous land, hey, hello, nice to meet you, I'm not you.* We stopped at a taco stand in Hatch, the famous capital of green chili, and sat eating our food next to a Lakota sculptor, who was bringing a tipi tied on the roof of his truck to a peyote ceremony. He went to his truck and called me over to give me a big handful of sage. *All my relations*, I said as a thanks.

Up from Hatch to Truth or Consequences in the passenger seat, I was thinking, *We've been too long just circling around our more private hearts. I'd like to turn and face Beth a little more. She's the one for life.*

Outside the window was a blur of speed. I turned to her and said, *Hello my dear, hello death, happy to travel with you.* Kindness is wild on these roads where we find each other. We're going to ride on out of this place—dogs, jack's o' diamonds, everything. The passenger takes the wheel, Willie's on the radio, dreaming in San Pedro colors, and we don't destroy the world we're living in anymore.

34

I HAD JUST spoken at the 2018 Horizons conference, on the bill with Michael Pollan, when my connecting flight in Dallas was canceled. There were no flights out for two days, so I decided to take a bus home, stopping in Lubbock to walk around for a day.

I recommend riding on a Greyhound bus through West Texas while high on mushrooms. As I stepped off the bus, the sun reflected off the sand-colored, retro architecture buildings and hit my tripping eyeballs. I began walking down Buddy Holly Boulevard, passing antique stores with taxidermy animals and mattress stores, down to where the industrial-size nightclubs cluster near the freeway, as they do in a dry town. I crossed the tracks like Wilma must have done a million times, into a neighborhood where the yards were kept like Southern graveyards. I snapped pictures of garden gnomes. A Black man on a porch invited me inside for a beer as I walked by. I declined, too high to meet a stranger.

The sidewalk crumbled, then fell away, and I continued walking in wet grass until the colorful resin surfaces of giant three-dimensional cartoon animals called me over to a yard behind a cattle fence. It was packed with circus detritus, actual props and sets from actual circuses that gave off the sweat of oil money, country music, and the drugs and alcohol that fueled what made it. I felt the presence of all the people who ever saw Lubbock from the vantage point of tripping, which is a lot of people. They were with me as I walked further by open fields of grass and towering cotton mills made of corrugated steel, old enough that Wilma must have seen them too when she walked down this road, on her way to meet Dr. Joel Prince at Caviels, the first African American-owned pharmacy in the United States. It was a little white building that now housed an African American History Museum. It was closed that day.

My search over the years to uncover any details of my grandmother's history and that of Joel Prince has gleaned almost no results. Over the years, I've written emails to historical societies and spent hours in the library archives and nothing.

But there are other ways to investigate one's origins— psychedelics being one of them. I know what happened. All around me, in me, in the language of ecstatic feeling, Wilma was imparting her knowings. Stark train tracks in the too-bright sun, a narcotic math—this is the crossing where my medicine lives. I know what happened, but that doesn't cure my longing to find another person to say they know what happened too.

Downtown, a barber shop on the main strip advertised shoeshines. My boots were a mess from walking in the wet grass. I went in and sat in the red vinyl king's chair and put my foot up like a boss. The old man who gave me the shine complimented my boots, and yes, they're good ones, dark brown with stitching that resembles a mushroom. Five guys were sitting around talking; it was a regular hang-out spot. One had just been to Colorado and was talking about weed, weed laws, weed legalization, and how people were going crazy on edibles and the kids were getting hooked, but whatever, it was bringing in money and he was all for it.

The barber, a young Latino man with a meticulous buzz cut, said weed had helped him, but it wasn't really his thing.

"It's okay, but yeah, I can't really do it, like, when I'm around other people," said another. I'd had the same conversation many times—people putting down weed in order to talk about weed because they love weed.

"Weed's not really my thing, either," I said, lying.

"I have PTSD," the barber said. "I'm a combat veteran and I've tried a lot of things to help me with it."

"There are studies on MDMA for PTSD in veterans," I said.

"I know. They love to use us for those studies."

"Nobody doesn't want to help a veteran," I said. One of the guys in the shop echoed the sentiment with a grunt and a nod.

I was really trying not to bring up mushrooms. The topic tends to open the door to other subject matter that is transgressive-lite and people, including myself, tend to overshare.

"I know MDMA could probably help," the barber said. "I mean, I did it once, you know, at a party, and it was fine, but it's a chemical. I'm more interested in psilocybin mushrooms."

It's surreal, no? That he said this? My excitement triggered an autistic flood of words about the shady history of MDMA, how it was trafficked from Israel to intentionally flood the U.S. market by players who have a stake in the corporate game.

"Getting people dosed on it on a mass scale could have been part of an advertising campaign," I said. "I don't trust that the CIA and DEA aren't tied up in it and they bust people just to make it seem like the only safe way to obtain it is from your doctor."

The barber knew all about it. He added more details and facts, obviously having read more than just the single article I was referring to. I told him I'd just spoken at a psychedelic conference and that I used to grow mushrooms in my house in New Mexico.

"I need to do that for my PTSD. I have a room and everything to do it in. I don't like doctors. I don't trust them. Especially as a veteran. It's a joke trying to get any assistance at all and then they say they have this new thing out there and it's like, *yeah, we know, so just do it already.* I can just get it from a drug dealer if I need to. Or even better, just grow mushrooms at home in my closet."

I shared with him some tips on growing, gave him some names of online spore companies. The old man resurrected my boots beautifully with a shade of brown he mixed himself from multiple containers he fished out of his box. He was quiet the whole time, taking it all in.

The barber asked for my contact information and I gave it to him, saying if he had more questions about growing, I'd be happy help him out. I stepped into the sun in my bad-ass boots and took a moment to observe my own blown mind.

Why was it blown?

Our conversation countered a message I hear all the time within the movement—that psychedelics must be destigmatized in the minds of mainstream Americans, that we should take out the association with the counterculture and educate them that mushrooms can be, if used in a clinical setting with a trained professional, a miracle medicine for our epidemic-level ills.

Who exactly are these uptight people they say we need to educate? Not these men. Working-class people, who are often living at ground zero of the opiate epidemic, who are familiar with the drug culture of the military and the commerce of dealing, tend to be very smart about drugs. They can't afford not to be. The population that is uptight about psychedelics, from my own experience—if I may be so vulgar as to use this label—are the liberal elite. They are acquaintances who give me that *Are you okay?* look when I fill them in on what I've been up to. They are Michael Pollan, who preaches that we are not ready to decriminalize psychedelic mushrooms because more studies need to be done and thus are potentially dangerous and should be used only in a clinical setting with a trained professional. They are Rick Doblin from MAPS (Multi-Disciplinary Association for Psychedelic Studies), who knows better but keeps silent and allows this doctrine to persist, because this is the lie upon which his lifelong project of corporate medicalization depends.

Psychedelic plants and fungi have had their proving ground for thousands of years and the evidence of their effectiveness as a medicine already exists, noted in anthropological texts and artifacts, and more importantly, in living traditions all over the world. We know this already.

How many capitalist projects actively depend on human beings forgetting what they already know and possess in order for it to be sold back to them for a price?

What my heart says is this: The mushrooms don't like it done that way.

Our intention has been to demagnetize ourselves from the machinery of the failed project. Exist in interstitial zones. Be available to the intelligence of the mycelium. There are species of mycelium that eat plastic. Others absorb oil and radiation. If there's any hope at all for sustaining human civilization on earth beyond what is writ, it will have something to do with the mushrooms, I am sure of that. *There's nothing that a mushroom can't fix*, said Kai Wingo. It's been scientifically proven that psilocybin mushrooms can help treat depression, addiction, and OCD, and while I'm positive the mushrooms have done all these things for me, that's not why I've taken them. I eat them to prepare my soul for this world.

Psychedelic experience offers us nothing less than decentralized access to knowledge. Forces of subjugation and control have always existed alongside their use. I get it with the law, but I didn't expect the level to which I would encounter it within the psychedelic movement itself. The discourse around medicalization versus decriminalization is heated and emotional because this isn't just a battle of ideologies. They're illegal, people are incarcerated, and the whole way we proceed with our lives alongside these consciousness-expanding substances is informed and polluted by this fact, and it's been that way so long, going far back into history, to the point we don't know what it would be like if it was different. We have no point of reference for freedom.

ON A TENSE night in May 2019, an initiative decriminalizing psilocybin mushrooms in Denver passed by a small margin. I was in shock. I had no idea it was coming.

"Not So Fast on Psychedelic Mushrooms," read the headline of Michael Pollan's scolding op-ed in the *New York Times* a few days later.

It *was* fast. That's how it moves with the mushrooms. Once they're released, so many spores fly around that you can't count them, let alone control them. In old times, it was usually a small group of elites in any given culture that used entheogens—cabals of mystics, priests, and medicine people who served their communities. The majority of people didn't do them.

It seems that now, a lot more people are going to be eating psilocybin mushrooms. What this will look like I have no idea. I'm more curious as to why the mushrooms are surfacing *now*, at this time in our human evolution, and what exactly they are here to do. It's about more than just quitting smoking and treating PTSD. They seem to be here to do what mushrooms do, which is help organisms be in balance with the ecosystem as the earth changes, but that's just me.

It won't be long before psilocybin-assisted psychotherapy in a clinical setting is legalized in some places. Mushroom retreats are popping up in Mexico and Jamaica, and underground in the United States, led by "trained facilitators." The definition is vague—having attended a women's retreat in Mexico, I can speculate on the myriad of things that can go terribly wrong, simply from the fact that at this uniquely well-staffed retreat, miraculously nothing did. While I appreciate such grand experiments in psychedelic culture-making, mixing mushrooms with a spa vacation package comes with its own can of worms.

Timothy Leary talked about the importance of set and setting. I can think of no better way of accomplishing this than keeping a mushroom trip free of capitalism. Ceremony is often the only space we have where we get to experience this. A capitalism-free zone is a part of keeping a space "clean," spiritually.

35

OR, THE END

I HAD NEARLY let myself give up writing completely.

"There's nothing more dangerous than a writer who is not writing," a friend said to me. My life was living proof that this is true. Rather, it's a sense of the end having already arrived, bodily and as real as day.

Dear reader, may I suggest you not stray far from your own life when seeking out the psilocybin mushroom? You'll miss out on the best part. When you do them in nature or at home alone, with another, or in a small group of friends, you get to set up your own altars, play your own music, work with your own ancestors and spiritual practices. What is born from the experience will be completely unique and yours, sovereign and unmediated by power structures and power trips.

The path of the mushroom has no teacher. It's the way of un-forgetting. In psychedelic space, we get to see our programs, the thought forms we have taken on from the outside world, belief systems and ideas about the way things work. We get to figure out if they really fit. Maybe they aren't even ours. We can shake them off and create something new through unmediated access to decentralized knowledge—a great talent of the mushroom.

No wonder those in power want to control these things, how we access them, how it is to be done "properly." Meanwhile, the biggest psychedelic revolution since the '60s has already had its day in the liquid sunshine and has gone unmentioned for the most part. Silicon Valley is made of LSD and her chemical siblings. The machines eroding our souls were invented by people who used psychedelics, with Steve Jobs as king angel. The prohibitionists cite the hippie counterculture as a cautionary tale lest we allow the unwashed masses to have access. But Silicon Valley doesn't really count.

Whenever psychedelics have spilled into a segment of the population, incredible advances occur on the landscape of both culture and invention. Evolution goes nuclear. It's already happening; urban farmers, rural homesteaders, anarchist chemists, eco-scientists, cyber insurgents, Indigenous activists, queers, Santeros, Jewish mystics, Buddhists, witches, gnostic Christians, Afro-futurists, veterans, mothers, fathers, teachers, artists, writers, musicians, everyone—when the people do mushrooms with one another, it is a revolutionary act. It's stealing power.

Culture is an outward manifestation of a people engaged with the machinations of their own souls. What motivates me the most is the joy I feel when I find my people, the ones with whom I am dreaming a world into being. Become the mycelium with your people—or better yet, recognize that it already is so. We are evolving into higher consciousness as one organism.

We are here to save each other.

Nudgers and shovers
In spite of ourselves.
Our kind multiplies:
We shall by morning
Inherit the earth.
Our foot's in the door.
   —Sylvia Plath, "Mushrooms"

ACKNOWLEDGMENTS

I THANK the late Kai Wingo, whose faith would not allow me put this project down; Ariana Reines, poet, prophet and friend in any state of emergency; Kathleen Harrison for her generous big-sister vibes and for being my psychedelic hero; Clement Hil Goldberg, artist and road-partner, for offering up the phrase "ambassador of the mushroom"; the skillful Marianne Morris for her alchemy of breakthrough; Mike Jay for walking into our store, bringing his knowledge of Peganum harmala; Bia Labate for inviting me into the "movement"; Jen Berkowitz, Dean Smith, and Mike Kitchell for their friendship; and to all the people I have tripped with—I'm humbled and honored to have been on the journey with all of you. Thanks to Sadaf Rassoul Cameron and the Kindle Project for the Makers Muse Award, to Victoria Carlson, Morgan Honeycutt, Ken Baumann, and Elisa Kier for giving me honest feedback on drafts and Haydyn Jackson for her skillful early copyedits that saved me months of toil. Margaret Wrinkle, my one and only writing partner, listened to me read out loud and her insight catalyzed the endurance it took to bring the first drafts to final ones. I am a very fortunate cat to have had the poet CA Conrad bless this book with a tarot reading upon its completion. They assured me an ally would come along to help bring it to publication. That person was Michelle Tea, seen in psychedelic space as a kind of luminescent glue that holds queer literature to the earth plane. She stood by this work and helped guide it to Dottir Press and the smart and gentle hands of my editor, Jennifer Baumgardner, and Dottir colleagues Larissa Melo Pienkowski, Charis Caputo, Drew Stevens, Mike Perry, Kait Heacock, and Amanda Trautmann. Lastly, without my partner Beth Hill, there would have been no psychedelic life to write about. I thank her for her continual editorial genius and for dreaming the world into being with me.